Mini Performance Manual

First published in 2003

A catalogue record for this book is available from the British Library

ISBN 1 85960 880 9

Library of Congress catalog card no. 2003104827

Published by Haynes Publishing, Sparkford, Yeovil, Somerset, BA22 7JJ, UK

Tel: 01963 442030 Fax: 01963 440001
Int. tel: +44 1963 442030 Int. fax: +44 1963 440001
E-mail: sales@haynes.co.uk
Web site: www.haynes.co.uk

Haynes North America, Inc.,
861 Lawrence Drive, Newbury Park,
California 91320, USA

Printed and bound in England by J. H. Haynes & Co. Ltd, Sparkford

Mini Performance Manual

Tim Mundy

contents mini performance manual

The car that probably started it all for me: my parents' second Mini, 745 VFC, pictured here with my father in 1965.

My first and all-time favourite Mini, MBW 501L, which is at the time of writing undergoing full restoration and further modification. (For updates on progress see monthly issues of *MiniWorld* magazine. Website: www.miniworld.com.)

There really is nothing quite like a Mini; especially a personalised or modified Mini. Over 42 years, the enthusiasm for Britain's favourite car has grown into something far beyond anything that Alec Issigonis could have imagined when he first sketched the design. Tuning the Mini began very early on, almost as soon as it went on sale, and competition success by the Abingdon and Cooper works teams fuelled the enthusiasm of many an owner to tune their road car. It was this that brought about the huge accessory and tuning industry that surrounded the Mini then, and which has grown even bigger today. Overall, the use of the Mini has changed over the years, as for the first three decades most were used as everyday transport. Today, many still are, both by enthusiasts and those who simply want easy-to-maintain transport, but a large number of Minis are now weekend cars, kept in the garage and built up and enjoyed by enthusiastic owners in their leisure time.

My own involvement started really with my parents' Mini. I worked on it as a teenager and was desperate to modify it but was not allowed to, alas! The first Mini that I actually owned quickly became modified. I still own it nearly 30 years later, and it is currently being further modified and restored. Needless to say, I have owned and modified many more Minis along the way.

This book is about modifying A-Series and A-Plus-engined Minis, primarily for road use. It cannot possibly contain everything in absolute detail. That would take many volumes, if indeed it would even be possible to assemble. There are many, many ways of modifying Minis and many methods; a modified Mini is every bit as individual as its owner. Hopefully, there is something here for everyone – a reference manual for those in the know, and a guide to what is possible for those new to the game.

The Mini, an all-British car, is the only car, as far as I know, ever to be responsible for a new word in the dictionary, and surely it is the most modified car of all time. Long may the trend continue.

Tim Mundy
January 2003

acknowledgements

Many people have helped me in putting this book together and it would be impossible to mention them all, but those who I feel deserve a special mention are as follows:

My parents George and Jean Mundy, as if they had not bought a Mini new in 1960 and again in 1964, I might never have become an enthusiast.

My wife Julie and sons Tom and William for putting up with me and my cars.

Monty Watkins, Editor of *MiniWorld* magazine, for recognising my potential as a motoring journalist.

Mark Hughes and Steve Rendle at Haynes. Also Jon Pressnell.

Also, in no particular order, the following friends for technical help and advice:

Keith Dodd, Justin Jeffery and all the team at Mini Spares Centre

Rob Walker of Rob Walker Engineering

Bryan, Neil and Ian Slark of Slark Race Engineering

James Sutton and everyone at Mini Speed

Bill Richards of Bill Richards Racing

Tim Harber of Mini Mail

Neil Booth and Richard Hawcroft at Mini Spares North

Chris Wooden of The Mini Shop

Pete Hines and Graham Phillips at Somerford Mini Specialists

Ian Hargreaves of Avonbar

Trevor Langfield of Wizards of Nos

Spam at Spamspeed

Steve Whitton and all the staff at MED

Introduction

Modified Minis come in all shapes and sizes. This is a particularly immaculate Mini Cooper lookalike.

Minis have been modified almost from day one. The first name to be associated with Mini tuning was Downton, who were later involved with the development of the Cooper and Cooper S models in the 1960s. Many of the BMC Special Tuning conversions were manufactured by Downton.

Every enthusiast wanted a Cooper, and if they did not have one they wanted their 850cc Mini to be as 'Cooper-like' as possible; this became even more so when the works teams proved so successful in rallying and racing. The Mini must have encouraged more people into motorsport than any other car before or since, and it went further; for those who did not race on the track built themselves a fast Mini for the road. Tuning companies have come, some have gone, some have gone and come back again. This is all part of the huge tuning and accessory market which grew from humble beginnings into the multi-million-pound industry that it is today.

A highly
modified
1,340cc MkI.

A furious
1,430cc
Clubman.

The rally look is popular, but this one is genuine.

Everyone has had a go with a Mini Hot Rod, including Rover.

What are you trying to achieve?

The possibilities when modifying a Mini are almost endless, but one thing is certain: whether you intend simply to fit a Stage 1 kit and a set of alloy wheels, or go for a full ground-up build with radical body mods and a 1,430cc engine, there is something for everyone, and all of it can be enormous fun.

Really the first thing to do is to decide upon the style of modified Mini you would like: classic, modern, rough-and-ready, rally or race replica, smooth lines, deseamed body, and so on. You may prefer to buy a ready-modified car and improve upon it, or buy a standard car and start from scratch. The other thing to consider is whether to build a concours Mini or an everyday user; perhaps both. The great thing is that a Mini is small and it is often possible to have a couple (or even more) – one that you don't mind using and parking, and one for 'best' or to take to shows.

Mini-based kit cars were popular in the 1970s.

A real cooking version – some Minis are hotter than others…

Buying the right Mini to modify is important. There are lots of good cars for sale, but there is also some terrible rubbish about. Worse still, there is the rubbish that is made to look good and fool the untrained (sometimes even the trained) eye.

The simple fact is that Minis rust absolutely everywhere, and it is important to check all the vulnerable areas fully, whatever type of Mini you are buying. The older the car the more important it is to check thoroughly for rust, but even Minis as new as five years old can have holed sills and rear valances.

Accident damage can happen to any Mini, and so can poor quality bodged repair work. It is important to buy a Mini which is structurally sound or can be made to be, and this is even more so when the car is destined to be modified, as greater stresses are imposed upon both the body and the mechanicals. Make a decision at this point as to whether you want a car requiring some restoration, one that is sound or one that has already been restored properly.

Distinguishing marks

The style of modifications carried out to a Mini ideally need to be in period with the age of the car. Here is a quick guide to what was made when.

MkI 1959–1967

Engines: 848cc standard. Coopers: 997cc, 998cc. Cooper S: 970cc, 1,071cc,1,275cc.
Gearboxes: Three-synchro; 'magic wand' gear lever; Coopers had remote change. Green flashing light on indicator control.
Brakes: Single-leading-shoe drums to August 1964, twin-leading-shoe thereafter. Cooper 997cc, 998cc: 7in discs. Cooper S: 7.5in discs and rear spacer-drums.
Suspension: Saloons: dry rubber-cone suspension to September 1964, then Hydrolastic suspension. *Estates and commercials:* 'dry' suspension throughout.
Grille: Rounded radiator grille with moustache and ends.
Body: External door hinges, large interior pockets, sliding windows. Door handle bosses from 1966. Rear side windows when opening use piano hinge. Smaller rear window and smaller rounded rear lights. Hinged rear numberplate.
Interior: Vinyl upholstery, no padding to lower dash rail, 'magic wand' gear lever; Coopers have remote change. Green flashing light on indicator control.

MkII 1967–1969 ('1275 S' to 1970)

Engines: 848cc, 998cc. Mini Cooper: 998cc. Cooper S: 1,275cc.
Gearbox: Three-synchro, then four-synchro from September 1968. Mini 850: 'magic wand' change; Mini 1000: remote change.
Suspension: Saloons: Hydrolastic. Utilities: dry. Steering has improved turning circle.
Brakes: Twin-leading-shoe. Cooper and Cooper S: 7in and 7.5in discs respectively.
Body: Bolder bevelled grille, external door hinges, larger rear lights, larger rear window.
Interior: More sumptuously trimmed. Deeper padding to lower dash rail, indicator stalk now controls the horn, indicators and headlamp dip/flash.

MkIII 1969–1976

General: Austin and Morris names deleted, Mini Clubman, Clubman Estate and 1275GT introduced; 998cc Cooper, Countryman/Estate, Riley Elf and Wolseley Hornet discontinued.
Engines: 848cc/998cc. 1275GT and Cooper S: 1.275cc.
Gearbox: Mini 850: 'magic wand'. Other manual models: remote change. Rod gearchange on all models from January 1973.
Suspension: Mini 850 and 1000 saloons 'dry' suspension. Clubman Saloon, 1275GT, MkIII Cooper S: Hydrolastic until July 1971.
Brakes: Twin-leading-shoe drums. 1275GT and S: 7.5in discs.

Body: Internal door hinges, restyled bootlid with larger body-colour numberplate light.
Interior: Wind-up windows; door pockets deleted.

MkIV 1976–1984

As MkIII but with the following modifications:
Suspension: Front subframe rubber-mounted, rear subframe rubber mountings enlarged; softer springs.

Body: From July 1977, Mini saloons from 1000 upwards fitted with Innocenti-style rear light clusters with built-in reversing lights. Gutter drip-rail deleted and plastic trim fitted from 1979. Extra sound-deadening material fitted to the floorpan areas from 1980 onwards.
Interior: Twin column-mounted control stalks. New switch panel with different hazard-warning-lights switch. Larger pedals from the Allegro.

MkV 1984–1992

Shell as Mk IV. Standardisation of front 8.4in disc brakes, and fitment of 12in wheels and Mini Special wheelarch extensions. From 1986 onwards, side repeater indicators on front wings. Engine 998cc until 1990, when 1,275cc unit reappears in A-Plus form, first in RSP (Rover Special Products) Cooper.

MkVI 1991–1997

1.3i fuel-injected engine in Cooper, with three-way catalyst. Non-Coopers had carburettors until 1995. Modified front subframe, engine moved forward, and internal bonnet release from late 1992.

MkVII 1997–2000

Twin-point injection, front-mounted radiator, driver's airbag, side impact bars in doors. Sports Pack with 13in wheels optional.

What to look for: body

- Check the paintwork, looking for differing shades and patterns in the paint, and varying levels of shine. Inspect the car as a whole: does it look right, or does it appear to have been bodged?

- Similarly, look at the rear end and boot-lid alignment.

- Check the floor, inner sills, and wheelarches for rust, filler, damp and rippling from accident damage. A raised floor indicates trolley-jack damage; if the floor is sound it can be beaten out. Bodged repairs are common.

- Do the same to the rear floor and inner sills, paying attention to the seat-belt mounting points.

- Look under the rear seat cushion for corrosion on the seat pan and right underneath at the heelboard.

- Lift the rear pocket liner, and inspect inside. If rust here is bad, the subframe and road beneath will be visible.

- The metal behind the dash by the fresh-air vents also corrodes. It is difficult to inspect as the dash covering needs to be removed or at least pulled back, which is not easy without damaging it. This area is worth checking if suspect, though, as it is difficult to repair, and is often bodged with filler or seam-sealer.

- Look at the outer sills. MkI and MkII should have four vents, and MkIII onwards six vents. Oversills are common, and are fitted because they are cheap to buy and less work to fit than genuine sills. Unless the old panel and all rust were removed before fitting, horrors are usually hidden behind such panels. Sometimes, indeed, several layers of oversill are present. The door steps which form the top of the sills can suffer too.

- Inside the boot, check the floor – in particular at the rear, where the wiring for the rear lights is fitted, and in the corners. Look all around the battery box, and at the box itself. Look at the rear wheelarch around the damper mounting. Only one side is visible in regular saloons, while on twin-tank cars both sides are hidden. On vans, pick-ups and estates both mountings can be seen.

- The rear wheelarches should be checked thoroughly, including the area around the top damper mounting.

■ Examine the rear subframe mounting points, including those at the rear of the frame. In some cases, the front mounts at the edges of the heelboard will have all but disappeared!

■ The rear subframe itself should come in for close scrutiny. If it needs replacing, this is not a problem, provided the mounting areas on the body are sound.

■ Check the rear valance and the closing panels which form the rear of the arch.

■ MkI, MkII, and van/pick-up doors rust in the pockets and around their lower frame. MkIII internal-hinge doors rust first, as a rule, along the bottom edge of the door skin. Door skins can be replaced, provided that it is only the skin that is rotten and not the frame itself. Sometimes it is just the frame, and the skin appears OK, but in all cases, filler bodging is common.

■ On MkIII and onwards, the door area by the check strap can crack, and on pre-1973 cars the strap mount can pull out. From mid-1973, doors were strengthened at this point. Rust is also a problem where the door hinges mount to the car; in bad cases the top hinge can pull out completely, and the door will drop off.

■ Mks I and II A-panels (between the door and front wing) rust around the external hinges while MkIII and later A-panels rust along their edge, in front of the door. On Mk III and later panels before this happens, though, the spot

Check the floor both sides at the front...

welds 'pull', as a result of corrosion causing internal swelling, and a series of dents appears down the panel. Corrosion occurs also in the wheelarch near the A-panel.

■ Front wings need examining for poor fit and poor welding if they have been replaced, and also for filler and rust. Inner wings need checking around the top damper mount and inside the engine compartment along the front edge. Accident damage and corrosion both occur here. The same applies with the front panel.

■ Front subframe mounts sometimes corrode.

■ Roofs can rust in the corners and particular care is needed when a vinyl roof is fitted, as on the Mini 1100 Special, because the panel rusts under the vinyl.

■ Gutter upright trims are not structural, but do rust and look unsightly. If rust is present on the body, paint repairs can be expensive.

■ Rust often starts around the rear opening window; this is more of a problem on later cars, where the join in the window frame fouls the body. Even if there is only slight evidence of rust, it is best to open the window and check, as rust holes quickly develop.

■ Good chrome adds value and improves all Minis.

The legal side

■ The vehicle identification number (VIN) is located on the offside front wing on later Minis, and at various points on and around the inner wings and front panel on older Minis. Check that the plate has not been tampered with. It is very important to confirm the identity of any Mini, particularly when buying privately. The registration document should have the seller's correct name and address, and it is worth checking past MoT certificates, service history (if there is one to verify), the mileage, and that the car is genuine. To avoid buying a car with a hidden history, particularly if it is a newer Mini, it is worth contacting the AA or HPI, who will check the vehicle for you for a fee before you buy. This will ensure that it has not been recorded as an insurance write off, or been involved in a major accident, and that it is not stolen, or has outstanding finance attached to it.

What to look for: mechanicals

■ When going to look at a Mini, take a trolley-jack and axle stands if possible and ask the owner if you can jack the car up at each corner. Make sure that the car is properly chocked and supported.

■ During the test drive make sure that the car runs smoothly, and the engine is responsive.

■ Ask the owner to drive the car away from you on a quiet road, and check the car is running in a straight line and not crabbing. Crabbing can be caused by either bodywork or mechanical problems.

■ The engine should run smoothly, with no undue tappet noise. Listen carefully for timing chain rattle at the radiator end of the engine, and noisy main/big-end bearings – the symptoms of which are knocking or rumbling from the bottom end.

■ Check the engine mountings by grasping the rocker cover and attempting to rock the engine back and forth.

■ Take a look at the condition of the radiator, the fan belt and the cooling system as a whole, including the heater valve and radiator and heater hoses.

■ Look for oil leaks, particularly around the head gasket and timing-cover areas. Remove the oil filler cap and look for condensation and creaminess both on the bottom of the cap and by feeling the underside of the rocker cover; be careful, though, as some have sharp edges. If 'cream' is present, it is a strong indication that the oil has not been changed regularly.

■ Remove the dipstick and check the oil for level, freshness and creaminess within the oil, this last indicating water content caused by head gasket problems or worse.

■ The clutch should be free from judder and slip. Synchromesh should be in good order, so pay particular attention when changing down from third to second. On automatic cars make sure that all gears engage and change cleanly, with no slip or clunking. Check for oil leaks, especially at the back of the gearbox on rod-change cars. Look at the sump drain plug: leaks can be an indication of stripped threads.

■ Drive the car on full lock in both directions to check for CV joint wear: if the joint is worn it will click or knock.

■ Inspect the front subframe for any damage or rusting. Subframe mountings can be inspected visually for deterioration and then the bodyshell rocked from side to side – in bad cases the body of the car will move and the subframe will not.

■ Check the rear subframe for rust and damage. Also look at the subframe mountings, particularly the larger type fitted to post-1976 Minis. Check the flexible fuel pipe from the tank where it passes through the boot floor, and ensure that the rubber grommet is present and correct.

■ With estates, pick-ups and vans check the condition of the fuel tank – see if you can smell petrol, as the tanks rust out on top.

...and also at the rear.

Check the sills
(right)...

...the front
wings (right)...
and A-panels
(far right). . .

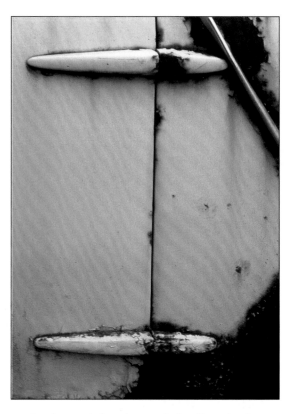

Check the fuel lines underneath, particularly
the union on the tank.

- Look at the ride height all round and from
  side to side. Measure the distance between
  the top of the tyre and the bottom of the
  arch. Some variation is common, with the
  driver's side being lower.

- Check the tyres, for quality, tread depth and
  general condition.

- Brakes on all Minis from 1984 are 8.4in discs
  at the front, and they should stop the car well
  and in a straight line, as should earlier disc-
  braked Minis with the Cooper S 7.5in discs.
  Twin-leading-shoe drums should also stop the
  car in a straight line, and a sharp pull to one
  side indicates leaking or seized wheel
  cylinders. Veering to one side often means
  adjustment is out of balance, it can also mean
  a leaking or seized rear cylinder.

- Jack the car up at the front end and check the
  steering swivels, the track-rod ends and the

steering rack for play, and also the wheel
bearings; at the same time inspect the CV-
joint rubber gaiters for splits. Examine the
flexible brake hoses for splits and the dampers
for leaks. At the rear, check for play in the rear
radius-arm bearings by trying to move the
wheel in and out while watching the bearing.
Wheel bearings can be checked by holding
the wheel at the top and bottom and rocking.
The handbrake must be off to check wheel
bearings.

- Don't forget the rear tyres, and if you can
  remove the wheels it is worth checking the
  condition of the rear flexible brake hoses.
  Check the clearance between the inside of
  the tyre and the shock absorber, it should be
  the same on both sides of the car.

- Hydrolastic models are more softly sprung.
  Check that Hydrolastic cars sit level: if one side
  is low there is probably a leak in the system.

- Try moving the steering wheel up and down to
  check the steering column bushes for play.

Check the rear seat pan (far right...

...and wheelarches/ heelboard (right).

Check for free play in the steering by turning the steering wheel slightly and watching the wheels. Also check that the steering self-centres.

■ On high-mileage cars check the clutch and brake pedals for sideways movement, indicating worn bushes. Look for signs of hydraulic fluid leaking down the brake or clutch pedals, particularly on early Minis.

■ Check that all instrumentation and warning lights are in working order. During your test run, keep an eye on the water temperature and oil-pressure gauges if fitted, and make sure that the heater controls work, and that the heater actually heats. Try the lights, indicators, hazard warning lights, wipers and washers, and both the front window winders.

■ Take a look in the boot at the battery, and the spare wheel for condition and tyre tread depth. Check that the boot lock works.

Specialist suppliers

Mini enthusiasts are lucky in that there are a large number of parts and accessories suppliers, and also engineering and tuning companies specialising in the Mini. Many are very good. There are also some very good restoration companies for those who do not want to carry out body repairs themselves. Both new and second-hand parts are in plentiful supply as are genuine and reproduction body panels.

Safety

This book is all about altering your Mini. Some of it is cosmetic, some mechanical, much of it aimed at improving the performance – which means not just making your car go faster, but making it corner and brake in a suitably uprated manner too. Fitting a 1,275cc engine gives a sizeable performance increase, but so does fitting twin carbs and a modified head with suitable exhaust to your standard 850 Mini. It is important in either instance that the brakes and suspension are fully up to the job. Indeed, they need to be upgraded before any serious tuning work is undertaken, and front drum brakes should ideally be replaced by a disc installation. The great majority of modifications and improvements detailed will affect the safety of the vehicle if the work is not carried out properly by a competent person. If you have any doubt as to your ability to do the work, then you should entrust it to a qualified specialist.

Insurance

Upgrading the performance of a Mini will affect the insurance so it is essential to obtain a quote from your insurance company before carrying out any such work. There are a number of specialist Mini insurance companies who can offer competitive premiums.

02 the engine

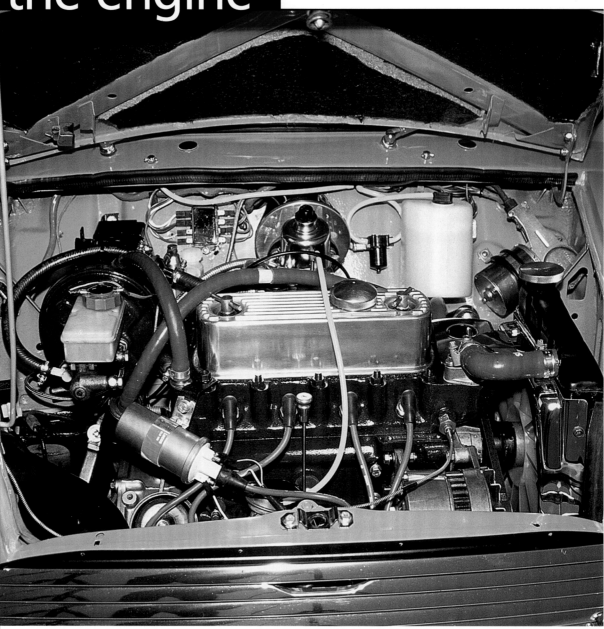

A general view
of a modified
Mini engine.

Tuning a Mini does not necessarily mean removing the engine and carrying out a
full rebuild and uprating performance at the same time, and it does not mean
that your 998cc engine must be thrown away in favour of a 1,275cc unit.
Provided that the engine and transmission are in good, sound condition it is
possible to bolt on additional power. Engine tuning for a long time has been
broken down into stages, the only problem with this being that different tuners
work to different specifications as the stages go up. Stages 1 to 3 are normally
bolt-on while Stage 4 and upwards require a cam change and therefore at this
point the engine should also be rebuilt and balanced.

Stages of tune
Stage 1 kits
Stage 1 kits are available from just about every Mini specialist and are a very worthwhile fitment. The kit consists of an uprated exhaust manifold which can be either a Cooper freeflow or an LCB, depending upon the kit supplier and engine size, an uprated inlet manifold, a K&N air filter or similar, plus a richer carburettor needle, and a decent exhaust system which is usually a Maniflow or an RC40. Most kits claim around a 20 per cent improvement on a 998cc engine. In a *MiniWorld/Keeping Your Mini Alive (KYMA)* test we managed to get 51bhp from a 998cc Mini which was standard apart from electronic ignition using a kit from the Mini Shop. The exercise certainly backed up the claims.

Stage 2
To go from Stage 1 to Stage 2 is a case of fitting a modified head. In the case of 1,275cc engines this will probably mean retaining standard valve sizes. A carburettor needle change will usually be required too.

Stage 3
Stage 3 involves fitting a larger-valve head and uprating the carburation.

Stage 4
Stage 4 and beyond will involve a cam upgrade. This requires the engine to be removed from the car and a full engine rebuild which should include strengthening the crankshaft and balancing all rotating components.

A 998cc Stage 1 tuning kit.

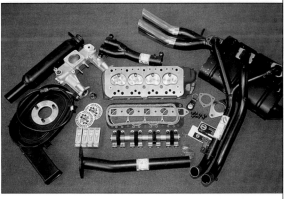

A Cooper 90bhp tuning kit.

Changing engines
Engine selection

Original A-Series engines were available in the following forms. All these engines are relevant to the Mini, but those in brackets were originally fitted to the 1100/1300 range.	*In A-Plus form the engine line-up is:*
848cc	998cc
997cc Cooper twin-carb	1,275cc with HIF38 carb
998cc single-carb	1,275cc with HIF44 carb (both Mini and Metro)
998cc Cooper twin-carb	1,275cc single-point injection 53bhp
970cc Cooper S	63bhp S, and 1,275cc multi-point injection
1,071cc Cooper S	
1,098cc single-carb (1,098cc twin-carb)	
1,275cc single-carb, (1,275cc twin-carb)	
1,275cc Cooper S	

Original engines

cc	bhp	Carb (in)	Fitted to	Tunability	Availability
A-Series					
848	34	1¼SU	Mini Mks I, II, III	good	average
848	36	1½ SU	Mini Mks III, IV	good	average
997	55	Twin 1¼	Cooper MkI	average	poor
998	38	1¼ SU	Elf/Hornet Mini 1000 Mks II, III	v. good	good
998	55	Twin 1½	Cooper Mks I, II	v. good	poor
1098	45	1¼ SU	Austin/Morris 1100	good	average
1098	45	1½ SU	Clubman 1100	good	good
1098	55	Twin 1¼	MG 1100 etc.	good	poor
1275	60	1½ SU	1275GT, 1300	v. good	good
1275	70	Twin 1¼	1300GT, MG 1300	v. good	poor
Cooper S engines					
970	65	Twin 1¼	970 Cooper S	v. good	v. poor
1071	70	Twin 1¼	1071 Cooper S	v. good	v. poor
1275	75	Twin 1¼	1275 Cooper S	v. good	v. poor
A-Plus engines					
998	40	1½ SU	Mini, Metro	v. good	v. good
1275	55	HIF38	Metro 1.3	v. good	v.good
1275	70	HIF44	MG Metro	v. good	good
1275	50	HIF38	Mini 1.3	good	v. good
1275	53	SPi	Mini 1.3i	good	good
1275	63	SPi	Mini Cooper 1.3i	good	good
1275	70	MPi	Mini and Cooper	good	good
1275	93	Turbo	MG Metro Turbo	v. good	average

Which engine is best?

The above chart is an overall guide only. There are often variations within groups, an example of this being the twin-carburettor 1,275cc non-'S' engine fitted to the 1300GT and MG/Wolseley/Riley/Vanden Plas 1300 variants. The GT engine is close to Mark III Cooper S specification, and the same engine is used in some MG 1300 models. Other MGs have a twin-carburettor engine with the smaller-valve single-carb head, and this same unit was found generally in the Wolseley/Riley/VP cars.

Which engine is best? Very few people tune 850s these days – unless building a period Mini, although this can be great fun and should not be dismissed. The 998cc unit is not as popular as it once was, mainly because of the easy availability of 1,275cc engines. Again, though, it really should not be overlooked as it is considered by many to be the most tuneable Mini engine. The 998cc engine is the sweetest revving, and very respectable power can be achieved – especially when a 12G940 1,275cc head is fitted. The project Mini used in a 998cc build with Slark Race Engineering for *Keeping Your Mini Alive* magazine achieved 82.1bhp at the flywheel when fitted with a special cam and a modified 12G940 head. The 1,098cc engine can be considered as a long-stroke 998cc, the advantage being the extra 100cc. In the past, 1,098cc units have been largely dismissed because of this long stroke, but if they were not the best engine for the race track, they are very good on the road. That said, the '1275' is the way to go for extra capacity and all-out power.

A-Series and A-Plus – the differences

A-Plus engines are visually different as well as being slightly technically different from the original A-Series. The blocks of both 998cc and 1,275cc engines are stiffened and the strengthening ribs are clearly visible even when the engine is in the car. They are most noticeable by the dipstick hole just below the core plugs on the front of the block; while 998cc A-Plus engines have tappet side covers, 1275 engines have a solid wall block. This is also true of A-Series engines: the 850cc, 998cc, and 1,098cc engines have tappet cover plates, but 1,275cc non-'S' and most MkIII 'S' engines do not. However, the 970cc, 1,071cc and 1,275cc Cooper S engines all have these side covers.

Engine Swaps

A popular way of uprating a Mini is to fit the engine and transmission unit from an MG Metro. MG Metro and other 1,275cc Metro engines are readily available from breakers as well as privately. It is a good idea to recondition the Metro engine before fitting.

There are a considerable number of minor differences between a Metro unit and a Mini unit which need to be corrected before installation in a Mini can take place. The main changes are as follows:

■ Mini engine mountings should be used.

■ Metros were fitted with non-Verto hydraulically operated clutches until 1985. If the Metro unit is non-Verto and the Mini to which it is being fitted is also non-Verto there will be no problem. If a later Verto Metro unit is being fitted to a Verto-clutch Mini, the Mini operating lever will need to be fitted, and the easiest way to do this is to fit the Mini clutch cover. Verto and non-Verto system parts should not be intermixed: if necessary, convert to one or the other. The Mini master cylinder is common to both types but the slave cylinder and flexible hoses are not.

■ A Mini pre-engaged starter or inertia-type

starter must be used as the Metro one will not fit in a Mini. Pre-engaged starters are a lot more expensive to replace when they go wrong, which may be a consideration, but changing to the earlier type starter – which I prefer – will also mean changing the starter ring gear.

■ The MG Metro carburettor is an HIF44, and it is suitable for use on a Mini. Most people use a K&N filter and a richer needle.

■ The cylinder head will need to be drilled to accept the Mini heater valve.

■ The thermostat housing needs to be changed for a Mini item.

■ The breather timing cover can be retained, but the Mini fan and pulley will need transferring. Spacers are usually needed to prevent the fan fouling on the Metro 1275 timing cover breather.

■ The electronic distributor can be wired into the Mini's electrical system, but a far better alternative is to use a new distributor with the correct advance curve from the specialist range offered by Aldon Automotive.

■ Dispose of the oil filter assembly and fit the Mini filter assembly.

■ The gearchange linkage is straightforward if you are fitting it to a rod-change Mini: you simply transfer the Mini's rod-change mechanism with all its bracketry. It is worthwhile replacing the oil seal to prevent leakage.

■ Driveshafts are no problem if you are fitting them to a Mini with pot joints, as the Mini ones will fit. If fitting to an earlier Mini the shafts will have to be changed for later Mini shafts with pot joints. A Mini rod-change will also be needed, together with the necessary bracketry to fit the change to the floor when a remote-change or automatic Mini is involved.

Off-the-shelf engines

An alternative to tuning the existing engine in a Mini, or rebuilding a Metro engine, is to buy an off-the-shelf engine from one of the engine specialists. Many will want an exchange unit, and most will not be prepared to accept a 998cc in part exchange for a 1,275cc engine. Prices for off-the-shelf engines vary considerably, and so does specification and quality. Do your homework before buying.

Really wild conversions

There is a growing trend amongst some enthusiasts to fit non-Mini engines. Most common are the K-Series, Honda Vtec, and also occasionally motorcycle engines. The question of whether a Mini so equipped is still a proper Mini is up to the individual to decide. Such conversions are a subject in themselves and therefore are not covered in this book.

Balancing

Any A-Series engine will benefit from being balanced. It does not actually increase power or the rpm potential of the engine to any significant degree, but it does make the engine run considerably smoother and this reduced vibration should help make the engine last longer. Pistons should be balanced unless supplied ready balanced as in the case of Omegas, the crank and flywheel/clutch assembly should be balanced, and the rods balanced end-for-end, so that the ends of all four rods are matched in weight, as well as having the weight equalised overall. It is also worthwhile balancing the crankshaft damper.

Automatics
Tuning automatics

The main problem when tuning an automatic is that the standard camshaft must be retained or the engine will not pull away from rest cleanly. Tuning in the form of a modified head, inlet and exhaust system is beneficial, but the improvement is not as marked as with a manual-transmission car.

A way of gaining more power in a 998cc auto is to fit the 1,275cc auto engine and box from either a later Mini or a Metro automatic. This can be increased in size to 1,380cc, and

Removing the engine.

An MG Metro engine ready for reconditioning.

A Honda Vtec engine in a Mini.

A motorcycle engine being installed in a Mini.

given a modified head and a decent exhaust system. A number of mods need to be carried out when fitting a Metro auto unit into an earlier Mini. These are along similar lines to fitting an MG Metro engine, and involve changing the engine mountings and the torque converter cover. The subframe also needs to be modified to clear the larger selector valve on the Metro engine.

Converting an automatic to manual
Automatic Minis can be converted to manual transmission. The automatic subframe differs from the manual in that it is wider in the engine mounting area to accommodate the automatic 'box. Although it is possible to make up and use spacers on the engine mountings, the best way is to fit a manual subframe. A manual power unit including engine, gearbox and gearchange mechanism will be required. The hole for the gearchange in the floor is the same, there being no difference in the bodyshell. A manual pedal box, clutch master cylinder and relevant pipework are also required.

Balancing the crankshaft assembly.

Dyno tuning

When any engine tuning is carried out on a Mini it is essential to have the car fully set-up on a rolling road. Fully rebuilt, tuned engines can also be set up and tested on a bench dyno before being installed in the car, where the tuning company has this facility.

The benefits of proper setting up cannot be over-emphasised, not least because if this is not done serious engine damage can result. Even if you haven't tuned the car and it is still standard (perhaps you need to build up an insurance no-claims bonus), it is worth visiting a rolling road for a tune-up – you will be surprised by the results.

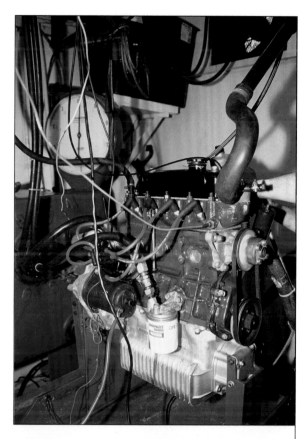

The bench dyno at Slark Race Engineering.

Peter Baldwin's rolling road.

the cylinder head

Fitting a modified head to a Mini is very rewarding. It is the next step after fitting a Stage 1 kit, and it will further increase the power considerably. Even gas-flowing and porting the standard head while retaining the standard valves will make a big difference.

Small-bore Mini engines can have the standard head modified and larger valves fitted as well, but a better alternative is to fit a 12G295 head as originally used in the 998cc Cooper – if you can find a good one. The 12G295 is similar in design to the 12G940 '1275' head, and bolting one on in standard form will be good for 7bhp or more, provided that the compression ratio is adjusted accordingly by removing metal from the head face. In recent times, partly due to a reduced number of 12G295 heads in circulation, it has become fashionable to fit 12G940 heads to 998cc Minis. In standard form this produces very good power, and when the head is modified the results are even better. When a '940' head is fitted to a small-bore block, pockets need to be cut in the block to prevent the valves from hitting the block face at full lift.

The 1,275cc (and larger) engine benefits from a modified 12G940 head, and as the level of tune increases larger valves are beneficial too.

A good performance head is fully ported and gas-flowed, with the chambers modified, reshaped and polished. Another important requirement is to burette the chambers (by filling with a measured amount of liquid) in order to equalise them and to calculate the compression ratio. To enable this to be done, information on the bore size and piston type and height for the particular engine is required. Valve height must also be set accurately: I have seen a number of cheaper heads on the market which are very bad in this respect.

There are many companies that supply modified heads, and some of them are very good indeed.

Original heads

Engine	Casting No	Inlet	Exhaust	cc
848cc & 998cc	2A628 & 12A1456	1.0625	1.00	24.5
998cc A-Plus	CAM4180	1.0625	1.00	25.5
997cc & 1098cc	12G202	1.156	1.00	26.1
998cc Cooper	12G206 & 12G295	1.218	1.00	28.3
1275cc non-'S'	12G940	1.3125	1.156	21.4
MG Metro & MkIII S	12G940	1.401	1.156	21.4
MkI S	12A185	1.401	1.218	21.4
Mks I & II S	AEG163	1.401	1.218	21.4
MkIII S	12G1805	1.401	1.156	21.4

The 12G940 is fitted to 1,275cc A-Plus including the MG Metro and Turbo.

Crack testing a 12G940 at Oselli Engineering.

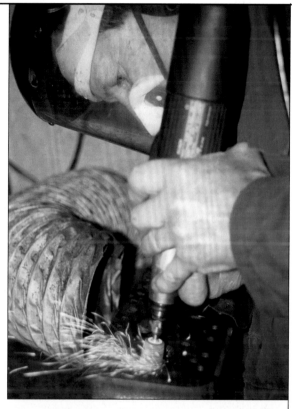

Far Left:
Refacing a
cylinder head.

Left: Modifying
a Stage 3
12G940.

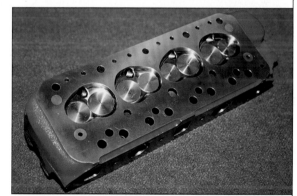

Far Left: A close-
up of the mods
taking shape.

Left Above: The
finished Stage 3
head.

Left below: A
close-up of the
chamber.

The block modification required when fitting a 12G940 head to a 998cc block.

Modifications for unleaded fuel

Minis with 998cc engines from the Mini 30 onwards (1989) should be able to use unleaded petrol without modification. 1,275cc engines from some time in 1989 onwards should also be fine for unleaded, and all 1990s 1,275cc Coopers are definitely able to run on unleaded. All fuel-injection Minis and all those fitted with catalytic converters must only use unleaded of course, which can be 95 octane Premium or 97/98 Super Unleaded.

When engines designed for leaded fuel run on unleaded the exhaust valves suffer seat recession. The inlet valves are cooled by the incoming fuel, whereas exhaust valves are heated by the outgoing exhaust gasses. Unleaded fuel burns hotter, and there is no build-up of lead to protect the seats. The remedy is to fit hardened inserts to the seats of the exhaust valves.

These are the parts that are needed to convert a Mini to run on unleaded petrol. They include hardened inserts for the exhaust seats, new valve guides, and a good-quality head-gasket set.

Octane numbers

The octane rating is the 'knock' rating of the fuel – or to put it very simply, the lower the octane number, the greater the risk of pinking, and so higher-octane fuel is important for performance. Most pre-1990 Minis in theory require 98 octane fuel, but they normally run perfectly happily, even when performance-tuned, on 97 octane fuel. Factory unleaded Minis are designed to run on 95 octane Premium Unleaded, but converted Minis need to either run on Super Unleaded or have the timing retarded to compensate – which will in turn reduce power slightly.

Fitting inserts is, technically, the only conversion work that is required to enable the engine to run on unleaded fuel. In practice, though, the cylinder head will need to be fully reconditioned at the same time and new valve guides will also almost certainly need to be fitted unless the originals have covered only a nominal mileage. Fitting valve-seat inserts is a highly skilled operation and if not done correctly the results can be disastrous. Pick the engineering company to carry out the work carefully, or if buying a ready-made unleaded head check that it originates from a reputable source. Unleaded heads can be modified in exactly the same way as leaded heads.

Over-the-counter modified heads

Many Mini specialists sell ready-modified heads over the counter. The standard of these is on the whole good, and many are produced by top head specialists. Buy only from a reputable specialist. Many will still want an old head in exchange.

Seven-port and eight-port heads

Eight-port heads manufactured by Arden and used on some of the works Minis are available again from Mini Spares, made on the original tooling. Eight-port heads went out of favour a few years ago as five-port power caught up, but recently eight-port technology has been further developed by Bill Richards Engineering and today some spectacularly high power outputs are obtainable. The eight-port head is a crossflow design with the carburettors mounted at the front of the Mini power unit. Four Amal carburettors, or twin Webers, normally provide carburation and a special four-branch exhaust

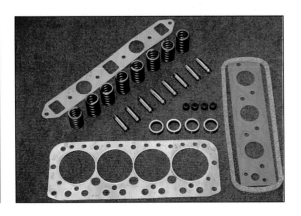

manifold is used. A number of engine modifications are required and special eight-port camshafts must be used.

Seven-port heads were developed in the 1960s in Denmark and at the time proved very successful, but production stopped and little was heard about them for a long time. They are now making a comeback and could become the next 'big thing' in Mini tuning. Seven-port heads are crossflow, like the eight-port, but there are only three exhaust ports, as per the five-port head. This means that a conventional LCB exhaust system can be used; the valve sequence is also similar to a five-porter and similar camshafts can be used. The centre cylinders exhaust at 360° intervals and so there is no sharing of exhaust time (ie more than one cylinder producing exhaust); therefore the seven-port head makes a great deal of sense. Very high power outputs are achievable too.

16-valve twin-cam conversions

Sixteen-valve heads for Minis are produced by KAD and Jack Knight. Fitting a 16-valve head is not a simple bolt-on conversion; the engine must be removed and cut-outs have to be machined in the block. The bottom end of the engine also needs to be strengthened to cope with the additional power. KAD produce two versions of their 16-valve head: the first is capable of producing power outputs of 110-120bhp, and the second produces 140–150bhp. The 110bhp version requires a tuftrided A-Plus crank and centre main strap, preferably the four-bolt variety. The higher-output version imposes much more strain on the bottom end of the engine and therefore a billet or forged crank with special rods and a four-bolt centre main strap are needed. A periodic stripdown is necessary as is normal with most competition cars. The Jack Knight head is not so common and is very expensive. It was fitted to Rover's one-off Mini Hot Rod.

Studs

When fitting a modified head it is best to replace the head studs and nuts. For mild-to-mid tune, a new standard set is perfectly adequate, but very highly tuned engines will benefit from specialist upgraded head studs

The KAD 16-valve head.

and nuts. Competition head stud sets are manufactured by APT and Mini Spares.

Gaskets

Good-quality gaskets, particularly the head gasket, are a must. I have always used Payen gaskets, as used by most engine builders. In most cases, gaskets can be purchased from the machine shop modifying the cylinder head. Turbos require special gaskets which are harder to find, the best bet being to go through a Turbo specialist such as Avonbar.

Compression ratios

Compression ratios today need to be around 9.75:1–10:1 for the road, 10.5:1 for very fast road, and 12:1 for full-race engines. A compression ratio of around 10:1 is really considered to be about the safest upper limit for running on 95 octane fuel, although some people successfully run slightly higher. Engines running on 97 octane fuel can go higher, but remember that it is a lot easier to raise the compression ratio than to lower it.

The Jack Knight 16-valve head installed in Rover's Mini Hot Rod.

valves, guides and rockers

There is quite a lot of power to be gained from modifying the valve train on an A-Series engine to complement a modified cylinder head. Upgrades to the rocker gear are among the most popular engine mods today.

Fitting larger valves

Fitting larger valves and modifying the cylinder head accordingly is very good for performance. The 12G940 head, which most people use today for the 998cc as well as the 1,275cc engine, comes in two versions. The standard has 1.3125in (33.3mm) inlet valves and 1.156in (29.4mm) exhausts, while the MG Metro/MkIII 'S'/late Cooper version has 1.401in (35.6mm) inlets and 1.156in (29.4mm) exhausts. The smaller-valved version can be easily fitted with the larger, 1.4in (35.6mm) valves and modified by an engineering shop.

The need to modify heads to cope with unleaded fuel has generally restricted the use of very large valves, and many machine shops will not fit exhaust valves larger than 1.156in (29.4mm) to an engine to which valve seat inserts have been fitted. However, some machine shops will go up to 1.218in (30.9mm) exhaust valves, with 1.401in inlets, bringing the head up to the old AEG163 Cooper S valve specification.

Valve sizes in performance cylinder heads vary slightly depending upon the specialist. To give an example, MED, who supply a large number of both fast road and race heads, fit the following size valves to their heads:

Head application	Head	In	Ex (mm)	Notes (mm)
Mild road 998cc	Std	29.3	25.4	997/1100cc sizes
Fast road 998cc	12G295	30.9	26.5	std sizes 12G295
Fast road 998cc	12G940	35.6	29.4	std 12G940
Tuned 1275/1293cc	12G940	35.7	30	unleaded
Tuned 1275/1293cc	12G940	35.7	31	leaded
Big bore 1380cc+	12G940	35.7	30	as 1293cc
Semi-race	12G940	37	30	
Full-race	12G940	38	31	offset valves

NB: *Later valves sizes are quoted in millimetres, not inches.*

A 12G940 unleaded head, with 1.401in (35.6mm) inlet and 1.218in (30.9mm) exhaust valves.

Rimflow valves

Rimflo valves provide anything between 5 per cent and 15 per cent more flow than most other performance valves, depending on the application. This is achieved by a flat back and modifications to the valve stem to reduce the bulk and therefore the amount of obstruction to the airflow. Rimflo valves are made out of EN214N stainless steel and they have chrome-plated stems so that they can be used with iron valve guides.

Valve guides and stem seals

Worn valve guides cost power and increase oil consumption and have no place in a performance engine. The standard valve guides are made of iron and are perfectly suitable for performance engines even when larger valves are fitted, provided they are in good condition.

They are not however suitable for valves made of EN214N steel – with the exception of Rimflo valves as detailed above.

Bronze guides are required when iron guides cannot be used, and these can also be used with most types of valve. They have traditionally been fitted to high-performance and competition engines, and I always have bronze guides fitted to all performance cylinder heads used on my own Minis. Different bronze guides are required for eight-port heads.

Top-hat valve stem seals should be fitted to inlet valve guides because there is a downwards pull caused by induction. They should not be fitted to exhaust valves because the pressure is outwards and little oil passes down the valve stem.

Valve springs

Performance valve springs should be stronger than the standard items to prevent valve bounce, but not too stiff or power will be lost. A range is available from specialists, and it is often a good idea to buy from your cam supplier. For example, Kent offer three types of spring: VS1 Iskendarian for road use, VS2 for road use, and VS39 for race. Different retainers are required for different springs: VR1 spring retainers are suitable for road use, and VR9 for race use with VS39 springs. Valve springs are included in the camshaft kits available from both Kent and Piper.

When dual valve springs are used, bottom spring locator collars should be fitted. These are available in standard form suitable for cams with up to 0.300in lift, and in competition form for cams with higher lift.

Rocker gear

The last part of the valvetrain before the valves themselves is the rocker gear. Three types of standard rocker were produced by the factory. The first was the Cooper S forged rocker which is incredibly strong but notorious for ratio inconsistency, which will vary the amount of lift, and the second was the pressed-steel rocker which was standard on most Minis until the 1980s. These do not look very high performance, but on a road car they are perfectly satisfactory. The third type is the A-Plus

Pressing in a bronze valve guide.

A valve stem seal.

Kent Cams valve springs and caps.

The standard A-Plus rocker gear.

The three types of A-Series rockers. Left to right: A-Plus, Cooper S forged (this one has been lightened) and pressed steel.

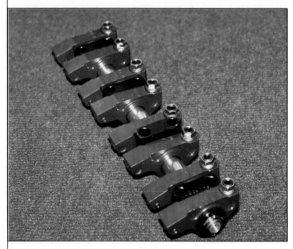

Kent Cams roller rockers.

sintered variety. These are fine for mildly tuned road engines and have the advantage of being cheap to buy. Whatever type you are using, make sure that they are not worn, and preferably use a tuftrided thick-wall rocker shaft. S-type forged rockers can be rebushed, but will then need honing to size.

High-lift rockers
The standard factory rocker ratio is 1.245:1. Higher-ratio rockers are available and they are ideal for use with a modified head. Fitting a set of 1.5:1 ratio rockers is the equivalent of going up to the next specification of camshaft, and a 1,275cc engine will gain around 4-5bhp.

Roller rockers of 1.7:1 ratio, as installed.

Forged high-lift Cooper S 1.5-ratio rockers are available as a set, together with a thick-wall rocker shaft, from Mini Spares.

Roller rockers
A further upgrade, which reduces friction and also looks attractive when the rocker cover is removed, is to fit roller rockers. There are basically two types available, with three different ratios. The two types are full roller rockers with roller tips and needle-roller bearings, and roller-tip rockers which, as the name suggests, have rollers on the tips only and have bushes rather than needle-roller bearings. These are a lot cheaper than full roller rockers and are absolutely ideal for road use. Ratios available are 1.3:1, which is ideal for most small bore engines; 1.5:1 for 1,275cc and big-bore engines, and 1.7:1, intended for big-bore and race engines. Rollers of 1.7-ratio are used in some injection Mini performance kits such as the Mini Sport 90bhp twin-point kit.

blocks

Reboring and overboring

When an engine is reconditioned, the block is rebored and new pistons fitted. Confusion sometimes exists regarding the difference between reboring and overboring. Reboring is when the block is bored by the minimum amount to clean the bores and remove all traces of wear. Reboring always means fitting new pistons: you cannot, as some people seem to think, simply fit larger rings. Standard oversize pistons come in +0.020in, +0.040in, and +0.060in sizes. Reboring does give a slight increase in capacity, and for the oversize pistons mentioned above, in a 1,275cc engine the increase will be to 1,293cc, 1,312cc, and 1,330cc respectively. There is nothing to be gained in going straight to the maximum rebore: it is far better to remove the minimum, as this way, on a standard block, two more

Checking a block for bore wear.

rebores are usually possible. If a block has already been bored to the maximum oversize and is in need of a further rebore, two things are possible; either liners can be fitted, or the block can be overbored.

Liners are actually made of better material than blocks themselves and after high mileages there will be less wear. Engine blocks needing liners that are being prepared for competition or for high-performance engines should be step-linered; this means that the lower part of the liner is machined to create a 'step' while the block is bored accordingly so that the liner cannot move down the bore. Incidentally, a number of Minis left the factory with linered blocks, particularly 998cc units. Blocks must be fully cleaned chemically before boring.

Overboring means going above the standard oversizes and fitting special pistons. This is almost always done with the intention of increasing power. In the past, when 1,275cc engines were thin on the ground, it was not uncommon to bore out the 1,098cc engine to 1,220cc. Nowadays it is not worth overboring the small-bore engines – it is far easier to start with a 1,275cc unit.

The standard bore size of the 1,275cc engine is 70.61mm. If it is bored to 73.5mm and the standard stroke crank of 81.28mm is retained, the capacity will be increased to 1,380cc. To improve reliability, most engineering shops offset-bore 1,380cc blocks to maintain as thick a wall as possible between the centre two cylinders. This means that the two bores on one side of the block are moved towards the water-pump end, and the other pair towards the oil pump. Increasing the bore size to 74mm will increase the capacity to 1,399cc. However, the bores are already quite close enough in a 1,380cc engine, and if another 0.5mm is added to each cylinder things become very close indeed. Some cheap big-bore Mini engines are not offset-bored, so it is important to check this before buying.

Overboring always carries a risk of breaking through into the water jacket and rendering the block scrap. The best blocks for overboring are A-Plus, as they are the strongest of all – with turbo blocks being the ultimate. However, if a

Far Left: Reboring, in this case +0.020in from 1,275cc to 1,293cc.

Left: Rebored and finish-honed, this is a Rob Walker 1,380cc engine.

Centre main straps, four-bolt, centre mains, studs and nuts

On a high-performance engine the bottom end can be strengthened by fitting a centre main strap. This is well worthwhile on all except Cooper S blocks, and helps to hold everything firmly together – reducing the chance of the centre main cap, which is the most highly stressed of the three, from giving trouble. In order to fit the strap the centre main cap must be milled flat. The strap requires two longer bolts to hold it in position.

Capacity chart

Standard	Rebore			Overbore	
	+0.20in	+0.40in	+0.60in	73.5mm	74mm
848cc	862cc	876cc	890cc	–	–
970cc	984cc	999cc	1012cc	1050cc	1065cc
998cc	1015cc	1030cc	1050cc	–	–
1071cc	1086cc	1102cc	1117cc	1160cc	1176cc
1098cc	1115cc	1130cc	1150cc	–	–
1275cc	1293cc	1312cc	1330cc	1379cc	1399cc

very long-stroke crank is being used, it is often better to use a late pre A-Plus block for clearance reasons.

In the past, Triumph 2.5 pistons were fitted to 1,275cc blocks with a bore size of 74.7mm, giving a capacity of 1,426cc with a standard-stroke crank. Such extreme bore sizes are rarely used today.

Honing

Pistons should never be run in a block which has only been bored: the block must be honed. All good engineering shops will do this as a matter of course.

Four-bolt centre main straps are normally only fitted to very high-performance engines to hold the sides of the block together. Gearbox clearance needs to be checked when these are fitted.

Often, when a centre main strap is fitted, it closes the centre main bearing housing slightly. This must be checked, or the crank will not turn freely when the engine is assembled and premature bearing and crankshaft wear will result. The remedy is to line-hone the block.

Good quality studs and nuts should be used, such as those made by ARP and Mini Spares.

Block preparation

Cylinder blocks should be finished off with a reface followed by a very thorough clean – particular attention being paid to the oilways. Threaded gallery bungs can be fitted to the oilways in the block, these being easier to remove than the press-fit brass type, should any attention be required in the future. Gallery bungs should be fitted last, after all machining and cleaning has been carried out. New core plugs should be fitted too.

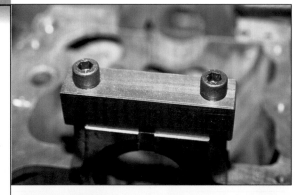

A centre main strap.

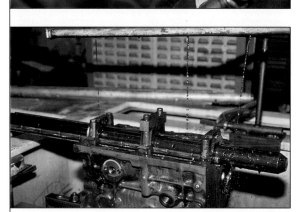

Line-honing after fitting a centre main strap.

Fitting threaded oil gallery bungs.

A fine-art block, in this case the work of Bryan Slark.

cranks, rods and pistons

Crankshaft identification table

Casting No.	Notes	Application
22A62/63	Early 850 1.375in diameter tail	848cc
22A298	Early 850 thin nose 1.375in tail	848cc
12A670	850 with 1.5in diameter tail	848cc
12A298		997cc
12A375	Oil feed hole for primary gear	997cc
12A595	Early casting	998cc
12A1451	Later casting	998cc
BHM1436	A-Plus 1985 on	998cc
12G82		1098cc
AEG330	EN40B not cross-drilled	970cc
AEG171	EN40B not cross-drilled	1071cc
12G1287/8	EN16 1.625in con rod journal	1275cc
12G1505	EN16 1.75in con rod journal	1275cc
12G1683	12G1505 casting tuftrided 1.75in	1275cc
CAM6232	A-Plus 1.75in	1275cc
AEG315/6	EN40B not cross-drilled nitrided 1.625in	1275cc 'S'
AEG479/480	EN40B cross-drilled nitrided 1.625in	1275cc 'S'
AEG623	EN16 tuftrided 1.625in	1275cc 'S'

Note: *Cranks from in-line A-Series engines cannot be used in transverse engines.*

Standard crankshafts and bearings

Cranks normally need to be reground when the engine is rebuilt. New standard bearings are available and oversize bearings are available in 0.010in, 0.020in and 0.030in oversizes. Cranks ground to the maximum undersize are not desirable on a performance engine, and if possible, you should go to 0.010in only. This will prove difficult with 'S' cranks due to their age and scarcity, and in this instance, larger undersizes are acceptable. Good-quality preferably steel-backed lead indium copper heavy-duty bearings should be fitted. When the crank is ground it is well worth having it tuftrided.

Tuftriding and nitriding

Tuftriding, or nitro-carburising, is a specialist process which dramatically improves fatigue strength. The process darkens the colour of the crank and leaves a somewhat dull finish, and the journals need to be repolished afterwards. Crankshafts must be checked for straightness after tuftriding, as occasionally they bend slightly in the process. Balancing can then be carried out.

Comparison of transverse (top) and in-line A-Series cranks.

Checking a main bearing journal for size.

It is important to check for wear at the primary-gear end of the crank. Primary gears themselves can be rebushed.

Left: A tuftrided crank.

Far Left: Regrinding a crank.

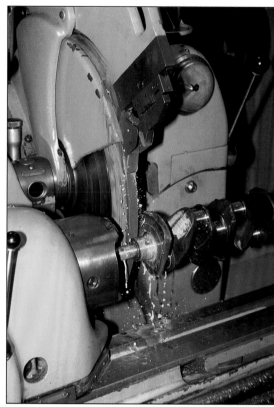

Nitriding is a very different process, which is carried out on EN40 steels only. Billet cranks (machined from a parallel billet of EN40 steel rather than a casting) are supplied nitrided, and they can be so treated again following machining work.

Stroking

It is possible either to reduce or lengthen the stroke of a 1,275cc engine crank. Reducing the stroke and increasing bore size is sometimes used to give a 'squarer' engine, and is known as de-stroking. Short-stroke engines are much better for higher rpm. Alternatively, the '1275' crank stroke can be increased to give a greater engine capacity. Both can be achieved by making use of the difference between 1275 'S' and non-'S' cranks. The 'S' crank has big end journals of 1.625in in diameter. Most non-'S' engines, because the crank was made of a lesser material had 1¾in big end journals. Using a standard non-'S' crank, and offset-grinding the big-end journals can be brought down to 1.625in diameter, and together with a set of

Cooper S or MG Midget con rods and a block bored to 73.5mm, results in a capacity of 1,425cc. Although the non-'S' crank is not as strong as the 'S' item, it is still strong enough to take the modifications, provided that it is tuftrided. Engines of this capacity have been built that will successfully rev to 8,000rpm. Billet crankshafts are required for a stroke of over 84mm, and the maximum possible with a billet crank is a 91mm stroke, which with a 73.5mm bore, results in a capacity of 1,544cc. Most people do not go this far as the billet crank plus steel rods, forged pistons and so on, work out somewhat on the expensive side.

'S' and non-'S' cranks

Cooper S cranks can be fitted into non-'S' blocks and vice versa with the relevant connecting rods, provided that special thrust washers are used. In the case of an 'S' crank into a non-'S' block, the thrusts need to be thinner; with non-'S' into 'S' they need to be thicker. Standard oversize thrusts are also available for worn cranks.

Stroking chart, 1,275cc capacity with:		
Crank stroke length mm	Oversize bore diameter mm	
	73.5	74
58.9	999cc	
75.5	1299cc	
76.5	1299cc	
81.3 (std)	1380cc	1399cc
84.0	1425cc	1445cc
85	1442cc	1463cc
86	1459cc	1480cc
87	1476cc	1497cc
88	1493cc	1514cc
89	1510cc	1531cc
90	1527cc	1549cc
91	1544cc	1556cc

The offset grinding can be seen by looking carefully at the position of the big-end journal in this picture.

EN40B Steel-nitrided cranks

EN40 nitrided steel is considered the best material for a crank and is the material of which Cooper S cranks were made. New forged cranks are available with 76mm, 81.3mm, 84mm and 86mm strokes. Most are available to fit both 'S' and non-'S' blocks, and the standard 81.3mm stroke cranks are available for both 'S' and 1300-type rods.

Cross-drilling

Very high-revving engines (over 8,000rpm) can suffer from oil starvation of the main bearings as a result of centrifuging action causing more oil to flow to the big ends. Cross-drilling the big end journals by plugging the normal oil exit hole and drilling another at right angles significantly reduces the problem. It can be carried out by competent Mini engine-machine shops, and ready cross-drilled cranks are available from some specialists. Most EN40B 'S' cranks are cross-drilled.

Wedging

Wedging involves removing metal by milling the crank webs on both sides, resulting in a more triangular appearance. The work is not often carried out on small-bore cranks but is common on 1,275cc cranks. It reduces the weight of the crank slightly and improves counter weighting. This results in smoother running.

Crankshaft dampers and retaining bolts

The crankshaft damper is particularly important when a lightened flywheel is fitted. If the standard damper shows signs of breaking up it should be replaced immediately. The standard damper is only just adequate, so it is much better to fit a Cooper S damper, these being available in reproduction form from Mini Spares.

The damper retaining bolt is quite short and has been known to work loose. Longer bolts and a large washer are the answer, and again these are produced by Mini Spares.

Wedging a crank.

Rods

Rod types

All A-Series rods are quite heavy. Many of the early small-bore rods use a clamp-type little end which can under some circumstances give trouble. Early 998cc and other small-bore rods have a fully floating gudgeon pin, and when these are used in a performance engine it is important to fit a PTFE pad to prevent circlip damage to the cylinder bore. The later 998cc rod with press-fit gudgeon pin is better for fast road use. With modification it is possible to use Cooper S rods in a 998cc engine, but unless you are building the ultimate '998' it is not really worth it for a road engine.

Large-bore rods come in five varieties. The best of all is the Cooper S rod, AEG521. This is made of EN24V and is extremely tough. 'S' rods are available new from Mini Spares.

Next on the list is the Sprite/Midget rod, AEG625. This uses the same big end journal size as the 'S' and although not fitted to Minis originally can be used with stroked 1,275cc cranks. The material, EN21, is slightly inferior. The remaining three types of rod are all large-big-end-journal 1300 types. The best, but rarest, is the type fitted to the Austin/Morris 1300GT and to Innocenti Minis. These are made of EN19 and are distinguished by a small strengthening web between the two beams, while the balance pad on the bottom is nowhere near as large as on the next type of rod, the 1300 type which was fitted to the Mini 1275GT. These are made of EN19 until the early 1970s when they were downgraded to EN16 and they are the heaviest A-Series rods of all. They are easily recognised by the aforementioned large balance pad. The last type of rod is the 1275 A-Plus. This is considerably lighter than the 1300 type and is made of EN16. Having said that, it is still a good rod, and is fully up to the job for a performance engine.

Before fitting, rods should ideally be bead-blasted and then balanced to achieve equal weight. The big end housings need to be checked for size and honed if found to be slightly oval.

'S' rods on stroked 1,275cc cranks

When 'S' rods are fitted to a non-'S' crank – usually when the crank has been offset-ground to reduce or increase the stroke – the 'S' rod needs to be modified. 'S' rods are 0.030in wider than the standard '1275' type, and to enable them to be fitted to the 1,275cc crank 0.015in needs to be machined from each side of the big end.

Modifying rods

Although it is not really necessary in a road-tuned engine, reducing the weight of the rods and pistons will help acceleration and the general smooth running of the engine. Small-bore rods can be lightened by up to 25 per cent, and all the 1,275cc rods including those of the 'S' can be lightened, although those that demand it most are of the '1300' type. All lightening needs to be carefully carried out, with all grinding up and down the beam and not across. Also, there must be no sharp edges, or cracking may result. Lightened rods should ideally be shot-peened afterwards to relieve stress and improve their appearance. Upgraded rod bolts, preferably ARP or similar, should be used and modified rods need to be checked for ovality and alignment and then balanced both end-for-end and for overall weight.

Pistons

It is essential to use good-quality pistons. Good quality means Omega, Mega or AE Hepolite. Oversize pistons are still available for 850cc and 1,100cc engines, for anyone wishing to build up one of these, while for 998cc units a very good purchase is the flat-topped AE 22463 piston. These were used in the KYMA project car for *MiniWorld* magazine and with a 10.2:1 CR they produced exceptional results. They are press-fit.

The 1,275cc piston comes in the usual 20thou, 40thou and 60thou oversizes and both AE and Omega are available. The 21253 is the best of the AE range and is a 9.75:1 CR piston.

It is even more important to use a good-quality piston in an overbored engine. Here, I would recommend either Omega or the Mini Spares Mega range which is made by AE Hepolite to the old Powermax specification. Both are excellent and I use both types in my own Minis. Ford pistons, which can be used in a 1,400cc engine, should be avoided in a Mini. These are very cheap but are not up to the job on a fast-revving, tuned Mini engine.

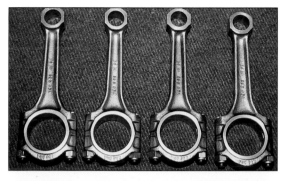

Far Left: Cooper S rods.

Left: A 998cc flat-top piston, as used by Mini Seven racers.

Far Left: These are Mini Spares Mega 1,380cc pistons made by AE to the original Powermax specification.

Left: Fitting pistons to press-fit rods using a special machine.

Far Left: Fitting the piston and rod to the block.

Left: Completed bottom end with wedged crank produced by Rob Walker Engineering.

When pistons are fitted to stroked engines, they need to be machined by the correct amount at the crown, otherwise the longer throw of the crank will push them out of the top of the bore.

Pistons are available with differently sized dishes in the crown. A 6cc dish is suitable for competition or road engines where a higher compression ratio is required, while 11cc dished pistons give a lower compression ratio and are normally only used in road engines. Turbocharged engines require very high quality, low-compression pistons.

the camshaft

Left: A performance cam, in this case a Kent Cams 286.

Far Left: The pin-drive camshaft.

Left: The star-drive or spider-drive cam, complete with spider in the foreground.

Far Left: The slot drive, or spade drive. This is also referred to as a Metro drive.

Camshaft profiles

Selecting the correct camshaft is an important decision which needs to be right first time. Choosing the wrong cam profile for a rebuilt engine will cause disappointment, so deciding what you want from your performance engine and where and when you drive your Mini are critical factors in arriving at the right decision, especially as there is now a bigger range than ever to choose from, from very mild to extremely wild.

There were lots of standard factory profiles over the years but only a handful of these are commonly found today. The original profile of the cam in the engine is largely irrelevant when you are upgrading to a performance cam, but the oil pump drive is important. There are two types of oil pump drive used in the original

A-Series engine. The first uses pin drive, and is found in all 848cc, 998cc and 1,098cc engines, and also in 970cc, 1,071cc and 1,275cc Cooper S engines. Most of these cams have ⅜in-wide lobes, but the 'S' engines have ½in wide lobes and use a longer-pin oil pump than the rest of the pin-drive engines.

The second A-Series drive is the star or spider-drive cam, which uses a separate 'spider' fitted on to the end of the oil pump and into the end of the cam. This type of drive was only ever used as standard in the 1,275cc non-'S' A-Series engine, and the lobes are again ½in wide. With the advent of the A-Plus engine, both 998cc and 1,275cc units moved to the new slot or spade drive, together with ½in-wide lobes. The differing cams (with the corresponding oil pumps and spider where relevant) are interchangeable, but on most engines there is no real gain in doing this – really it is best to stick with what you have got, as for example, fitting a spider-drive cam to a 998cc block involves using spacers. If you do want to change, it is best to fit the latest type A-Plus spade-drive cam and oil pump.

Scatter-pattern cams

Scatter-pattern cams are becoming increasingly popular in the A-Series engine. A scatter-pattern cam has different timings for each pair of cylinders, and reduces the possibility of one cylinder in the pair robbing the other through the siamesed inlet port when both inlet valves are open together – as they are for a short time when a long-period cam is fitted. The scatter-pattern cam cuts down this 'shared time' through the siamesed inlet ports. Scatter-pattern cams are superior, both in terms of bhp and torque, but they are at their best on 1,275cc and above large-valved A-Series engines.

Camshaft re-profiling

Performance cams can either be profiled from second-hand units or from brand-new blanks. Although there is a visible difference between the two, the performance is exactly the same and there is no real benefit on a road engine, in particular, in opting for a cam made from a blank. Cams which have been re-profiled have the benefit of being considerably cheaper than those cut from a new blank.

Cams which are in good condition, with no lobe or bearing damage, can be re-profiled to create a higher-performance cam as detailed above. They can also be re-profiled to the same original profile if for any reason a standard camshaft is required. If there is minor wear or damage to a performance cam that has been re-profiled it can be ground again to the same profile to freshen it up. The profile cannot be changed, however, as there is insufficient metal to allow this.

The Kent Cams cam profile library. Each disc represents a profile for an inlet or exhaust lobe.

Core – or second-hand – units undergoing re-manufacture at Kent Cams.

Grinding a Kent Cams cam.

Cam chooser chart

Cam	Power band	Suitability	Note
Kent Megadyne cams	**(rpm)**		
MD256	1000–6000	Mild road	Smooth-idle
MD266	1000–6500	Fast road	Smooth-idle 1,275cc
MD274	1000–6000	Fast road	Single-point injection
MD276	1500–7000	Road/Rally	Lumpier-idle 1,275cc
MD286	2000–7500	Rally Supersports	Lumpy-idle 1,275cc
MD296	3250–8000	Race	Competition only
MD310	4000–8500	Full race	Rough-idle 1,275cc
MD315	4500–9000	Full race	Rough-idle 1,275cc
Kent scatter-pattern cams			
274SP	1500–6500	Ministock	Scatter-pattern
286SP	2000–7500	Rally	Scatter-pattern
296SP	3250–8000	Race	Scatter-pattern
310SP	4000–8500	Full race	Scatter-pattern
Piper cams			
BP255	1000–6000	Mild road/Turbo	Smooth-idle
BP270	1500–6500	Fast road	Smooth-idle
BP270i	1500–6500	Injection	Smooth-idle
BP285	2000–7500	Road/Rally	1,275cc and larger
BP300	3000–8000	Rally/Race	1,275cc and larger
BP320	4000–8500	Race	1,380cc Race cam
649+	3700–8500	Race	Upgraded 649
457	3000–7500	Ministock	BRISCA
466	3000–7000	Ministock	Spedeworth

All Piper cams are available with scatter lobe angles.

'Works' and other profiles			
500	1500–6000	Mild road/Turbo	Pin-drive 450
567	2000–6500	Mild road	Pin-drive 948 also known as 88G229
600	2000–7000	Fast road	Pin-drive 550
800	2500–7000	Fast road	Pin-drive 731
643	2500–7000	Fast road/Rally	Pin-drive 544
530	3000–7500	Race	Pin-drive 649
Sprint 598	3000–7500	Race	
Supersprint 595	3000–7500	Race	
895	3000–7500	Rallycross	
475	5000–9000	Race	

Choosing a profile

Choosing the correct cam profile is very important, but at first can seem a little daunting. The choice of profile can quickly be narrowed down, according to what the car is used for, and the size of the engine. When used in 998cc or 1,098cc engines all cams will be slightly hotter and have a slightly less smooth idle than when they are installed in 1,275cc engines.

So which is the right one for you? If you want to stay traditional and opt for a reproduction factory or ST cam there are a couple that are worthy of mention. The 997cc Cooper cam, usually referred to as a 948cc cam or an 88G229, was at one time the best all-round fast-road cam to have, and it is still up to scratch today, particularly in 998cc or 1,100cc engines. The other good cam is that used in the MG Metro, and again, this is a worthy fast-road cam for a 1,275cc engine. All the same, most people fit one of the newer-generation specialist performance cams, as these have been developed for road use and offer a far better combination of flexibility and performance.

If the car is used only on the road, it pays not to go too wild, and under normal circumstances the Kent 286 is probably as hot as anyone should consider for all-round tractability. Most popular are fast-road cams such as the Kent 266 or 276: the 266 is a very good all-round road cam, whereas the 276 is lumpier at idle, particularly in smaller-bore engines. My own mild-tune favourite is the Kent 266, which is good in 998cc, 1,098cc and 1,275cc engines. For something a little hotter, the KYMA cam, designed by Bryan and Neil Slark and produced by Kent, works very well, particularly when a 12G940 head is used on a 998cc engine. Moving on a little, the Piper 270 is particularly good in 1,275cc engines and up to 1,430cc big-bore units; in fact, there are those who consider it to be the best all-rounder ever. For something hairier though, the Kent 286 scatter-pattern cam works exceptionally well in large-capacity engines. My favourite classic profile is the 544 (544 in pin-drive, 643 in spider-drive) which is the old Formula Junior cam. Although it was originally designed for small-bore A-Series engines it works very well in classic tuned 1,275cc and larger engines.

With competition engines, sometimes the cam is specified; if not there is usually a right one for the job, and really it is a matter of researching what the other competitors use. Competition engines can take much hotter profiles where regulations permit. Many people use hotter race-type profiles on the road and this can be fine provided that the car is mostly used on the open road and not driven in traffic to any great extent. A fast road car should remain drivable in all situations; if it is not, some of the enjoyment will be lost.

It is often better to buy a complete cam kit which includes followers and valve springs. This is a Kent Cams 266 kit.

Piper also produce similar kits. This is their 270 kit.

Cam followers.

Cam followers

Cam followers are made of cast iron. The bottom face, which bears against the cam, is chilled in the casting process to harden the surface. It is absolutely essential to replace the cam followers every time that you change the cam, even if they have only done say, ten miles. Cheap cam followers will often fail, and when they do they have a habit of destroying the cam and sometimes the rest of the engine too. Kent CF1 and Piper FOLMIN followers are chill cast and of the correct hardness.

Camshaft installation

Installing a new camshaft must be carried out with precision and care. Cleanliness is of paramount importance as is the need to insert the cam in such a way that the cam bearings in the block are not damaged by the lobe edges. Some people find it easier to install the cam downwards with the block on its side to help prevent this. Cam bearings should be replaced too, especially if there is any sign of wear, and in any case they should be replaced as a matter of course when a full engine rebuild is undertaken. If a performance cam is being fitted into an 848cc block, cam bearings should be fitted, as in standard form two of the cam journals run straight in the block.

The block can be line-bored and bearings fitted by any competent engineering shop. In the case of all 1,275cc non-'S' blocks – both A-Series and A-Plus – the followers must be fitted before the cam. With all the other engines the followers can be inserted through the tappet chest apertures in the side of the block after the cam has been installed. Always use plenty of cam lube, and never remove the phosphate coating on the camshaft. If the engine is not going to be run for some time after assembly it is often better to use an engine assembly grease rather than cam lube as it will not drain off. Old cam followers must never be re-used, unless they are unworn, the same cam is being refitted, and they are being used on the same lobe. When a new cam is fitted and the engine is first fired up, it is very important not to let it idle – run it at around 2,500rpm for 20 minutes or so to allow the cam and followers to bed in properly.

Installing the cam on a fast-road 1,275cc single-point-injection engine at Rob Walker Engineering.

Camshaft drives

The cam drive is one area that very much needs attention on a performance Mini engine, particularly if it is one of the earlier examples. This is not a problem as there are many different upgrades available. The majority of Minis, with the exception of the Cooper S and 1275GT, are equipped with a 'simplex' timing chain – in other words a single-row chain. On early cars the chain is tensioned merely by two neoprene rings fitted to the camshaft gear. As wear sets in, which it does after around 10,000 miles, the chain stretches, the neoprene rings harden and become less effective, and the result is that cam timing deteriorates. A worn timing chain quickly becomes noisy and produces the familiar rattle from the radiator side of the engine. Some Mini engines indeed have no tensioning system at all, which means that the problems begin even earlier. Later Minis, with A-Plus engines, have a proper tensioner which works well, but even so, once the tensioner has worn through the chain becomes very noisy. A slack timing chain reduces power output, and is highly undesirable on a tuned engine, and a noisy chain is equally undesirable.

The Cooper S and 1275GT engines have a duplex (twin-row) timing chain, which virtually eliminates most of the problems mentioned above. Duplex chains are a tight fit, and are far less prone to stretching – fortunately, as no tensioner is fitted. The Cooper S set-up has lightweight steel timing gears, whereas the 1275GT uses cheaper sintered gears, and both types make an excellent (and in the case of the 1275GT set-up) a very cheap upgrade for road engines of all capacities which are not so equipped.

Finally, there are two main types of timing cover. The A-Series engine has an oval-shaped cover. A-Plus engines, meanwhile, use a strange-shaped cover in order to house the tensioner.

Upgrades – the options
Non-adjustable chain drives
The standard simplex chain and gears are acceptable for original standard engines only.

If you want to retain a single-row chain for cost reasons on an A-Series engine, fit the tensioner from an A-Plus power unit. To do this the front plate, tensioner and timing cover from an A-Plus engine will be needed. A far better route for both A-series and A-Plus is to fit the standard duplex as used in 1,275cc A-Series engines. This works particularly well on all 850cc, 998cc and 1,098cc engines, and on Metro 1,275cc engines, even when they are tuned. The tensioner on A-Plus engines can be retained with a duplex timing chain, and can be fitted to earlier engines being converted to duplex using the parts detailed above.

Faster and more highly modified engines will benefit from the Mini Spares ultra-lightweight duplex set-up, which is the modern-day equivalent of the original BMC Special Tuning gears.

With all of the above non-adjustable cam drives the only way to ensure accurate cam timing is (where required) to use an offset cam key. Keys are available in 1° increments up to 9°. In cases where the timing is out by a massive amount – which can be the case when a different upgraded cam is being fitted – the camshaft gear can be moved round one tooth. Offset keys can be fitted either way round, so in all cases it is possible to time the cam correctly.

Adjustable chain drives

Accurate cam timing is much easier with a vernier-adjustable arrangement, and today most performance Mini engines are so equipped. There are a number of systems available, with a choice of chain, belt, or geared drive. The vernier-adjustable lightweight duplex is the most popular system. Two types are available. The first, produced by Mini Spares, uses a dowel-adjustment system giving fixed, 1° adjustments. This is preferred by some engine builders, as there is absolutely no chance of any movement. The second type, produced by Kent, Piper and Mini Spares, uses an infinitely variable screw adjustment system, which in theory, provides even more accurate adjustment. If you are a

The Mini Spares ultra-lightweight duplex.

Kent vernier-adjustable duplex.

timing chain fan, both of the above systems are excellent.

Belt drive

If you are not in favour of timing chains there are two options available. The first of these is the Mini Spares belt-drive kit. This is a complete kit which replaces the timing chain with a belt and which is vernier-adjustable. The great advantage over a chain is noise reduction. The kit is available with adjustment by dowel or by screw and either type is available with an alloy or a plastic case. Cam belts need to be changed at regular intervals.

Geared drive

The second option makes it possible to do away with the timing chain or belt altogether. The Slark Race Engineering conversion

replaces the timing chain with a transfer gear which transmits the drive from crankshaft to camshaft. There are three new gears which are straight-cut and also lightweight (2lb 4oz/1.020kg) against a vernier set-up including the chain which weighs 3lb ½oz (1.375kg). Although intended primarily for competition engines, the conversion is also suitable for highly tuned road engines. The only downside is increased noise. Fitting is a lot more involved than with normal duplex gears and chain, and therefore fitting with the engine in situ in the car is not recommended. Because the transfer gear casing uses the bolt holes for the timing chain tensioner, and therefore takes up more room than a regular A-Series untensioned timing chain, the SRE conversion can only be fitted using an A-Plus timing cover.

A Mini Spares belt drive.

Right: The SRE transfer gear conversion.

Right: Where to modify an A-Plus timing cover.

Far Right: Establishing full lift on No. 1 inlet.

Duplex conversion

Duplex gears and their matching chain can easily and cheaply be fitted to A-Series and A-Plus engines. Both engines will need the front plate countersinking to accept Allen screws, as the standard bolts foul the wider duplex gears. This can be done easily using an electric drill. When carrying out this conversion, the A-Plus timing cover needs modifying close to the edge of the casing, on the right of the oil seal, to prevent the chain from rubbing. There is a section of steel tube welded to the outside of the casing which causes the problem. Careful reshaping from inside with a hammer is the way to correct the situation. In addition, the 1,275cc breather-type of timing cover needs the metal area behind the breather removing.

Finally, always fit a new oil seal, and use gasket sealant on the lower sections of the timing cover gasket to reduce the possibility of leaks when you reassemble – this was recommended by Rover.

Timing the cam.

Duplex conversion with the engine in the car

A standard engine can easily be converted to duplex with the engine in the car. Adjustable drives are more complicated to fit and really they should be done at the time of build, with the engine on the bench. Begin by removing the bottom hose from the water pump and disconnecting the heater hose from the bottom hose, and then remove the radiator, the fan, the pulley, and the fan belt.

Next remove the alternator and place a trolley jack under the gearbox. Remove the two bolts securing the gearbox to the engine mounting bracket and support and raise the engine on the jack. Also remove the mounting from the subframe by removing the two nuts and bolts. Knock back the locking tab on the crankshaft pulley and remove the bolt. Do this by putting the car in gear and applying the brake. Undo all the bolts securing the timing cover, remove the tensioner from A-Plus engines, and the oil thrower from the crank timing wheel. Knock back the tab on the camshaft sprocket nut and remove it. Ease the timing gears off the crankshaft and camshaft at the same time. Remember not to turn the engine once these have been removed.

Remove the engine front plate and counter-sink the two bolt holes behind the crankshaft pulley with an electric drill. Remove any traces of the old gasket from the plate and the block with a scraper. Refit the engine front plate, using Loctite or similar when fitting the new countersunk Allen screws. Also, centre-punch the heads into the front plate as an added precaution. Fit the new timing wheels first without the chain and check alignment with a straightedge, and then use shims to correct if necessary. The gears can then be removed, and the chain fitted, aligning the timing dots carefully, followed by reassembly of the rest of the components.

Camshaft timing

Accurate cam timing is essential on a performance engine. This is never more important than when an uprated cam drive, particularly one with vernier gears, is being fitted. The standard method is to align the dots on the crank and camshaft gears. If the cam is more than 2° out a power loss will result, and because of manufacturing tolerances, the dot-to-dot timing method can be up to 15° out.

Timing in the cam is considered by many to be far too difficult to contemplate. In fact, as long as you have the correct basic equipment available, it is very straightforward:

Step 1 Line up the new gears off the engine using the original gears as a guide and then fit them. If vernier gears are not being used an offset camshaft key will almost certainly be needed to correct the timing.

Step 2 Fit the camshaft timing protractor and make up and fit a pointer out of some wire.

Step 3 Turn the engine until No. 1 piston is at TDC, using a dial gauge to ensure absolute accuracy. Set the protractor to TDC.

Step 4 Fit a pushrod to No. 1 inlet. The dial gauge is then used to establish when No. 1 inlet lobe is at full lift. Once this has been accurately established the dial gauge is set to zero and the engine turned backwards around 100thou on the dial gauge (not degrees on the protractor). It is then turned forwards to 5thou before full lift, and a reading taken off the protractor. Another reading must be taken from the protractor, 5thou after full lift, and the two figures added together.

Step 5 Divide the result by 2 and the figure that results is the number of degrees that No. 1 inlet reaches full lift after TDC. Taking two readings establishes more accurately where the centre of full lift occurs.

Step 6 The vernier can then be adjusted to correct the cam timing, or in the case of a non-adjustable set-up, an offset cam key can be used. Check the timing readings again.

the oil system

In the early days, Mini engines were filled with thin multigrade oils, a common choice being a 10W/30. The use of these thin oils often led to piston scuffing and gearbox problems. Things improved enormously with the introduction of a heavier, 20W/50 multigrade. The requirement in a Mini is for an oil that will both lubricate the engine and protect the transmission: a Mini transmission does not require an EP-type oil, as a good-viscosity multigrade is sufficient to do the job.

So what engine oils should and shouldn't be used in a Mini engine? First, the oils not to use in Minis are fully synthetic oils such as Mobil 1. Fully synthetic oils are excellent if you drive a 1990s or a later design of engine, but the A-Series is an older type and the wider tolerances and by modern standards somewhat old-fashioned oil pump means that fully synthetic oil will tend to leak past the oil seals. A thicker oil such as a 20W/50 will not.

For many years I always used Castrol oils in Minis – on one occasion when I did not, the engine failed. I still do sometimes use Castrol today, but more recently I have used Penrite. Penrite specialise in oils for older vehicles and they have gone a step further than traditional 20W/50 with their HPR 20W/60. Penrite recommend this oil for all Minis regardless of age, because it does not contain any friction modifiers, and offers very good 'pumpability' when cold, combined with exceptional viscosity when hot. Although this oil is designed for older cars, it uses modern technology to enhance protection, and it contains an anti-wear additive.

HPR20W/60 is the oil that Penrite recommend for all Minis, but for anyone driving a low-mileage Mini Penrite also offer HPR 15W/60 which is semi-synthetic. Once the engine has covered 30,000 miles or so, it would be better to use the HPR 20W/60 however. Most of the top Mini engine builders today recommend using 10W/40, 15W/50, or a reputable 20W/50 or 20W/60 oil. Older engines should always use the thicker oils. With any good-quality oils of the above viscocities you should not go far wrong.

Running-in

Brand-new or newly built engines need oils without additives to allow proper bedding in of the components. When choosing running-in oil it is important to avoid the use of oil containing friction modifiers as the characteristics of the oil prevent the piston rings from bedding in properly. The result would be high oil consumption for the life of the engine. Running-in oil and most cheap 20W/50s do not contain friction modifiers. Avoid very cheap engine oil with no API (American Petroleum Institute) or ACEA (Association des Constructeurs Européens d'Automobile) designation. Engines filled with running-in oil should be driven gently and the oil level checked even more regularly than usual.

Recommended oil change intervals

BMC's original recommendation was that under normal circumstances Mini engine oil should be checked and topped up every 3,000 miles, and then changed every 6,000 miles. Things changed over time, and the last recommendation from Rover was that the oil and filter should be changed every 12,000 miles or 12 months. Even though oils have improved, in a Mini the oil is shared by the engine and transmission and personally I always change both the oil and the filter in a Mini, regardless of age, every 3,000 miles, or six months.

Oil pumps

There are six main types of oil pump fitted to transverse A-Series engines. These are as follows:

1) Pin-drive, as fitted to 850cc, 1,000cc and 1,098cc.
2) Long pin-drive fitted to early 'S'.
3) Star-drive for 1,275cc pre-A-Plus engines.
4) Slot-drive for A-Plus 1,000cc and 1,275cc.
5) Slot-drive Metro Turbo high capacity.
6) Automatic Mini.

Within these categories there are a number of different makes and types of pump; some are two-bolt fixing, some three-bolt and some four-bolt. The only reason to change the type of

pump is if a camshaft with a different drive is being fitted. Metro Turbo engines use a high-flow oil pump, but this should not be fitted to non-turbo engines as it is unnecessary, and the excess oil pumped will be dumped back through the oil-pressure relief valve.

The A-Series pump is very reliable and failure under normal usage is quite rare. As mileages increase, the pump wears, and as a result loses efficiency. The early oil pumps were lower output – a higher-flow pump was introduced with the Cooper S and this improvement was later adopted through the range, regardless of the drive of the pump. There is no need to upgrade a standard Mini oil pump. When an engine is being rebuilt, a new oil pump should be fitted. In some cases, though, if a low-mileage unit is being stripped and checked it is permissible to re-use the pump, but the cover should be removed and the degree of wear checked with feeler gauges – details of this are given in workshop manuals. If the pump is of the type fitted with a large O-ring seal inside, it is very difficult to reassemble, and replacement is often the only option. When fitting a new

Good-quality running-in oils from Castrol and Penrite.

The three main types of A-Series oil pumps: Metro-drive, star-drive or spider-drive, and pin-drive.

Oil filters

There are two types of oil filter fitted to manual transmission Minis, the older paper element type, and the later, screw-on metal canister. Both work well, but the latter type is more efficient, and it is certainly a great deal less messy and easier to change. Converting an earlier engine to this type is straightforward and entails fitting a new filter head and pipe. Always fill both types of filter with oil before fitting – this reduces the time for oil pressure to return after an oil change. Automatic Minis are fitted with a different filter assembly.

The later, screw-on type of Mini oil filter.

Mocal Mini oil coolers and hoses. The cooler radiators are 10-row for most tuned road engines, 13-row as fitted to the Cooper S, and 16-row for competition in UK only. Clubman models and Minis with a pre-engaged starter will need longer hoses.

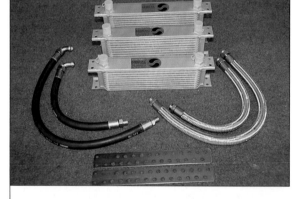

pump it is a good idea to dismantle it and check it internally. Although some manufacturers recommend that you do not do this, I have in the past found swarf from machining present inside a new pump. Always prime the oil pump with engine-building lube before fitting.

Modifications to the lubrication system

The lubrication system on a Mini works well, and does not need any real mods to improve it, even when the engine is highly tuned. However, there are two improvements that can be made, other than fitting the K&N breather filter (see opposite) or the later type of filter already mentioned. These modifications are essential on seriously tuned engines, and are as follows.

Oil cooler and piping

An oil cooler helps to control oil temperature particularly at high speeds and when the engine is under load. They were popular in the 1960s and '70s, but are not so necessary today because engine oils are of far better quality. Mini engines producing less than around 90bhp do not need an oil cooler under normal circumstances. If you do fit a cooler make sure that the oil is not being over cooled. Do this by covering the oil radiator in the winter, or by fitting an oil cooler thermostat which will prevent oil flowing through the cooler until it has reached around 80°C. If the oil is too cold it will lead to excessive crank, bearing and bore wear. The traditional Mini oil cooler is an oil-to-air cooler. Some Metro engines are fitted with an oil-to-water cooler which is fitted between the oil filter housing and the oil filter. Using one of these is not a good idea on a Mini as the radiator in most cases is already overworked. If you are fitting a Metro engine which is sufficiently tuned to require a cooler, dispose of the oil-to-water cooler and fit a traditional oil-to-air Mini oil cooler instead.

Centre oil pick-up pipe

Cornering a Mini hard can cause oil surge, resulting in loss of oil pressure. Overfilling with oil up to the 'X' of the MAX mark on the dipstick was a partial cure recommended in the past, but the problem can be completely resolved by fitting a centre oil pick-up pipe which draws oil from a central position at the lowest point of the gearbox. The gearbox must be dismantled in order to fit the modified pipe. This is another area where it is essential to buy a good-quality item from a reputable source: some centre pick-up pipes are not at all well made, and will need to be heated and bent to the correct shape to enable fitment and to prevent fouling on the gears. Owen Developments produce the best centre pick-up.

Pressure regulator kits, pressure springs, and valves

For most modified Mini engines the standard oil pressure valve and spring will do a perfectly adequate job. If a stronger spring is required the Cooper S spring can be fitted, this being both shorter and stronger. Some people also replace the standard bullet-shaped oil pressure relief valve with a ball bearing. This is ideal if debris is likely to become trapped around the standard valve and cause it to stick. Going beyond this, it is possible to fit an oil pressure regulator kit, which allows adjustments in pressure at the turn of a knob. The oil pressure does not need to be higher than 60-65psi to protect the bearings.

Magnetic sump plugs, oil traps and taper plugs

The standard Mini sump plug has a magnet built into it and is quite alarming to see the 'Christmas tree' of iron filings attached to the magnet when it is removed during an oil change. The magnet must of course always be wiped clean and the rag disposed of properly. A sump plug with an extended nose is available for more efficient collection of debris from a more central point in the gearbox. It is a good idea to fit one of these when a centre oil pick-up pipe is fitted. Magnetic oil traps with and without a filter are also available.

It is not unusual for the thread of the sump

Crankcase ventilation

It is important to pay attention to the engine breathing system as neglect can lead to poor performance and excessive oil consumption. Worse still, blocked engine breathers can cause failure of the flywheel oil seal, causing oil seepage which will eventually contaminate the clutch and cause it to slip. The oil filler cap is part of the breathing system on many models, so make sure that it is not blocked or dirty, and that if the rocker cover is replaced the correct type of cap is fitted. The factory recommendation is that that the oil filler cap should be replaced every 12,000 miles.

Regarding breather mods, when a 1,275cc engine is fitted the flywheel-housing breather should also be fitted if the flywheel clutch housing from the original small-bore engine is retained. The 1,275cc breather will fit, but a hole must be made in the casting. Breather filters of the K&N type look very good and they work well, but they can cause a film of oil to be sprayed over the engine, as engine breathers do just that, sucking and blowing air, fumes and oil. Bear this in mind before fitting this type of breather to a concours engine.

drain plug in the gearbox casing to strip, especially on older Minis. The normal reason for this is if the plug has been over tightened at some point. A tapered-thread sump plug is an ideal semi-permanent answer when the thread is stripped, as it is extremely difficult to repair the thread with a helicoil when the engine and gearbox are in situ.

Far left: A centre oil pick-up pipe in the gearbox.

Left: A taper sump plug produced by Paynes.

03 engine ancillaries

Fuel systems and manifolds

The earliest Minis were fitted with a single 1¼in SU HS2 carburettor. This remained a standard fitment on 848cc and 998cc Minis until May 1974, when the 1½in HS4 replaced it. The Cooper and Cooper S sported twin 1¼in carburettors throughout production, and the automatic Mini was always equipped with a 1½in HS4 SU, as was the 1275GT. The Clubman started out with the 1¼in followed by the 1½in SU which was also fitted to the 1,100cc model. Next came the RSP Cooper with an HIF44 single SU, as fitted to the MG Metro, while 1.3 pre-injection non-Cooper Minis were fitted with an HIF38. The '38' and '44' are measurements in millimetres, and are equivalent to 1½in and 1¾in respectively. The HIF, which stands for horizontal integral float chamber, is not a complicated carburettor. The mechanics are more simple than the HS types, the main difference being in the design of the float chamber – on the HIF it is integral and located underneath the carburettor body as opposed to being mounted on its side, as on the HS unit.

The Coopers went over to fuel injection from October 1991, and all other Minis followed in 1995.

Changing and modifying Mini carburettors has long been a popular pastime. In the early days the 1¼in SU could be improved by modifying the piston to the quick-lift variety and further improved by cutting off the protruding part of the screws from the throttle butterfly, and gas flowing the inside of the carb a little. When a ram pipe was fitted as well, a couple of bhp would be gained. Nowadays it is easier to fit a larger carb and/or change the needle. Fitting a 1½in HS4 to a 1¼in-equipped Mini using a standard manifold is good for around 2bhp. The 1½in cast manifold must be used – this being different from the 1¼in type – together with a new exhaust system. But change to a decent inlet and exhaust manifold and system, along with an improved air filter, and the gain will be 10bhp or more on a 998cc engine.

On a Mini which is tuned to any extent, carburation improvements become desirable, and as levels of tune go higher they become essential. The question is whether to stay with an SU set-up and use a larger single, or twin SUs, or change to something different such as a twin-choke. SUs and Webers have always been the most popular choices, but a few other carbs have appeared from time to time.

SU – single or twins?

There are certain advantages with both single-carb and twin-carb set-ups. Twin SUs look excellent and often feel more responsive and willing than a large single carb. With any single-carb set-up, the outer two cylinders will run much richer than the inner two. Fuel distribution is far superior through twin carburettors, and as a result all four cylinders will receive about the same strength of fuel mixture. When air is sucked in through a small aperture it travels in much faster than through a larger opening, and this is a definite advantage, particularly lower

The classic favourite: twin 1¼in HS2s.

down the rev range, making twin 1¼in SUs excellent for mild to mid-tuned road engines. Engines in a higher state of tune, or those used for competition, will benefit from the larger twin 1½in SUs.

Having said that, larger-capacity road engines, from '1275' through '1380' and '1430', work well with a single HIF44 provided that not too wild a cam is fitted. The HIF44 is also a good upgrade for a tuned '998' with a modified large-valve head: it worked particularly well on the Slark-built 998cc KYMA project engine with a 12G940 head. It performed badly, however, when the standard unmodified 998cc head was used. With twin SUs it is best to fit heat shields: these are available in the original black finish, or in stainless steel, and differ according to the size and type of SU with which they are used.

Correct needling or jetting is a must with any carburettor. Rolling-road tuning is the only way to determine this.

The HIF44 1¾in SU carburettor.

As fitted to the works rally Minis, a twin 1½in H4 set-up – the stud pattern is the same as that of the HS2.

Carburettor suggestions
(See also original engines chart, Chapter 1.)

Capacity	Tune	Carb options
848cc	Mild	single 1½in SU, twin 1¼in SU
848cc	High	twin 1¼in, twin 1½in SU
998cc	Mild	single 1½in SU, twin 1¼in SU
998cc	High	twin 1½in SU, single HIF44, Weber
1,098cc	Mild	single 1½in SU, twin 1¼in SU
1,098cc	High	twin 1½in SU, single HIF44
1,275cc	Mild	twin 1¼in SU, single HIF44, Weber
1,275cc	High	twin 1½in SU, single HIF44, twin HS6 SU Weber
1,380cc	Mild	single HIF44
1,380cc	High	twin 1½in SU, single HIF44, twin HS6 SU, Weber
1,430cc	Mild	single HIF44, Weber
1,430cc+	High	twin HS6, Weber
Eight-port	High	twin 45DCOE, Amal

Note: *This is only a guide, and not the last word! Cooper S 970cc and 1,071cc engines are similar in their requirents to 1,275cc units. Weber, or other carbs, can be fitted to all engine capacities, but generally speaking, engines in a lower state of tune will require the 40DCOE, while those more highly modified, the 45DCOE. For many applications an upgraded throttle cable will be needed: longer, non-stick cables are available from Mini Spares.*

Weber carburettors
Popular back in the 1970s was the Weber 28/36 DCD (dual choke downdraught). This carb, when suitably jetted, was a good match for all engines from a standard 850cc unit right through to a tuned '1275'. It is now obsolete, but second-hand examples can be found and all spares are available for rebuilds. It is a good alternative to twin 1¼in SUs but finding an air filter to fit can be a problem. The popular

The 45DCOE Weber carburettor.

Split Webers.

Twin DCOE Webers on a KAD 16-valve head.

Weber today is the DCOE, and the 40DCOE is suitable for highly modified 850cc Minis through to cars with a mildly tuned 1275cc engine. Power outputs of around 80bhp and beyond will need the 45DCOE, which is good for both competition and road use and again can be used on any engine from 850cc upwards.

For those who want something really exotic it is still possible to buy the split 40 Weber conversion from Richard Longman. Split Webers became famous on the works rally Minis. Splitting involves cutting away part of one

carburettor and using only one choke on each carburettor. Split Webers do not provide any more fuel than a single twin-choke Weber, but fuel distribution is much better as the throttle barrels are wider spaced than they are on a single twin-choke carburettor and are (on split Webers) directly in line with the ports. Consequently, the mixture is constant and performance is improved – and the carbs look absolutely fantastic, too. Twin (non-split) Weber DCOEs using both chokes on each carb are an ideal set up for eight-port (although bonnet mods will be required) and 16-valve heads.

Amal carburettors
Another famous works Mini set-up, which is still available today, is four Amal motorcycle carburettors. Needless to say, this is only suitable for eight-port heads. Phenomenal power can be achieved, but camshaft selection is vital with Amals if the engine is to run properly. Bill Richards Racing are the specialists when it comes to eight-port Minis.

Inlet manifolds
If you are changing carburettors for a different type, then it is also necessary to change the manifold. For HS4 and HIF44 carbs, water-heated manifolds have much improved gas flow.

Twin HS2s and HS4s require different inlet manifolds as the stud pattern is different, although the older, works-type H4s use the same manifold as twin HS2s. When changing the inlet manifold, it is essential to change the exhaust manifold and system too. Most inlet manifolds can be modified to improve flow, thereby liberating more power, and the twin-HS2 mani-fold responds particularly well to modification.

When fitting a 40DCOE or 45DCOE Weber, manifolding has to be chosen carefully as bulkhead surgery is required in order to fit the best type: 'swan neck' manifolds, which will fit without any modification, tend to restrict gas flow.

Fuel injection
Two types of fuel injection have been fitted to Minis. From October 1991, single-point injection was fitted to Cooper models. This was later fitted briefly to non-Cooper models

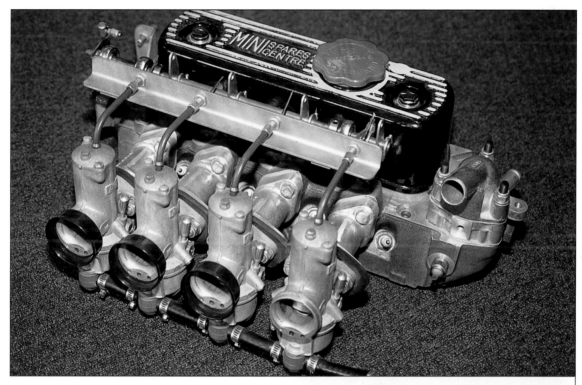

The four Amal set-up on a Mini Spares eight-port head.

before all Minis went over to twin-point, or multi-point, injection in October 1996. Single-point injection is just that: there is only one injector which discharges fuel into the air stream in the same place as a carburettor. Multi-point injection usually means a separate injector for each cylinder, but in the case of the Mini the inlet ports are siamesed, hence the system uses two injectors and is known as twin-point injection. 'S' versions of both injected Coopers were available from John Cooper Garages.

Modifications to the injection system itself were rarely carried out when the cars were current. Inlet manifolds can be modified to improve flow slightly, and with mildly uprated twin-point-injection Minis, such as cars with the Cooper 90bhp kit, it is best to fit an uprated fuel pressure relief valve. The Rover injection system is not programmable and therefore mods to engines so equipped are somewhat restricted.

For really serious mods to an injection engine it is necessary to fit an upgraded programmable system such as Weber Alpha injection. This system was fitted to the Mini Cooper Grand Prix Special Edition produced by Cooper in 1994 and was also used on the Monte Carlo Minis of the

An HIF44 inlet manifold.

1990s. With a programmable system such as Weber Alpha it is possible to build very high output injected engines indeed. Reliability is excellent. Recently, other programmable systems have come on the market.

Converting from injection to carbs

It is also possible to convert a fuel-injection Mini to use carburettors. Fitting a carb to the injection engine is only possible with single-point injection Minis and will cause problems with wiring and other ancillaries. There will also be problems with any Mini which legally requires a catalytic converter. The best way round this is to fit an

Modifying a twin HS2 manifold at Swiftune.

earlier engine, such as an MG Metro unit, in which case it will be necessary to fit a complete new wiring loom as well as the petrol tank from an older Mini. A mechanical fuel pump or Facet electric pump will be needed. With any conversion like this, the catalyst should be removed – provided you can prove the age of the engine. Current MoT and emissions regulations should be studied beforehand.

Air filters

All Minis will benefit from an air filter upgrade. In any case, running without an air filter is not

Fitting injection to a carb car

Fuel injection can be fitted to an engine which was previously fed by carburettors. Numerous changes need to be made to the car, and the fuel tank and the wiring looms from an injected car are needed, so the easiest way to go about this conversion is to buy a crashed or scrap injection Mini and use all the necessary components. Any other way is likely to be very expensive.

A modified twin-point-injection engine.

recommended, even under most competition conditions. Today, there are four main companies manufacturing performance air filters – K&N, Pipercross, ITG and Green. All these companies have a good reputation and the filters are proven both in competition and on the road. There are two main types available: foam and cotton.

K&N filters are constructed with oiled surgical cotton gauze sandwiched between fine epoxy-coated aluminium wire. Both replacement elements and bolt-on units are available. K&N claim up to 40 per cent extra flow, and up to 100,000 miles before needing any servicing.

ITG's 'reticulated polyester foam' technology uses various thicknesses of finer or coarser foam to create the optimum design for each application. The Pro-filter replacement-element filters never need cleaning, and will last five times longer than a conventional paper element. A variety of bolt on road/competition Megaflow filters is also available.

Pipercross filters are made from a multi-layered reticulated polyurethane foam lattice which is impregnated with a dirt retention additive. The layers of foam contain pores of differing sizes with larger dust particles being

trapped in the outer layers. Both replacement elements and bolt-on units are available.

Green's cotton air filters are constructed with a double layer of cotton gauze made up of a medium and a fine layer and held in place by a strong fine mesh. The green colour is so that any dirt build up is visible and it is therefore apparent when the filter needs cleaning. Replacement elements and bolt-on filters are available. The filters come with a 100,000-mile warranty.

Bolt-on filter or replacement element?
With many applications there is a choice of an extra unit or a replacement element which fits

The modified 3.5-bar fuel pressure relief valve (right) on a twin-point-injection Mini compared with the standard 3.0-bar valve. The different shape alters the pressure rating.

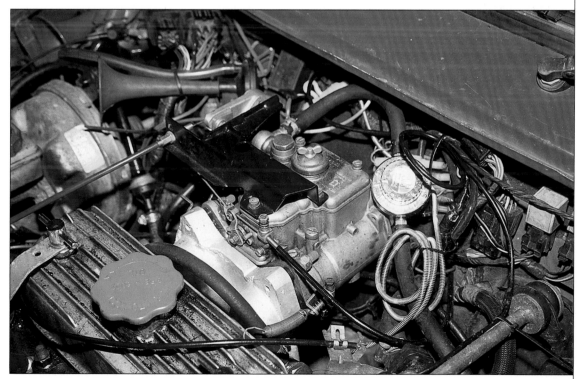

A Weber 45 fitted to a single-point-injection Mini.

into the standard airbox. Bolt-on filters provide superior flow, but there is an increase in sucking noise, this being particularly noticeable on Minis with a central speedo. If you drive only on the road and especially if you make a lot of long journeys, a replacement element in the original filter housing may be the answer. The flow is still very good and there is only a little more noise inside the car in most cases than there is with a standard paper element.

Fuel filtration and regulation

Performance Minis benefit from a fuel filter. The Purolator in-line filter is made with toughened glass and is a very neat installation which is suitable for almost any application.

The original Filter King can also be fitted to Minis. It is a combined filter and regulator, allowing for adjustment of the fuel pressure. Correct fuel pressure is essential for optimum power and fuel economy as over-fuelling causes poor starting and idling and high fuel consumption, while too low a pressure can cause fuel starvation. The glass bowled Filter King is ideal for road use but is not permitted in competition, where the alloy-bodied version must be used for safety reasons. If an adjustable fuel regulator without a filter is required, dial-type adjustable regulators are available.

Fuel-injection Minis have a fuel filter fitted as standard, located on the rear subframe. The filter should be renewed every 24 months, or 24,000 miles.

Fuel pumps

Early Minis used an electric fuel pump mounted on the rear subframe. Burlen Fuel Systems manufacture replacement pumps of both the original type with points and an identical-looking electronic type – which even ticks like the original. The earlier type of mechanical fuel pump, as fitted from October 1969, which could be dismantled and fitted with a new seal and filter is no longer available, but the later sealed-for-life mechanical pump is still available new and can be fitted as a replacement. Standard mechanical pumps are satisfactory up to around 90bhp.

For power outputs above the 90bhp mark an upgraded electric pump such as a Facet interrupter is a must; these use transistorised switching to eliminate the points within the pump and are therefore more reliable. They are available in three different versions for Minis. The standard Silver-Top pump delivers 18 gallons per hour and runs at 4-4.5psi, and this is ideal for twin-choke carburettors, all single-SU and most twin-SU set-ups. A competition version of the Silver-Top is also available, delivering 5–6psi and 30 gallons per hour, and is suitable for higher-output engines running with the previously mentioned carburettors.

Finally, the Red-Top delivers 40 gallons per hour (6–7.25psi) and is suitable for big-bore and stroked engines with carburettor choke sizes

Ram pipes are only really suitable for certain types of competition. Socks are available from some of the filter companies to fit over them.

K&N, the favourite of many, and the filters that I use on my Minis. Green filters are of similar construction.

Pipercross and ITG filters are of the foam variety.

over 45mm or split Webers etc. All the above Facet pumps are suitable for negative earth only, and are internally filtered.

An alternative type of Facet pump is the solid-state variety. This comes in three versions: 'Road', which delivers 12 gallons per hour at 2.5–3psi, and is intended as a replacement for the standard mechanical pump; 'Fast Road', which delivers 18 gallons per hour at 4–5.5psi, and is suitable for single-SU and twin 1¼in SU set-ups; and 'Competition', which delivers 25 gallons per hour and runs at 6–7.25psi, this being suitable for carburettors up to twin 1¾in SUs. Solid-state pumps must be pre-filtered, and it is worth noting that a mounting kit to reduce vibration and noise is available for all Facet pumps. When fitting an electric fuel pump where a mechanical pump was originally used, it is necessary to fit a blanking plate to the engine block.

The fuel tank

Three main types of tank have been fitted into Mini saloons. The early type has a 5½-gallon capacity and the retaining strap running across its top. Later 5½-gallon tanks have the strap running across the side of the tank diagonally. In June 1974 the 1275GT was fitted with a 7½-gallon tank which was simply a fatter version of the later 5½-gallon type. In February 1980, this larger tank was fitted to all Mini saloons. Vans, pick-ups and estates have a 6-gallon tank which fits under the floor at the rear.

Tank capacity can be upgraded either by fitting the 7½-gallon tank to early cars or by fitting a right-hand tank. Unleaded petrol tanks have a restricted filler neck.

Fuel lines

The fuel lines on a Mini are flexible from the tank through the boot floor to where they join a metal pipe or the fuel pump in the case of cars with an electric pump. The metal pipe runs under the car to the engine compartment where a flexible section connects to the fuel pump when a mechanical pump is fitted. The pipes should be inspected regularly for damage, in particular the flexible pipe which passes through the boot floor: a rubber grommet protects the pipe from chafing, and it must be both present and in good condition. If the grommet becomes

An in-line fuel filter is the neatest solution.

Filter King units are available with a glass or an alloy bowl.

A Facet Red Top pump.

A Facet solid-state pump.

dislodged, the pipe can chafe through completely – with disastrous results. The best type of pipe to use on all flexible connections, including the carburettor, is the original Smiths braided type, with the correct type of clips.

boosting power

There are three different ways of boosting power output from a Mini engine in addition to the more traditional modifications. The first two are methods of forced induction, while the third – which can be used in conjunction with either of the first two – is nitrous oxide injection.

Forced induction

In a normally aspirated engine the cylinders are filled with air at normal air pressure. This is the case regardless of whether the engine is fed by carburettor or fuel injection. With forced induction, more air is forced into the cylinders at a greater pressure and when this happens, together with the arrival of more fuel, the result is more power. This is achieved by fitting either a turbocharger or a supercharger. The difference between them is that a turbocharger is driven by the escaping exhaust gases, while a super-charger is a mechanically powered device which these days is driven by a belt from the engine.

How does a turbo deliver its charge? What actually happens is that the exhaust gases which escape from the exhaust ports in the cylinder head are collected in the exhaust manifold, and are then passed over the vanes of the exhaust turbine in the turbocharger. Attached to the same shaft as the exhaust turbine, and therefore rotating at the same speed, but in a totally separate chamber within the turbo, is the inlet turbine. As the accelerator is pressed down, the engine sucks in more air/fuel mixture in exactly the same way as a normally aspirated engine. But as more exhaust is produced, so the exhaust turbine starts to spin faster, the result being that the inlet turbine, which is spinning at the same rate, forces the air/fuel mixture into the cylinders under pressure, which in turn produces the extra power. This explains why there is no turbo boost at idle or with low throttle openings and why turbocharged cars sometimes suffer from turbo lag (the time delay in the power coming through) as the exhaust has to be produced in the first place in order to spin the turbo.

The principle of operation is the same with a supercharger, but it is driven by the engine rather than by the exhaust gases.

Turbocharging

The turbocharging of Minis has become very popular in recent years on account of the 1989 ERA Turbo Mini, and the number of MG Metro Turbos which have been scrapped, thereby providing a cheap source of turbocharged A-Plus engines. Turbocharged Minis can be very quick indeed, but the work involved in building one does present a number of problems – first, the preparation of the bodyshell to create room for the turbo installation, secondly the modifications to the fuel system, and thirdly, the need to cope safely with the very high temperatures generated by the turbocharger. None of these problems is by any means insurmountable, but building a turbo Mini requires a number of specialist skills and it is not a conversion for the inexperienced.

The easiest way to build a turbo Mini is to buy a complete scrap MG Metro Turbo, as it will have the whole power unit and all ancillary items, including the $\frac{5}{16}$in fuel pipe. Turbo engines and gearboxes are best rebuilt before being installed, as many are high-mileage and most will have had a very hard life.

There are a number of differences to the turbo engine; solid-skirt cast pistons are fitted rather than the slipper variety, and some turbo blocks were linered by the factory in an attempt to cure oil consumption problems. Pistons for rebores are available in 0.020in, 0.040in and 0.060in oversizes, and it is possible to build a 1,380cc turbo engine although the boost must be kept to 8-9psi maximum.

The fuel and exhaust systems with a turbo installation are straightforward. The main requirement is the $\frac{5}{16}$in fuel pipe: if not fitted, fuel starvation will become a problem. It is also essential to fit a fuel pressure regulator. These are set at the factory to 4-4.5psi, but are fully adjustable and gauges are available to enable pressures to be set at home. The carburettor fitted to the Metro Turbo is a sealed SU HIF44, and there is no need to change it, but if turbo boost is increased, the carburettor needle and spring must be replaced. It is essential that the correct profile of needle is fitted or detonation followed by meltdown of the pistons can occur, this being the case in particular when the engine is used at anywhere near full throttle. Avonbar, who have always been at the forefront of Mini turbocharging technology, produce a range of special needles and springs for 8psi, 10psi and 12psi of boost. Needles for higher levels of boost can also be supplied.

Fuel tank mods are needed, and a fuel return pipe must be plumbed in, as high up on the tank as possible. The original roller-vane type of fuel pump must be used, and can be either the genuine component or the aftermarket equivalent. Facet-type fuel pumps will not work with turbo installations.

For the exhaust, use a Maniflow turbo link pipe coupled to a Maniflow 2in exhaust system with a single silencer box.

The turbo engine has a higher-capacity oil pump to that of normally aspirated A-Series engine. The oil-feed pipe comes out of the mechanical fuel pump mounting area, and when fitting a turbo power unit to a Mini, there is a problem in that the oil pipe is secured to the Metro Turbo block where the Mini engine steady bar normally fits. The pipe must be secured properly or it will fracture, but securing it with the engine steady is not the answer. The easiest remedy is to fit an Aeroquip braided oil pipe.

Heat is a massive problem with all turbocharged cars – but even more so with a Mini because of the extremely restricted under-bonnet space. Modifications must therefore be made to the car to keep the temperatures down as much as possible, and all pipework must be of the correct quality and properly routed and secured.

As far as radiators are concerned, at lower levels of boost the standard Mini side-mounting position can be used, but it is essential to fit an uprated two-core or four-core radiator. For higher levels of boost and uprated power levels, a late-type Metro Turbo radiator or a front-mounted late Mini radiator with electric fan can be fitted. An oil cooler should also be fitted, if you can find room for it!

Keeping the heat contained so that it can exit through the exhaust system can be aided by using a Thermotec blanket kit to wrap the exhaust. It is best not to wrap the turbo, as there have been some instances of the exhaust port cracking. As 95 octane unleaded petrol burns at 15–18° higher than four-star or Super Unleaded fuel in a turbo engine, 97 or 98 octane Super Unleaded should be used.

The ignition system for turbos is fairly straightforward, but decent spark plugs, such as NGK's B7 ECS with a retarded nose, should be fitted. Extended-nose plugs should not be used in a turbo engine.

The best distributor to use is one from a MkI MG Metro Turbo, or better still use the special distributor supplied by Avonbar. Make sure that you retain the Metro's wiring harness as new ones are now unavailable. The ignition timing should normally be set at around 9–10° before TDC at 1,500rpm, but it should be noted that all installations can vary slightly.

Body modification for turbo engine
There is not room in a Mini simply to drop in a Metro Turbo unit – it will not clear the bulkhead and so modification is required. First, it helps to use a late-type injection subframe, as the engine is mounted slightly further forward giving a little more bulkhead clearance – anything which allows more air around the turbo is a good thing. If using the non-injection frame it is possible to drill new engine mounting holes in the subframe approximately ½in further forward so as to move the engine unit accordingly. Again this will aid both installation and cooling. Secondly, a steel bulkhead box must be fitted into the Mini to make a housing for the turbo. The bulkhead must be cut out and the box securely welded into position, as a great deal of strength will be lost if it is not. On no account must the box be merely riveted into place. When the box is fitted to a road car, the heater support brackets need to be cut from the original panel and welded onto the back of the box. The heater will stick out further into the car as a result.

Fitting a turbo boost gauge is a good idea, but not essential.

Modifying and upgrading turbocharged engines

When modifications are carried out on a turbo engine, the first area to receive attention should be the cylinder head. The exhaust valves on the turbo engine are sodium filled for improved cooling, and have thicker stems, which require different valve guides; they are also expensive. Consequently, larger valves are not fitted as a rule, although it is possible, to fit bigger, Montego Turbo valves; in this instance the position of the collet grooves needs altering, and other modifications to the valve stems are also needed.

The head should be modified to a special chamber shape – if the 'beak' is left in it will glow red above 5psi, causing pre-ignition and detonation which will quickly lead to melted pistons. Compression ratios, meanwhile, are best kept around to 8-8.5:1 – ratios in the mid-eights are good for up to 10psi or 11psi of boost. Ian Hargreaves of Avonbar recommends that for a higher turbo boost of 8psi and upwards, it is better to run with an intercooler.

A Metro Turbo engine installed in a Mini.

Right: A Metro Turbo fuel regulator.

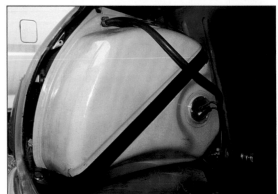

Far Right: A petrol tank modified with a fuel return pipe.

A popular mod is to use a dump valve: this vents away excessive turbocharger pressure when the throttle is closed and helps to keep the turbocharger spinning at lower engine rpm.

Adjustable boost valves are available from Avonbar, and together with a dump valve and a modified head they will give a considerable increase in power.

The next modification on the list is an uprated camshaft. Because the Garrett T3 turbo from the MG Metro is of a large size, power is restricted when under 3,000rpm. The Avonbar Phase 2 turbo cam will enable the turbo to work from around 2,600rpm – the improvement being due to changes in the overlap of the cam. The rpm figures are of course approximate, as all engines vary. This cam will help to reduce lag, and works particularly well when a dump valve is fitted. High-lift rockers should not be fitted to turbo engines as they increase turbo lag: 1.3-ratio rockers are the best.

For really wild turbo Minis, water injection kits are available. The water acts as a coolant for the fuel and reduces detonation. Water injection kits are expensive, but are straightforward to fit.

Supercharging

The alternative to turbocharging is to supercharge. Superchargers themselves have been around for a long time. In the past they have not been fitted to Minis to any great extent, but latterly, with the introduction of new kits, they have been gaining popularity. Supercharging offers some advantages over turbocharging, the main one being that it is much easier to carry out the conversion. The supercharger will fit 850cc, 998cc, 1,098cc, 1,275cc and larger Mini engines. It works best with long-stroke engines, 1,430cc units being particularly good. It will work with short-stroke engines, but the rev limit for the drivebelt is 7,500rpm maximum. Performance increase starts at around 30bhp on a standard 1,275cc engine.

It is essential that the engine to be supercharged is in good condition, and if possible it is best to carry out a full rebuild. Good-quality pistons are needed, ideally Omega

A Green turbo air filter, specially made for Avonbar.

A turbo exhaust downpipe.

Bulkhead modifications.

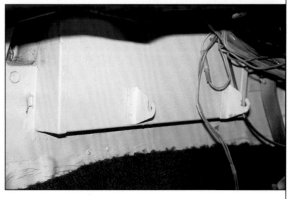

An internal view of the above, showing heater brackets.

or a top-of-the-range AE. Compression ratios have to be lower than with normally aspirated engines, and this is something to watch when the kit is being fitted to a previously tuned engine. The standard boost is 7psi, and at this level the compression ratio of the engine should ideally be dropped to around 9:1 to avoid pinking. An alternative wheel is available for the compressor which will give approximately 14psi boost, but at anything over 10psi boost the maximum CR possible is 8.3:1. Additional

engine mods are required at this stage, such as a tuftrided crank, a cam change, and head mods. Increasing boost any further would require the fitting of an intercooler, but because of the design of the supercharger unit this is not possible.

With all levels of boost a few further mods are required, in the form of an uprated radiator, a multi-bladed plastic fan or a six-bladed metal fan, a high-capacity water pump and a large-bore exhaust manifold and system. No changes are required to the ignition system other than that it will need to be retarded by around 5° to prevent the engine from running too hot; ideally electronic ignition should be fitted.

Finally, if a mechanical pump was fitted previously, it will be necessary to replace it with a Facet electric pump, as the mechanical one will not be up to the job.

The kit sold by Mini Speed is designed to use an early-type alternator with a small-diameter shaft. A later type can be fitted, but the pulley will need to be modified to suit, which is a job for a machine shop. The main part of the overall fitting procedure is converting the standard fan belt to a Poly V assembly to drive the manifold-mounted compressor. On most 1,275cc A-Plus engines the timing cover will have to be changed to the non-breather variety as fitted to the 998cc A-Plus, and a new breather will have to be fitted to the old fuel pump mounting to restore engine breathing. The standard breather will not fit, although it can be modified; alternatively a breather from a Maestro 1300 can be used.

After fitting a supercharger, the engine should be fully set up on a rolling road.

Body modification for supercharged engine
The body mod (yes, just the one) required to fit a supercharger is very minor indeed. The oil feed pipe into the top of the supercharger unit fouls the underside of the bonnet. The remedy is simple: the bonnet bracing needs to be slightly cut away to accommodate it. There is no work needed to the bonnet skin.

Nitrous oxide injection
Another method of boosting power is to fit nitrous oxide injection. This is totally different

An Avonbar-modified turbo head.

An internal adjustable boost valve.

The supercharger kit ready for installation.

The alternator and modified pulleys.

Far Left: The exhaust manifold used is a Maniflow LCB.

Left, top: The supercharger in position with the carburettor fitted.

Left, bottom: Modified bonnet bracing for supercharged Minis.

A completed supercharger installation by Mini Speed.

The solenoids, one for petrol and one for nitrous, need to be mounted in the engine compartment – anywhere that is dry and reasonably cool, in other words, but away from heat produced by the exhaust. Here they are fitted to the engine-steady mounting plate. Also in the engine compartment, the petrol solenoid is connected to the petrol pipe.

The largest part of the kit, the nitrous oxide supply bottle, is located on brackets in the boot.

from turbocharging and supercharging in that it is not forced induction.

Nitrous oxide (N_2O) was discovered by Sir Humphrey Davey, who is better known for inventing the miner's safety lamp. In the 18th century, nitrous oxide was used by dentists as a pain killer. It is soluble in water, alcohol, ether and benzene and is manufactured by the decomposition of ammonium nitrate by heat. It supports combustion better than air as it is made up of one third oxygen by weight, and can be broken down into its two elements, oxygen and nitrogen, at relatively low temperatures. When the oxygen is released, it can then be used for burning fuel; it is not the nitrous itself that produces the power – N_2O will not actually burn on its own. The power produced from fuel is limited by the amount of Oxygen that can be drawn in. The additional oxygen from the nitrous simply makes the fuel burn much more efficiently, and therefore produce more power. However, the correct mixture must be maintained – more oxygen needing more petrol – and for this reason a petrol solenoid as well as a nitrous solenoid is fitted. This way, N_2O

is injected into the manifold with petrol rather than on its own. So why use nitrous oxide rather than pure oxygen? Simply because the nitrogen content helps control the burn, and also because nitrous oxide can be stored at 700-800psi as opposed to oxygen which needs to be stored at 2,000-3,000psi.

The nitrous system suitable for fitting to both carburettor and injection Minis (it works equally well on both) is the Streetblaster 100C. When twin carburettors are fitted some additional components are needed. The system comes in 25bhp, 50bhp, 75bhp and 100bhp versions but even the fastest Mini in the world is only fitted with a 75bhp kit. The power increase is determined by the size of the nitrous jet. To begin with the manufacturer, Wizards of Nos, will only sell you a 25bhp kit, but once this has been fitted, and the results reported back to them, they will then consider supplying the parts to increase the power boost to 50bhp.

With power increases of 50bhp and above, the ignition timing will need to be retarded; better still, a Powamax progressive controller can be fitted, allowing a greater amount of usable power to be released.

The nitrous is switched on or off by means of a dashboard-mounted switch. The big advantage of nitrous is that it runs at full throttle only, so the car can be driven normally even when the system is switched on. The additional power comes in at any rpm when the throttle is floored – in a similar way to a kickdown on a car with automatic transmission.

Nitrous works very well on both totally standard and tuned cars. Anything that is normally done to improve the performance of the engine can be done when nitrous is installed. This includes turbocharging and super-charging, where it works even better than ever.

The main injector switch is located on the dashboard.

The throttle-activated switch can be fitted to the standard spacer block which is between the carburettor(s) and the inlet manifold.

A twin SU carburettor assembly, fully kitted for nitrous. Only one throttle-activated switch is needed. A T-piece is used to divide the supply pipe to both carburettors.

the exhaust

One of the more fundamental areas – perhaps the most fundamental – when tuning a Mini is improving the way in which exhaust gases escape. Many owners fit a Stage 1 kit to the engine of their Mini, and in doing so find a noticeable power increase. The reason for this is simple: the mainstay of the Stage 1 kit is an uprated exhaust manifold and system.

There are several different types of exhaust manifold to choose from and, needless to say, for maximum performance it is important to choose the correct one. The best one is by no means necessarily the largest one.

Probably the best-known name in exhaust manifolds is Maniflow. David Dorrington of Maniflow originally worked for Downton Engineering, and was involved in the design of the manifolds that were developed for the Cooper and Cooper S. The basic designs of the Cooper Freeflow and the LCB that are available today have remained virtually unaltered from the original design.

Apart from the eight-port system, the other important manifold is the three-into-one which was developed primarily for competition by Richard Longman, who is also an ex-Downton man.

Exhaust manifolds – the range and suitable applications

It is important to choose the right manifold for the size and power output of the engine. Here is a guide to what should be fitted to what.

Link pipes, or Magic Pipes

The cheapest way to fit a performance exhaust system to a Mini is to retain the cast manifold and to use a link pipe. The link pipe – or Magic Pipe, as it is called at Maniflow – effectively extends the length of the standard cast inlet/exhaust manifold to that of a Freeflow or LCB. The link pipe was produced originally for BMC Special Tuning who wanted a cheaper alternative to a Cooper Freeflow for inclusion in its Stage 1 tuning kits. The same link pipe is still available today for original Mini applications and it has also been developed for use on both carburettor and injection-model Coopers of the 1990s.

Cooper Freeflow

The Cooper Freeflow manifold is good for engines in a mild to mid state of tune, particularly the smaller engines.

Ideal for: 850cc, 998cc, 1,098cc and mildly tuned 1,275cc engines.

Pipe sizes: 1⅜in primary, 1½in centre and 1¾in tail.

The long-centre-branch manifold

The LCB, the most popular manifold for the Mini, is available in three sizes, small, medium and large. It is suitable for most Mini engines from mild to wild. LCBs for injection cars are the same design as for carburettor cars, but there is a threaded hole to allow the lambda sensor to be fitted. With a Janspeed LCB, because of the positioning of the lambda sensor, the standard sensor wire is not long enough to reach. This is overcome by means of an extension wire. Maniflow manifolds have the mounting point for the sensor in a similar position to that of the standard manifold and an extension is not required. A pipe to link the LCB to the cat is available.

Small-bore LCB
Ideal for: '850' through to 1275GT with engines producing up to 70bhp.

Pipe sizes: 1¼in primary, 1⅜in secondary and 1¾in or 1⅝in tail.

Medium-bore LCB
Ideal for: engines producing from 70bhp to 100bhp.

Pipe sizes: 1⅜in primary, 1½in secondary and 1¾in or 1⅞in tail.

Large-bore LCB
Ideal for: engines producing from 100bhp to 125bhp plus.

Pipe sizes: 1½in primary, 1⅝in secondary and 2in tail.

Three-into-one

The next stage up from the LCB is the three-into-one manifold. This is also available in small, medium and large sizes. Small is for

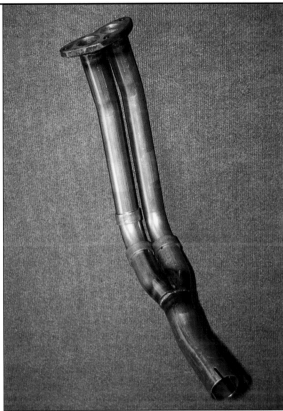

Far Left: A
Maniflow Magic
Pipe.

Left: A Magic
Pipe for injection
Minis.

road use, and medium and large are primarily
intended for competition. This is due to
the clamping of the pipes at the bottom
– the road manifold uses similar clamps to
an LCB, while the race versions have a quick-
release clamp. The size of the pipe dictates the
need for the different clamping methods.

Small-bore three-into-one
For road use on highly tuned 1,275cc engines
through to '1400' units.
    Pipe sizes: 1¼in outer two, 1⅜in centre and
1⅞in or 1¾in tail.

Medium-bore, three-into-one
For race application with camshaft durations of
over 300°.
    Pipe sizes: 1⅜in outer two, 1½in middle and
1⅞in tail.

Large-bore, three-into-one
For race application on '1400' engines where
camshaft duration is over 305°.

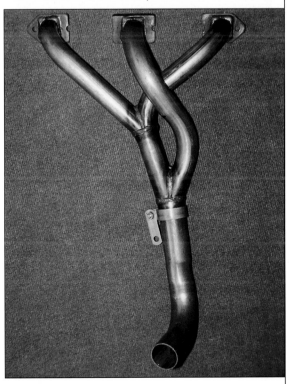

The Cooper
Freeflow.

Right: An LCB manifold.

Far Right: A three-into-one manifold.

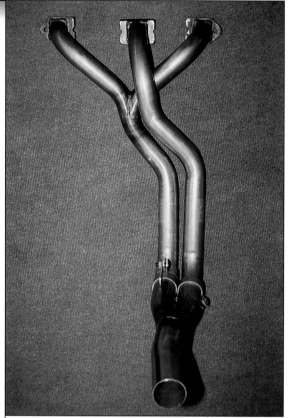
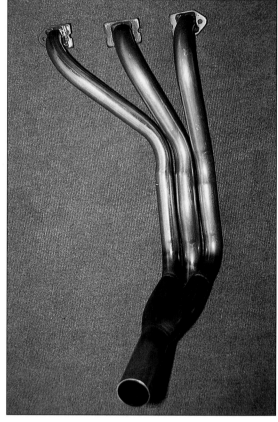

The Y-piece of the LCB runs close to the driveshaft. This is more of a problem with rubber-coupling shafts; pot joints, as here, have reasonable clearance.

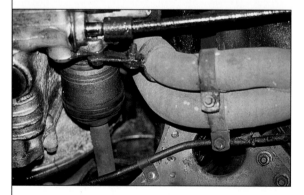

Pipe sizes: 1½in outer two, 1⅝in centre and 2in tail.

All sizes are outside diameter (o/d) except where two tail sizes are given, and this refers to inside diameter (i/d) and o/d for different size exhaust system fitment, i.e. on a medium-bore LCB the 1¾in system fits into the tail of the LCB, and the 1⅞in system fits over it.

Fitting performance manifolds

Fitting LCBs and three-into-one manifolds in particular can be somewhat fiddly. Care must be taken in correctly aligning the manifold to prevent the driveshaft contacting the manifold downpipes when the car is moving. This is particularly the case with the rubber-coupling type of driveshaft, where clearance is minimal at the best of times. Make sure that all engine mountings are in first-class condition to prevent any engine movement. The bracket which secures the manifold to the differential casing must always be used, or fracturing will almost certainly result. Most performance manifolds allow for the fitting of two sizes of exhaust system: the smaller size fits inside the tail of the manifold, and the larger one over it.

Turbocharged engines

Turbocharged engines use a special downpipe along the lines of a large-bore Magic pipe, but with a balljoint to reduce breakage.

Catalytic converters

Catalytic converters fitted to Minis are of the

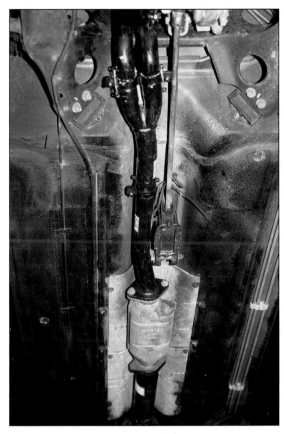

Far Left: A Janspeed exhaust manifold and system retaining the catalytic converter.

Left: This is how to rid a Mini of the cat. It is a Maniflow pipe, and substituting it for the catalytic converter will bring about an instant gain of around 3-4bhp which is constant regardless of the power output of the engine.

three-way type. There are two varieties of three-way cat, the open-loop type fitted to all carburettor Mini engines, and the closed-loop, which is fitted to both single-point and twin-point injection engines. Open-loop cats are regulated only once, at the carburettor. If the carburettor is incorrectly adjusted, this will impair performance of the cat.

Closed-loop cat systems continuously monitor the exhaust gases entering the converter. This is achieved by fitting a lambda sensor into the exhaust system, to measure the oxygen content of the exhaust gas. If the amount of oxygen differs from the pre-set level, the sensor will electronically adjust the electronic fuel injection unit to achieve the optimum fuel/air mixture. Injection cars must be fitted with the lambda sensor. If they are not, the engine may not run properly, risking severe damage.

It is important that only unleaded fuel should be used in any car fitted with a cat: 95, 97 or 98 octane unleaded are all satisfactory. The use of leaded fuel will render the cat inoperative by coating the monolith (internal coated honeycomb) with an impenetrable film. Performance exhaust manifolds and systems work well with or without a catalytic converter.

Removing the cat
In the UK, provided that a car was used before 1 August 1992, it will not be subject to a cat test at MoT time. If you are tempted to remove the cat on a later model Mini, and refit it in order to pass the MoT, remember that sometimes roadside spot-checks on emissions are carried out. Emissions spot-check regulations are the same as those for the MoT, but heavy fines can be imposed if a car fails.

The MoT, modified cars and emissions laws
Vehicles fitted with modified engines, in the UK, still have to meet exhaust emission requirements for the year of the car. There is however one exception to this. If the car is fitted with an earlier engine, it must be tested for the age of the engine, not the age of the car. So if you have fitted an MG Metro carburettor engine to a twin-point Cooper, it will – at least in theory – not be required to have a cat test at MoT time. However, the owner must be able to prove the age of the engine.

Exhaust systems
With an uprated manifold goes a performance exhaust system. Many types are available with the best usually regarded as being the Mini Spares RC40, the Maniflow and the Janspeed. A good system looks good, sounds good, and improves performance. Most good systems are

Left: A Maniflow tailpipe.

Far Left: This John Cooper Janspeed DTM twin tailpipe is particularly attractive.

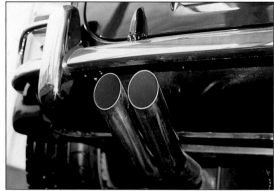

Extreme mods require extreme exhaust solutions. This is a twin-engined Cooper.

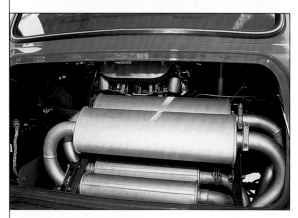

Exhaust mounts

When an upgraded exhaust system is fitted the mountings must be in good condition. Where rubber hanging mounts are used, on 1990 onwards Minis, these should be new; when the earlier type is fitted, the RC40 fitting kit or similar should be used. This is perfectly adequate for virtually all road applications. It is possible to further upgrade the early type of mountings by using reproduction 'works' mountings in the centre and at the rear. The centre mount is reinforced by having the bolt running right through the rubber mounting rather than being attached to the metal plate fixed to the rubber mount. The rear mount is a much more substantial affair than the standard cotton-reel type. Both 'works'-type mounts fit the standard mounting holes on the rear subframe, and the rear mount can be used for both side-exit and centre-exit exhaust systems.

available in centre and side exit form, and longer systems are also available to fit vans, estates and pick-ups. Some very large-bore systems are also available, which in most cases sound good and look the part if size is important, but a very large-bore system is usually not the best for maximum performance.

Tailpipe design is important, and a decision has to be made whether to have side or centre exit and if a single or twin tailpipe is required. DTM-style exhausts have become popular in recent times, and the side-exit systems look particularly good.

Twin silencer or single? Single-box exhaust systems are available for earlier Minis, and especially when used with an LCB – as in The Mini Shop's Stage 1 kit – they can sound absolutely wild. If you opt for a single-box system and use your Mini for long journeys, then a soundproofing kit will be essential!

the cooling system

The Mini's cooling system is conventional apart from the radiator being mounted at the side as opposed to the front of the engine (with the exception of 1996-onwards MkVII Minis).

This means that air passes over the engine, through the radiator (with fan assistance), and out through the nearside wheelarch. Although the air will be warmed as a result of being passed over a hot engine before it reaches the radiator, thereby reducing the cooling effect, this is offset by the fact that the engine is not surrounded by pre-heated air which has passed through a front-mounted radiator. In theory, the only problem with the Mini's cooling system is that there is increased likelihood of carburettor icing. This is why the air filter intake on a Mini is located near the exhaust manifold.

The cooling system consists of a radiator, water pump, thermostat and rubber hoses to link the components together. The radiator is cooled by air which is pushed through by a belt-driven fan mounted on the water pump. On 1990s 1,275cc pre-twin-point Minis there is an auxiliary electric fan in the front wheelarch to supplement the engine-driven fan.

The system works by circulating cold coolant from the bottom of the radiator up the bottom hose to the water pump, and then around the water passages of the block. From there it goes to the cylinder head to cool the combustion chambers and valve seats. Once the engine has reached normal operating temperature, the coolant passes through the opened thermostat into the top hose and back to the top of the radiator where it begins travelling downwards, cooled by the air passing through, and so on.

The original system used a three-core radiator with 13 gills per inch. When the Cooper S was introduced it had a larger radiator with 16 gills per inch. This larger radiator was fitted as standard to all Minis from 1980. Twin-point-injection Minis have the radiator located at the front, behind the radiator grille.

The cooling system needs uprating when the engine has been modified, and there are plenty of ways to do this. First, all parts of the cooling system must be in good working order.

Radiators
Early Minis with the 13-gill radiator should be upgraded to the later 16-gill type as an absolute minimum. This should be adequate for mild states of tune, particularly with small-bore engines. For engines in a higher state of tune, or of larger capacity, there are

Radiator upgrades, two-core and four-core.

It is possible to fit a front-mounted radiator. This works particularly well in the Clubman where there is more room.

Extra cooling in the form of an additional radiator.

two-core and four-core radiators available. The four-core rad increases water capacity by 25 per cent, and increases cooling efficiency by a greater margin. The two-core radiator from Mini Spares provides even greater cooling efficiency. It is designed for increased air flow, with large cores and V-shaped gills. Both of these performance radiators work well, and will cool most modified Minis. The two-core rad is of a more delicate construction and is not suitable for certain types of competition or for very rough and muddy roads.

It is also possible to fit the latest front-mounted radiator to earlier cars, as it is quite small and very light weight. This will entail fitting an electric fan, and requires some front panel surgery.

If overheating remains a problem, a heater matrix can be plumbed into the cooling system on very highly tuned cars to act as an additional radiator. This modification was offered as a kit by BMC Special Tuning in the 1960s and '70s.

Different radiator top brackets are required for different years and models of Mini, and will usually have to be changed when going to a larger engine, particularly when fitting a 1,275cc unit.

Water pumps

There are three types of water pump that are relevant. The first is the original, small-impeller pump for early cars, part number GWP132. The second pump is the later, higher-capacity version with the larger impeller, part number GWP134. If this pump is fitted to early (pre-A-Plus) small-bore engines, the impeller usually fouls the block. When a 12G940 head is fitted to a small-bore block the top edge of this pump needs to be modified along the top edge to allow the head to sit properly on the block. There should be a minimum of $\frac{1}{16}$in gap between the top of the water pump and the head. The third pump is No. GWP187, the Metro type which is also high-capacity with a blanked-off bypass hose take-off. If you are fitting a Metro engine, and wish to use a bypass hose, this pump can be drilled to suit. It is also the pump to use if the thermostat and bypass hose are removed. If you are not converting to a bypass, an expansion tank should be fitted.

Hoses

The correct hoses for the model (and engine) must be fitted. A 998cc top hose fitted to a 1,275cc engine for instance will be severely kinked and water flow will be much impaired.

Hoses for Minis, including heater hoses, are available in Kevlar and in silicon, these being much more durable and longer lasting. Kevlar hoses are reasonably priced, but the silicon ones are much more expensive.

Two types of bypass hose are available, the first being the straight, solid type, which is fitted as original equipment and should be used on all modified Minis. As long as this type of bypass hose is replaced at sensible intervals and checked regularly I have never known it to give trouble. The other is the concertina-type, which is made of thin rubber, and is intended to be fitted with the head and water pump in situ; it should only be regarded as a get-you-home repair. When fitting a bypass hose, use new clips of the correct type – jubilee clips should not be used.

Thermostats (and their removal)

Most Minis require an 88° thermostat. It can be removed to aid cooling on very high output engines but this mainly applies to race-spec engines. If a Mini is run with the thermostat removed, a hot spot will occur around number three and four combustion chambers in the cylinder head unless a blanking sleeve is fitted.

When this is done the bypass hose should also be removed and the resulting holes in the head and water pump blocked off. It is possible to run with a thermostat but with no bypass hose or expansion tank. The holes should be blanked off and four or six holes drilled around the periphery of the thermostat.

Metro engines

Metro engines do not have a bypass hose fitted. When a Metro engine is fitted into a Mini, a bypass hose can easily be fitted by removing the blanking plug from the cylinder head, fitting the correct outlet pipe and either fitting a bypass type water pump or modifying the Metro pump. The alternative is to run with a Metro style cooling arrangement and to plumb in an expansion tank.

Fans

The 11-blade fan, which is standard on most Minis, is quite efficient at low speeds but less so

Silicon hoses.

Bypass hoses – on the left the permanent type, on the right the get-you-home sort.

A thermostat with a blanking sleeve.

at high speeds, when it can restrict airflow through the radiator. A six-blade metal fan is more efficient all round, but it is noisier. A four-blade fan is good for fast road use, but is noisier still. Two blade fans are ideal under racing conditions, as they produce high airflow at high revs.

A Kenlowe electric fan conversion is available for both Mini and Clubman models if you prefer.

Fans: 11-blade, four-blade and six-blade.

Pulleys

There are two sizes of fan pulley. The larger one, which is fitted to the Cooper S and A-Plus engines, is more efficient and will help to reduce cavitation. However, if the head has been skimmed to any extent, as in the case of a 12G295 or 12G940 head fitted to the 998cc engine, the large pulley will foul the head. Toothed belt-drive systems are available for road and race applications, as is a poly V-drive system as fitted to most modern cars and to the twin-point Mini with front-mounted radiator.

Coolant additives

There are several cooling system performance improvers on the market, some of which are additives, and some of which are used without dilution as a replacement coolant. Benefits include decreased operating temperature, a quicker warm-up, and reduced sludge and corrosion.

Oil coolers – see lubrication section

An electric fan.

the electrics

It is vital that the engine electrics are up to the job on a performance Mini. This means ensuring that everything is in tip-top condition and, as higher states of tune are reached, upgraded as necessary to suit.

Distributors

Mildly tuned engines can usually retain the standard Mini distributor, provided that it is in good condition and preferably fitted with electronic ignition. If an engine from a later MG Metro is fitted the electronic distributor can often be successfully retained and wired into the Mini loom. Any more than this level of tune and the best route by far is to fit an Aldon distributor. These are supplied in several specifications and can also be individually tailored with a different advance curve to suit a particular engine specification. The vacuum advance, which is really a low-speed economy device, is best retained on most road applications where compression ratios are up to around 10:1 and camshafts up to a Piper 270 or equivalent; above this a non-vac distributor should be fitted. Low-vacuum and high-vacuum advance/retard units can be fitted to Aldon distributors. A final point to note is that A-Series and A-Plus engines have different distributor drives and retaining clamps which are not interchangeable.

Electronic ignition

A very good all-round way to upgrade a Mini is to fit electronic ignition. Provided the system is properly installed, the car will start more easily, fuel consumption will improve slightly, and you will have the benefit of a system that is maintenance-free and unaffected by dampness. The improvements are a result of increased efficiency and the fact that electronic ignition cannot go off-tune through wear or dirt in the contact-breaker points. Sideways pressure on the distributor shaft is also eliminated, so there will be virtually no future wear in the distributor, while existing wear (within reason) is overcome. Wear in the distributor shaft causes 'scattering' of the ignition timing: in other words, if the engine is correctly timed on number one cylinder, it does not follow that numbers two, three and four will be correctly timed.

An Aldon distributor, in this case an A-Plus non-vac unit.

Electronic systems on the market include the Aldon Ignitor and the three different Lumenition systems, called Magnetronic, Optronic and Performance. I have used the Ignitor and the Lumenition Performance and found both to be excellent systems. Fitting is very simple in both cases. The Lumenition Performance kit includes a new coil which is designed for easy removal and is ideally suited to high states of tune, but is expensive. For a tuned road car my recommendation would be to use either the Aldon Ignitor or Lumenition Magnetronic; both fit into the distributor itself and do not require a separate 'electronic box' to be fitted to the car. The part numbers of electronic ignition systems are different for the different distributors.

It is also possible to do away with the distributor altogether and fit a system such as the POLEstar management system. Developed in conjunction with Bryan Slark, this system – which uses a magnetically operated crankshaft sensor and a timing disc, which attaches to the crankshaft sensor – is successfully used on a number of racing Minis including Miglias.

Right: The Aldon Ignitor.

Far Right: The POLEstar management system.

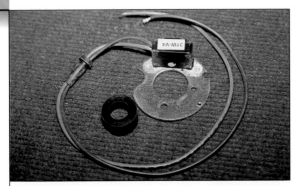

A Lucas sports coil.

brilliant ignition system will not work properly if the leads are past their best. Avoid very cheap leads, because they do not perform well and frequently fall to bits. Standard, good-quality Unipart-type leads are fine for lower levels of tune; above that, Lumenition Red leads are very good, and so are their Blue, pure-silicon leads with spirally wound stainless steel. The latter give 98 per cent suppression, but do have a tendency to turn brown, in my experience, which is not good on a concours Mini.

Coil

On most Minis the best thing to do is to replace the coil with a gold high-energy Lucas sports coil. This performs well, and also looks good. It is ideal with an Aldon distributor, but check the requirements of your car's specification before buying. Some electronic ignition systems, such as the Lumenition Performance, require a dedicated coil.

Plugs and leads

Check the condition of the HT leads, as a

Dynamo to alternator conversion

When carrying out this conversion, a Lucas 18 ACR alternator – which has a 45-amp output – is the best one to go for, provided that huge-output stereos and lots of additional lights are not being fitted. An alternator, brackets and pulley are needed. Positive-earth Minis will need to be converted to negative earth.

Alternators

The alternator fitted to the last production Minis

engine bay enhancements

A modified engine is definitely more pleasing if it also looks good. A clean engine bay is a good starting point, and is easily achieved if the engine is out being rebuilt, and the inner wings and bulkhead can meanwhile be resprayed if necessary. A good coat of paint on the engine in an appropriate colour is the next requirement, followed by the rocker cover and all the ancillaries such as the carburettors, starter motor and alternator being cleaned and painted or polished as appropriate when they are refitted. Beyond this are countless numbers of small items that are available to improve the look of the engine bay as a whole, for example, braided hoses and a fancy dipstick, but watch some of these, as they don't always fit. A smart engine can be further enhanced with items such as a stainless-steel coil bracket and wiper motor retaining bracket. Some items such as engine steady bars look good and at the same time, perform a useful function.

Engine steady bars

The bushes on the original engine steady bar – or bars, where a lower one is also fitted – wear out regularly and need frequent replacement. A quick check can be made by trying to rock the engine to and fro holding the rocker cover. This must be done when the engine is switched off, cold, and with the handbrake on. There should be virtually no movement. If there is pronounced movement, the bushes need replacement, and there are several options. The first is to replace them with standard bushes. These, in my opinion, are fine so long as you replace them regularly and with the proviso that original bushes are used: some of the aftermarket standard bushes break up very quickly. Secondly, the bushes can be uprated: there are several different types available, in varying degrees of hardness, and a sensible increase in hardness is a good idea. I do not like the totally solid bushes, as all they do is transmit noise and vibration through to the bulkhead – which is not good for the car or its occupants.

Lumenition leads and a Performance coil.

A Unipart heavy-duty battery.

had a 45-amp power output. This should be sufficient for most needs. Alternators with a greater output are available, but some are physically much larger, and you will need to check that there is enough space to enable one to be fitted. If the speed of the alternator needs to be reduced on a high-revving engine to avoid overcharging, this can be done by fitting a larger diameter, 5in pulley.

Starter motors

Two types of starter have been fitted to Minis: the early 'inertia' type was fitted up to 1995, after which a pre-engaged starter was fitted. No modification is necessary, but it is worth noting that the earlier type is lighter and much cheaper to replace if it goes wrong. Different flywheel ring gears are required for the two types.

Battery

The battery that is recommended for most Minis is barely adequate, and it is always worthwhile fitting a heavier duty battery. The MG Metro Turbo battery is the one to use and will certainly help eliminate starting problems. It will fit all Minis manufactured up until 1994.

Both upper and lower steady bars can be fitted with uprated bushes, and provided the engine mounts are in good condition, this should be sufficient to hold most engines in situ. If the angle of the engine needs to be altered slightly, adjustable-length steady bars are available.

If movement is still a problem – and this is more likely to be the case with rod-change gearboxes, as the gearchange extension on cars with the earlier remote gearchange is effectively a big steady bar in itself – then an 'ultimate' engine steady bar can be fitted. These come in a number of different versions for RHD and LHD Minis. These extra steady bars bolt to the thermostat housing and to the bulkhead. Some require the bulkhead to be drilled and a plate fitted (not welded) from underneath. Different bars are needed for small-bore engines and 1,275cc engines as the thermostat stud layout is different – and

where a 12G940 head is fitted to a 998 the 1275 type will be needed. Some types of steady bar cause problems with the breather canister on the tappet inspection cover on the back of the 998cc engine block and will require it to be modified. 'Ultimate' steady bars are available in a number of different finishes, including chrome, to tie in with the theme of the engine bay.

Engine mountings

The standard engine mountings on any Mini, but especially a modified car, must be in good condition or the engine will move about. They should be replaced when the engine is removed and at regular intervals thereafter. I have always used standard, genuine engine mounts and have never experienced any problems. They are not the easiest things in the world to fit and patience, screwdrivers and a pair of long-nosed pliers are required. Easyfit mountings with captive nuts are available, but I personally think they are in some ways harder to fit than the standard type. Although with these it is not necessary to hold the nut or bolt in position they are harder to line up with the subframe holes and it is easy to strip the threads in the captive nuts if you try to screw the bolt home when it is not fully aligned. Also, some of the Easyfit mounts that I have tried are too big, and the engine will not sit down far enough in the subframe to allow alignment; even squashing them in an engineering press has failed to do the trick. So if you do want to fit this type of mount, make

Standard and uprated engine steady-bar bushes.

Left: Standard engine mounts.

Far Left: All-metal engine mounts: these are bad news.

sure you buy from a reputable supplier. Solid metal mounts are available from some suppliers and are intended for competition use. They are noisy, hard and are generally horrible, so don't even think about using them on a road car.

Rocker boxes

If there is one thing that will set off an engine bay well, it is a smart rocker cover – even if the rest of the engine is not particularly clean. Various types are available, in a number of finishes ranging from crackle-black to polished aluminium. Many owners chrome plate the original rocker cover, but even painting it will make a big improvement, and actually, if the traditional look is important this can be the best thing to do. The alloy rocker cover fitted to the MG Metro looks very good , and is similar to those available back in the 1960s and '70s from firms such as J. V. Murcott – the same people who were responsible for the Minifin brake drum. The MG rocker cover will not fit if high-lift rockers are fitted, in which case a special, squarer design of cover will be needed – these are available from specialists.

Chassis, engine and rocker cover plates

A finishing touch to the engine compartment is to renew the chassis plates and also the stickers or plates affixed to the rocker cover where applicable. New chassis plates are obtainable from Mini Mail, who on production of your logbook as proof of ownership, will stamp the plates with the correct number. Rocker cover decals are available from a number of specialists, although they look their best on original, steel rocker cover boxes.

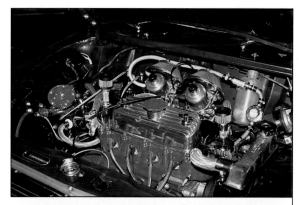

A well-presented engine bay, here showing the MG Metro/Minifin type of rocker cover.

Another exceptionally pleasing engine bay, this time with a chrome-plated standard rocker cover.

Sump guards

If a Mini is used for any type of off-road work or if it has been lowered a great deal, a sumpguard is a sensible precaution. There is a choice of types, ranging from very strong designs which are intended primarily for rallying – with an optional extension for even more protection – through to smaller and more decorative models. Two of the best for road use are the Mini Spares alloy sumpguard and the steel type as used on Italian-built Innocenti Minis. Both are relatively inexpensive. Do buy carefully as some sumpguards are not suitable for lowered Minis because they hang down too far beneath the gearbox.

04 the transmission

When tuning a Mini engine to improve the performance it is also important to consider the transmission. With the exception of very early Minis, the standard transmission will cope with engine tuning to Stages 1 and 2, provided that it is in tip-top condition. As levels of tune rise above this, upgrading will be required. Some of the upgraded components are small and inexpensive and are worth considering during a transmission rebuild, even on a hard-driven standard car.

The clutch

All manual gearbox Minis have a single dry-plate clutch which is operated hydraulically. There are three basic types of clutch which were fitted. Within those types of clutch, and depending upon the size and power output of the engine, different strengths of spring are used, meaning that there are several different part numbers for each clutch system.

Before considering any upgrading, it is important to determine which type of clutch is fitted to your Mini. The earliest Minis used a coil spring clutch which is very rare today and new parts are no longer available. In 1964, the coil springs were replaced with a diaphragm spring, and an improved diaphragm clutch was introduced. This was used up until 1982, when it was superseded by the Verto clutch which stayed with the Mini until production ended.

The main difference between the clutch systems is that on the coil-spring and diaphragm types the major clutch components – i.e. the clutch friction plate and the pressure plate, are fitted on the inside of the flywheel, whereas with the Verto clutch they are on the outside of the flywheel. The principle of operation is the same for both types but identification is easy: with the coil spring and diaphragm type (which are identical on the outside) the slave cylinder is mounted horizontally on the flywheel housing, while on the Verto the slave cylinder is mounted on a plate on the flywheel cover and points down-wards. The major reason for the change from the original diaphragm set-up to the Verto clutch was an attempt by the factory to eliminate clutch judder, a problem that to varying degrees has always plagued Minis. Unless all the Verto-clutch Minis I have ever

owned are exceptions, the venture was not exactly crowned with success.

Swapping clutch systems

It is perfectly possible to renew a Mini clutch or change the system with the engine and gearbox in place. The only special tool required is a flywheel puller, and these can usually be hired or bought from most Mini specialists and motor-accessory shops. On fuel-injected cars the ECU and all related components will need to be removed to gain access to the clutch area. As far as modifying goes, generally speaking, it is best to stay with the clutch system that is fitted to the Mini, but in some instances, such as if another engine unit is being fitted, or for personal preference, the system can be changed. If you are fitting a different flywheel make sure that the ring gear is compatible with the starter motor: there are different ring gears for 'inertia' starters and the later, pre-engaged type. The best way to check this is to count the number of teeth on the ring gear. The early, inertia-type flywheel has 107 teeth and the later pre-engaged type has 129 teeth. New ring gears can be supplied and fitted by an engineering shop.

Coil-spring to diaphragm

Coil-spring clutches are no longer available. It is possible to use a later diaphragm driven plate, provided that everything else is in order. It is only worth retaining a coil spring clutch on an original car, a 1071S for example: in all other cases with early cars fitting a diaphragm clutch complete is the way to go.

Diaphragm to Verto

There are many that would consider this a backward step! Generally speaking if you have a diaphragm clutch it is best to stick with it and upgrade it using modified diaphragm components as necessary. The main reason for converting to Verto will be when a later power unit is being fitted, in which case the Verto components should be used together with a Verto clutch operating arm, slave cylinder and flexible hose. Should you wish to convert an existing engine – perhaps because you have new or modified Verto components – you will also need a flywheel, pressure plate/spring, the relevant retaining bolt and keyplate, thrust sleeve and release bearing.

Verto to diaphragm

This is a more common conversion as a lot of people, myself included, prefer the earlier type of clutch, not least because more can be done to improve and uprate it. Again, it is a case of replacing the flywheel, pressure plate, clutch plate, diaphragm, and release bearing. The clutch operating arm, slave cylinder, hose and release bearing must also be changed. Unlike the Verto system the pressure plate and diaphragm are two separate components, and a new pressure plate is not included in a new clutch kit.

Metro power units

Early Metros use the diaphragm clutch, later Metros the Verto clutch. If a Metro engine is being fitted into a Mini it is possible to retain the Metro clutch provided that the correct slave cylinder is used to operate it, in other words if you are fitting a Verto Metro unit into a diaphragm Mini you will need to fit a Verto slave and hose plus the necessary mounting plate and clutch operating arm, and vice versa. If the Metro had a cable-operated clutch the same applies: the correct Mini operating components must be fitted. Do not try to mix-and-match the systems, as in most cases the clutch will not work properly.

The flywheel

Standard Mini flywheels are heavy. This is true of both the earlier type and the later Verto clutch flywheel. Lightening the flywheel on a fast road engine is very beneficial because it reduces the amount of energy used when the engine is accelerating, and is an essential part of the tuning process of a properly uprated engine. The benefit is most noticeable when pulling away – the engine will pick up faster and therefore acceleration will be quicker. Flywheels should not be over-lightened though, or the idle will be uneven. All the same, quite a lot of metal can be removed from the standard flywheel, particularly from the non-Verto type, with metal removed from the outer areas of the flywheel having the greatest effect. The flywheel fitted to the 1300 saloons and the early 1275GT is the heaviest and most in need of attention. If metal is removed in a lathe from the face to which the driving straps are bolted (which it should be on a properly lightened flywheel) then spacers of an equivalent thickness to the metal removed must be made up and fitted.

The flywheel weight chart shown below, supplied by Mini Spares, gives an indication of the amount of weight that can be lost. Standard flywheels should not be overlightened for safety reasons and competent engineering shops with experience of Minis know the sensible maximum to remove.

Lightening the standard flywheel is fine for engines up to a middle state of tune – say around Stage 3. Beyond this, it is best to invest in one of the steel flywheels which can be bought from Mini specialists. The steel flywheel should be supplied with the correct distance pieces for mounting the pressure plate, and Mini Spares recommend that when fitting their steel flywheel three clutch driving straps are used per location, to minimise stretch on high-performance engines. The road spec flywheel should be used on all but the most extremely tuned engines on the road – the ultra-light flywheels are in the main too light, as they are designed for full-race engines. When buying a light steel flywheel it is important to remember the ring gear – as previously stated, a different gear is required for pre-engaged starters. A light steel outer section which is nearly 4lb lighter than standard is available for Verto flywheels and this is well worth considering if you are running a Verto clutch. A version of this flywheel is available with a reluctor ring for fuel-injection Minis.

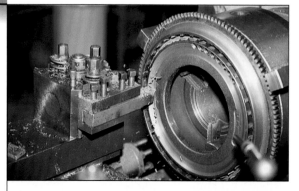

Lightening a Verto flywheel.

A non-Verto lightened clutch and flywheel assembly. Note the spacers.

The Mini Spares Verto lightened outer flywheel section.

Flywheel weights

	lb	kg
Standard diaphragm	16.71	7.58
Lightened standard	13.36	6.06
Fast-road lightened steel	11.02	5.00
Standard Verto outer section	12.83	5.82
Steel Verto outer section	8.84	4.01
Ultra-light steel race	8.83	3.8

Clutch backplates

Non-Verto clutches have a separate pressure plate or backplate which is not usually renewed

when a new clutch kit is fitted, and is not included in the kit. It is possible to reface the original pressure plate if needed when fitting a new or uprated clutch plate. If the flywheel is being lightened, the pressure plate should be lightened at the same time.

There are two types of standard backplate used with the diaphragm clutch. The most common is the 22A598, which was fitted to virtually all Minis. The exceptions were the Cooper S, 1275GT and most 998cc Coopers, which were fitted with the 22G270 backplate.

The 22G598 can be lightened to a degree, but not anywhere near as much as the 22G270 which is the backplate to use for serious power outputs. The 22G270 was made of far superior material – a very high-grade iron. It has been unavailable new for a long time, but has been reproduced in lightened form (in the same material) by Mini Spares under the part number C-AHT230. Further lightening of this component is also possible. Backplates must be lightened by a competent engineering firm which knows the difference between the standard plates (the part number is cast in) as too much lightening of the '598' can cause it to explode at high revs, with obviously very serious consequences.

The Verto clutch has a backplate built into the spring assembly. It is similar in design to a lightened 22G270, and cannot be further lightened.

Clutch plates and diaphragms

The standard Mini clutch diaphragms and clutch driven plates are capable, as a general guide, of withstanding power increases of around 30 per cent without problems, provided they are in good condition. For power increases over this amount it is likely that upgrading will be required. The easiest way to upgrade a standard clutch system, whether Verto or not, is to fit the clutch kit from a more powerful engine from within the range. In the case of 850cc, 998cc and 1,100cc engines this will be the kit intended for the 1,275cc Cooper S. With some manufacturers this may well be the only part number now available.

For most upgrades of a Verto clutch the MG Metro Turbo clutch will be adequate,

Far Left: A
clutch
diaphragm. This
is a standard
Cooper S unit
from AP Racing.

Left: An AP
Racing paddle
clutch.

as it is good up to 7,000rpm. The Turbo's clutch plate differs from other Verto plates in that it does not have any springs built in and in fact looks more like a non-Verto plate. Many people fit a non-Verto plate to a Verto clutch assembly as a budget repair. It will work, but the pressure plate face must be in good condition; in my experience, even when this is the case the clutch becomes juddery when warm.

Very high states of tune will need a more specialist approach. For this the solution is a clutch kit manufactured by AP Racing. Three types are available: a Fast Road kit suitable for a torque figure up to 76lb ft, an organic driven plate similar in design to the normal road plate, together with an orange diaphragm, which is good for 119lb ft of torque, and a paddle clutch with a grey diaphragm which is again good for up to 119lb ft of torque. The first two kits are suitable for road use, the last is intended for race use although some people do use them on the road. The paddle clutch has a very much in-or-out operation as the plate gives very little cushioning. This can result in fierceness and judder and therefore it is not suitable for Minis which are regularly used in traffic. The components are available individually from Mini Spares and some other specialists.

Release bearings

There are two types of release bearing, Verto and non-Verto. Both are reasonably long-lasting and require no modification or upgrading.

Balancing

The clutch/flywheel assembly should be

Braided flexible hoses for clutch line

In the same way as brake flexible hoses can be changed for the more robust and better looking braided variety, so can the clutch flexible hose. A different hose is required for Verto and non-Verto clutches as the slave cylinder union is different. It is also possible to replace both the metal pipe and the flexible hose with one long length of braided hose which runs directly from the master cylinder to the slave. This not only looks good but also helps if the engine has to be removed as it is easier to tuck the slave cylinder out of the way once it has been unbolted from the flywheel housing.

balanced along with the crankshaft assembly when a performance engine is being created. It is particularly important to balance a flywheel and backplate that have been lightened; ideally the components should be balanced individually and then as an assembly.

Master cylinders

There is only one clutch master cylinder, this being common to both clutch systems. On a normally tuned car it should be in good working order of course, and no modification is needed. It is possible to rebuild the cylinder with new seals, provided that the bore is in good condition and not worn or corroded. The original cylinder, with a metal reservoir, is no longer available and the replacement has a rather nasty plastic reservoir, so if underbonnet looks are important it is well worth spending time rebuilding the original.

the gearbox

Building a really high-powered Mini engine is fine, but if you want to take full advantage of the extra performance it is essential to make sure that as much of the power as possible reaches the wheels, and continues to do so without anything in between breaking. The manual gearbox fitted to the Mini has never really been the strongest point of the car. The gearchange is good and the gearboxes are pleasant to use, but the box does have a tendency to wear quickly – and generally the more power that is transmitted, the faster it will wear.

The earliest Mini gearboxes were three-synchro only, with synchromesh solely on second, third and fourth gears, and this was the case with the Cooper and S boxes too. The gear lever was the long 'magic wand' on 848cc Minis, the very early ones being straight, the later type having a bend near the top. Cooper and S models had a remote change which had the advantage of improving engine stability because of the mounting-point at the end of the remote extension, as well as providing a much sportier and faster change. In 1968, the four-speed all-synchro gearbox was introduced, and again both 'magic wand' and remote levers were used, the 'magic wand' for 848cc cars while 998cc (Mini 1000) and upwards used the remote. Early in 1973, the last major update took place when the rod-change 'box was introduced, and from this point onwards all gearboxes were of this type. The rod change works in the same way as the remote, but has an exposed rather than encased operating rod under the car. It is in many ways the most precise of the change mechanisms, and is generally very reliable.

All the gearchange mechanisms work well – including the 'magic wand', which is actually perfectly acceptable once you become fully accustomed to it. Today, most people use the rod-change gearbox when building tuned Mini power units, largely because there are many more around than there are of other types. However, there are a fair number of Mini enthusiasts, myself included, who still prefer the feel of the earlier remote change and appreciate its engine stabilising qualities.

Gearchange modifications

If you are changing a 'magic wand' Mini to a remote gearchange, fit the remote-change unit together with this type of gearbox. Trying to fit a remote change to a 'magic-wand' box is more trouble than it is worth and there is also the risk of oil leaks developing. Fitting a rod-change gearbox and change to a pre-1973 Mini bodyshell is possible, but the mechanism runs very close to the central tunnel. Fitting a remote gearchange and gearbox to a later Mini shell (post-1973) is also possible, and straight-forward, but suitable bracketry needs to be made to support the rear mounting. It is not possible to fit a rod change to an earlier remote 'box or vice versa, as the casings and many of the internals are different.

The rod-change gear linkage can be moved inside the car as on some racing Minis. To do this, a hole needs to be made for the rod to go through into the car, and either one or two (two preferably) 'helicopter' joints need to be fitted to the rod to allow it to move to the new position. The static locating rod stays where it is under the car, and the mounting bracket for the box at the base of the gear lever is used inside the car complete with the rubber mountings.

Idler gear upgrades

Transmitting the power from the engine to the wheels begins with getting the power from the crankshaft to the gearbox. With a Mini's transverse engine this is more involved than a conventional in-line installation where the gearbox is behind the engine and is effectively an extension of the crankshaft. The transfer gears or drop gears have to deliver all of the power produced by the engine. With standard engines, or those in mild to mid states of tune, the gears can usually cope. But when power output is upped considerably, the drop gears also need to be uprated. It is the idler gear, located between the primary gear on the end of the crankshaft and the first motion shaft in the gearbox, which always fails first. When any engine tuning is undertaken it is important to ensure that the drop gears are in absolutely first-class condition and if necessary the

standard gears should be rebuilt with new bearings and set up to the minimum recommended clearance. The latter point is particularly important both for longevity and keeping noise to a minimum.

Attention should also be paid to the primary gear, which should be renewed or rebushed by a competent engineering shop if worn. The standard helical-cut drop gears are normally capable of withstanding a power output up to around 110bhp; for serious outputs above this, and also with most turbo and supercharger applications, straight-cut drop gears should be used. Straight-cut gears are much better for power transmission and longevity because helical gears naturally wind up. This action causes both radial and axial loads which gradually destroy the bearings in which the gears rotate. A way around this on high-powered engines is to use the Jack Knight idler gear which overcomes these problems by being made in two pieces. The shaft is stationary in the usual bearing housing and the standard

roller bearings which are normally fitted to both sides are replaced by one central heavy-duty bearing which is considerably larger than the standard item. This is fitted into the gear itself. Mini Spares sell a taper-roller-bearing conversion for the idler gear, which is another way of overcoming problems in this area.

The downside to using straight-cut gears is that they are quite a bit noisier than the standard helical-cut gears. This is not so much of a problem on a stripped-out race-replica Mini, but is food for thought if you intend putting a very quick power unit into a luxury Mini.

Improved gearbox internals

The first items that normally fail in a hard-worked Mini gearbox are the baulk rings and the synchro hubs. When any engine tuning is undertaken, the gearbox should be rebuilt, using all-new bearings to ensure that it is in first-class condition to cope with the extra power. If the level of tune is not too excessive, the standard box can be retained, but it is a good idea to incorporate a few upgrades while it is being rebuilt. This will add little to the cost but could save a lot later on in preventing the need for another rebuild. The first component to upgrade is the layshaft. These are available in upgraded material for three-synchro and four-synchro boxes, and in the case of four-synchro to suit both A-Series and A-Plus gearboxes. Competition-grade baulk rings are available but they are not really suitable for road use: new standard ones are actually better. The other item that should be upgraded at the time of a gearbox rebuild is the diff pin; an upgraded pin is available and this will be dealt with fully in the section on the differential.

Close-ratio conversions

The Cooper S, 1275GT and Austin/Morris 1300GT were fitted with a close-ratio gearbox. All factory gearboxes, including these, were helical-cut. To convert a standard gearbox to 'S' ratios it is necessary to fit the first motion shaft and the laygear from the Cooper S. These parts are reasonably easy to find second-hand, but

do check the condition of the gears carefully. The parts are also available new, but when new parts are being fitted to pre-A-Plus gearboxes the later type A-Plus mainshaft is also required. This type of 'box is ideal for a 1,293cc Stage 2/Stage 3 engine for example.

Straight-cut gear conversions

When the engine has been modified to give a really serious power increase, an upgrade to straight-cut gears is very advisable. Straight-cut gears will cope with much higher power levels than helical-cut gears and another advantage is that less power is lost through the transmission. There are a number of options available and they can be bought in kit form or assembled into your gearbox by some of the specialists. Manufacturers such as Quaife and Jack Knight also provide a build service. Straight-cut gearboxes have a reputation for being noisy, which is not a problem with competition cars, but a lot of gear noise is not really desirable on a road car. But while it is true that straight-cut gears are noisier than the standard helical-cut type, provided good-quality gears from a reputable manufacturer such as Quaife or Jack Knight are used, the noise increase should not normally present a problem. Most of the extreme gear noise that can be heard on race Minis comes from the straight-cut drop gears anyway.

Straight-cut gear ratios are closer-ratio than those in the close-ratio gearbox fitted to the Cooper S and 1275GT. Straight-cut gear sets intended for race Minis are closer still and are therefore not always ideal on a road car. The following table shows a comparison of standard gear ratios and the ratios used in the straight-cut gear sets available from the Mini Spares Centre:

Gear ratio comparisons, four-synchro					
Gear	Std 850/998	Std S/1275GT	Std A Plus	Mini Spares Clubman	Mini Spares ST
1st	3.52	3.32	3.64	2.583	2.54
2nd	2.21	2.09	2.18	1.711	1.731
3rd	1.43	1.35	1.42	1.25	1.258
4th	1.0	1.0	1.0	1.0	1.0

Five-speed conversions

Never available as standard from the factory, or even as an option, five-speed gearboxes have been made available for some while as an aftermarket modification. At the time of writing, Jack Knight are the only company producing five-speed 'boxes for the Mini, and these only in straight-cut synchromesh form. A finite number will be produced now that the production of Mini gearbox casings has ended, but no doubt they will appear on the second-hand market from time to time. Jack Knight has said that they will continue to sell spare parts for these gearboxes which are suitable for highly modified engines where five speeds are required. It can cope with flywheel power outputs of up to around 130bhp.

Dog 'boxes

Dog boxes are the ultimate, and are primarily intended for competition. They can be used on the road but are only necessary for road use when extremely high power outputs demand their use, – they can cope with power outputs of 190bhp and more. The laygear and mainshaft differ on dog 'boxes. A dog 'box does not have synchromesh, although the layout is similar to that of a synchro 'box. Changing gear is easy as long as the revs are correct at the time – this is something that comes with experience! All gears are heavy duty, and failure of dog 'boxes is extremely rare.

Building gearboxes

The rebuilding and assembly of a Mini gearbox at home is certainly possible for those with the knowledge and ability. As with all mechanical assembly, cleanliness is essential. Common problems following inexperienced DIY assembly include a blocked oil pick-up pipe caused by too much gasket sealant being used between the engine and gearbox – only a smear is needed – and broken gears brought about by jamming the gears with a screwdriver when fitting the input gear. The correct way to fit the input gear is to select two gears together which will lock the gearbox, allowing the nut to be torqued correctly.

The other point to remember is to install the 'O' ring in the gearbox casing. Forget it and

there will be no oil pressure when you try to start your new engine. When this happens the power unit must be removed, stripped down, and the 'O' ring installed – there is no other way around the problem. For anyone in any doubt about their abilities, it is far better to have the gearbox attended to by a competent Mini specialist.

A four-speed synchromesh straight-cut gear kit – a traditional favourite of many Mini enthusiasts. This is a Quaife set, and for remote changes the ratios are: 1st – 2.544, 2nd – 1.731, 3rd – 1.259, 4th – 1:1. For rod changes the ratios are:1st – 1.827, 2nd – 1.731, 3rd – 1,329, 4th – 1:1.

The difference between straight-cut and helical-cut gears.

A five-speed helical-cut synchromesh gearbox from Jack Knight. Sadly, no longer available, this gearbox copes with power outputs of 85-90bhp without problem, making it ideal for tuned injection Minis.

A Quaife dog-box kit.

A dog engagement.

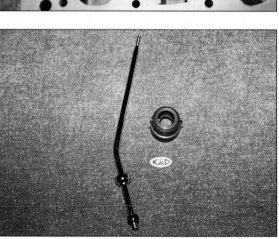

Fitting a central oil pick-up pipe.

Left: The KAD Quickstick for rod-change gearboxes.

Far Left: The Jack Knight Quickshift.

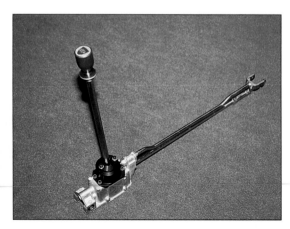

All performance gearboxes should be fitted with a central oil pick-up pipe, which needs to be installed during assembly of the gearbox. For more details see the lubrication section.

Quickshift gear levers

An excellent conversion for all fast road Minis with remote or rod-change gearboxes is a quickshift mechanism. Its purpose is to tighten the gate and thereby reduce the amount of travel between gears. It works by lengthening the lever below the pivot point, and thereby reducing the amount of travel above. There is more than one version available, but I have found those produced by KAD to be very effective and reliable. The KAD Quickstick comes in two different versions, one to fit the remote change and the other for the rod change. The remote version is a simple replacement part with the addition of a spacer. The rod variety requires a bit more work, but fitting is still surprisingly easy. Mini Spares also sell a shift bias lever for rod-change gearboxes. This improves the second-to-third gearchange.

A more expensive alternative to the Quickstick – but for rod-change gearboxes only – is the Jack Knight Quickshift system. Developed from the standard unit, it uses a modified gearchange housing with a turret machined from aluminium. Ball bearings are incorporated to give a very slick, smooth shift with reduced travel between gears. The unit is fully adjustable on the car to ensure perfect changes.

Gearchange rod seals

Virtually every rod-change gearbox leaks oil from the gearchange rod seal at the rear of the gearbox/differential casing. Some leak more than others, and some can leak to an alarming degree – sometimes even after a new seal has been fitted. Many people fit more than one seal in an attempt to cure the problem. A kit has been developed by Mini Spares which uses an alloy spacer fitted with an 'O' ring to centralise the rod; when used together with an original oil seal and dust cover, this will considerably reduce the occurrence of leaks, and the dust cover prevents grit getting on to the seal and damaging it. This kit is inexpensive and is well worth fitting, particularly when the gearbox has been overhauled, but it is also not difficult to fit with the engine and box in situ.

the differential

The purpose of a differential is to allow the two driven wheels to rotate at different speeds at the same time. For most of the time that the car is travelling under normal, straight-line conditions the Mini's front driven wheels turn at the same speed as each other, and it is only when the steering is turned that the diff starts its real work. The crown wheel and pinion are turning all the time that the car is in motion, and the planet gears come into action when differing wheel speeds are required.

The Mini differential is actually a very robust unit which is normally capable of taking quite considerable power increases and covering high mileages before giving trouble – provided it is treated with a reasonable degree of respect. Mini Miglia racers use standard diffs and they are very reliable, which shows that they can happily cope with high power outputs. Having said that, problems do come about through both use and abuse and these include noisy bearings and sometimes the thrust washers wearing through. The diff pin, on which the planet wheels rotate, also wears. Some people get through these at an alarming rate, others make them last almost indefinitely, and it is not always down to driving style, so maybe some pins are harder than others. On a properly built tuned Mini the diff should be rebuilt at the same time as the gearbox and items such as the diff pin and bearings replaced. Premature diff problems are often caused by aggressive driving, such as wheel-spinning out of junctions: this wears the planet gears and diff pin very fast, particularly when a powerful engine such as a 1,380cc is involved. Too much of this sort of treatment to a standard diff has been known to result in some of the components breaking and making a sharp exit straight through the casing without warning.

So if your engine is modified to any degree, or you are a very aggressive driver of a standard car, differential mods should certainly be on the agenda.

Changing standard diff ratios

Fitting a different engine, changing the diameter of the road wheels, or merely the type of use to which your Mini is to be put: all these may bring about the need to change the diff ratio. The

The offending area – the rod-change where it enters the gearbox.

crown wheel and pinion are the two components that are referred to when changing the diff. Crown wheels are normally stamped with the part number, and the number of teeth for both the crown wheel and pinion. The pinion is not stamped with the part number, but it should be remembered that it is essential to use the components in a correct pair, or considerable damage and failure may well result.

Probably the most common original-equipment differential fitted to the Mini over the years has been the 3.44:1, which went into the vast majority of 998cc cars and the Cooper S. For most applications this is perfectly acceptable and no change will be required. In fact, in many cases where a different standard diff is fitted, a change to the 3.44 is a good idea.

The 3.44 is without a doubt most people's favourite, including mine. However, if a Mini spends most of its time cruising at 70mph on the motorway or if you like long-legged acceleration and relaxed cruising, something higher, for instance a 3.1 or even a 2.9 diff, would be more suitable. The lower the numbers in the differential ratio, the higher the gearing of the diff, thus a 2.9:1 is considerably higher-geared than a 4.1:1. A higher-geared diff is often referred to as a 'taller' diff. To calculate the differential ratio, count the number of teeth on the crown wheel and divide by the number of teeth on the pinion. For example, if the crown wheel has 62 teeth, and the pinion 18 teeth this gives you 62 divided by 18, equalling 3.44 as the differential ratio.

It is vital that all parts of the diff are fitted and correctly shimmed as detailed in the Mini workshop manual. New bearings must always be fitted.

So which diff is best? Recommending diffs for particular applications is in fact a very difficult thing to do. Each case has to be treated individually, and it is the owner's preference and the main use to which the car is subjected, rather than the specification of the engine, that are the principal determining factors. A diff ratio has to be a compromise between good acceleration, relaxed cruising and good fuel consumption, and this is what, in theory, you get with the factory-fitted standard diff.

Ratios available:
2.9:1
3.1:1
3.2:1
3.4:1
3.6:1
3.7:1
3.9:1
4.1:1

Upgrading the differential

Competition diff pin

There are several upgrades that can be made to a Mini differential. The first is worth doing to any diff whether standard or modified when it is rebuilt, and that is to fit a competition diff pin. Manufactured by Mini Spares, the competition pin simply replaces the original pin, but is a lot harder wearing as it is made out of improved material and is subjected to upgraded heat treatment. The planet wheel contact area is increased and the surface is ground to a finer finish. This is an excellent mod; in fact for a standard diff it is a must.

Cross-pin diffs

If you want to have a virtually indestructible diff which is ideal for road cars, but do not want to go as far as fitting a limited-slip diff, the answer is a cross-pin diff. This uses four planet gears

A Mini Spares competition diff pin.

The Tran X cross-pin differential.

rather than the two used in standard diffs. It can be used with Hardy Spicer couplings, and pot joints, and has been well proven under racing conditions and in the RAC Rally; it is reasonably priced too. The original Tran X cross-pin diff is an exceptional unit, and I use one in one of my own Minis. It is available exclusively from Minits in the West Midlands. Mini Spares now manufacture their own unit under the name of Trannex, and other types are available from specialists such as Mini Sport. For most tuned road-going Minis this is without a doubt the ultimate diff upgrade.

Semi-helical CWPs

When the gearbox has been modified to include close-ratio straight-cut gears, the next stage of modification is to fit a semi-helical crown wheel and pinion. Mid-way between straight-cut and helical-cut, the difference in the angle of the teeth can clearly be seen if they are compared with the standard parts. When using semi-helical-cut gears, there is a reduction in the power loss that occurs through the standard helical-cut gears, but the penalty is increased gear noise. Semi-helical CWPs are primarily intended for competition cars when regulations permit.

A Jack Knight semi-helical crown wheel.

The Quaife limited-slip differential.

Jack Knight semi-helical ratios:
3.4:1
3.6:1
3.7:1
3.9:1
4.0:1
4.1:1
4.2:1
4.3:1
4.6:1
4.9:1

Limited-slip differential

Although few road-only Minis use them, for huge power outputs and for Minis used in competition – especially anything involving rough terrain or loose surfaces – the ultimate is to fit a limited-slip differential. In times past it was common practice to lock the diff on some competition Minis by welding the components together, thus maintaining the drive to both wheels all the time. This certainly overcomes the problem of losing traction over loose or slippery surfaces, particularly on corners when one wheel is loosing grip and spinning, but it also makes a Mini – or any front-wheel-drive vehicle – very hard to steer, and is totally unsuitable for road use. A limited-slip diff does not transfer power to both wheels permanently, but maintains the drive to the wheel which is gripping – unlike a standard diff which tends to transmit to the wheel which turns with the least resistance. The best-known classic design of LSD is that made by Salisbury, but it is not such a popular fitment nowadays. Currently one of the best LSDs is the Quaife. This is a limited-slip diff which is suitable for both very highly tuned road Minis as well as competition Minis, as the car remains very driveable. This diff is generally reckoned to be bullet-proof. The Quaife LSD needs to be fitted with a special crown wheel and pinion, as the standard variety will not fit. A number of different ratios are available and special output shafts must be fitted.

driveshafts

The drive from the differential on a Mini is transmitted to the wheels by a pair of unequal-length driveshafts, the left-hand shaft, when viewed from the driver's seat, being the shorter of the two. The various models of Mini over the years have used a number of slightly different driveshaft arrangements. All types are jointed at both ends to allow for steering and suspension movement.

There are actually six main types of driveshaft arrangement used as standard equipment on Minis – two types of outer constant-velocity joint, and three types of inner joint. The different types are as follows:

A) Standard drum-braked Mini with inner rubber-coupling joint. The 997cc and 998cc Coopers also use this shaft.
B) Cooper S with inner rubber-coupling joint.
C) Automatic Mini with Hardy Spicer inner joint.
D) Cooper S and 1275GT with Hardy Spicer inner joint.
E) Standard drum-braked manual/automatic Mini with offset-sphere plunging-type joints (known as pot joints).
F) Late-type 8.4in disc-braked manual/automatic Mini with pot joints.

Constant-velocity joints
At the outer wheel end of the shaft there are two types of constant-velocity joint fitted. These are:

A) Small outer CV joint fitted to all drum-braked cars and 997cc and 998cc Coopers; requires 1⅛in socket.
B) Large outer CV joint; 1⁵⁄₁₆in socket is required. The large joint is fitted to all other Minis with 7.5in and 8.4in front disc brakes.

Under normal conditions, even on a high-performance Mini, the CVs are reliable and do not often cause problems until they have covered very high mileages. The exception is when the rubber gaiters split, allowing water and dirt to enter – after which failure can be very rapid. A split or holed gaiter will mean MoT failure, and should be rectified immediately.

Universal joints
At the inner end there are three types of inner universal joint. These are:

A) Rubber coupling.
B) Hardy Spicer.
C) Offset-sphere plunging or pot joints.

The rubber couplings, which were fitted to Minis other than later examples of the Cooper S and early 1275GTs, will give long service provided that they do not become contaminated with oil leaking from the engine or differential oil seals. Worn engine mountings will also contribute to the coupling's early demise. These couplings generally have a bad name with many Mini owners – quite wrongly so. Inspect them periodically and you will have no problems, and they have one very big thing going for them: they are the easiest type of inner joint to renew.

This set-up remained until 1973 when the design was changed to the offset-sphere plunging type of joint – or pot joint as they are generally known – which brought it closer in concept to that of the outer CV.

Driveshafts
In between the two joints there are basically three types of driveshaft. These are:

A) Rubber coupling and Hardy Spicer, as fitted to drum-braked manual/automatic Minis and the 997/998cc Cooper.
B) Hardy Spicer upgraded Cooper S.
C) Pot joint drive shaft, fitted to all manual Minis 1973 onwards, and automatics from around 1977.

This is a guide to the main types of driveshaft. As with most things Mini, there are a few oddities and variations which tended to creep in: for instance the original Hardy Spicer shafts are slightly shorter than the rubber coupling type, although they are interchangeable. Automatic Minis were fitted with Hardy Spicers and at the changeover point to pot-joints on auto Minis a pot-joint diff was used with Hardy Spicer couplings. There are also some very thin pot-joint driveshafts around, which Leyland fitted for a year or so before reverting to the normal type. Although there is no evidence that these shafts break more easily, they are probably best avoided on a high-performance Mini.

Shaft interchangeability

Mini driveshaft assemblies can be interchanged to a degree, and also modified. When an LSD is fitted, modification to the assembly is essential.

The inner splined end is the same on both Hardy Spicer and on rubber coupling driveshafts and the sliding flanges are interchangeable provided that the diff output shafts and flanges are changed to match at the same time. Pot joint inner splined ends, meanwhile, will only fit into pot joints.

The disc-type CV joint will fit straight on to the drum-type driveshaft without modification, but the correct (larger) rubber gaiter kit must be used. All types of shaft will fit on to both the large and small CV joint which is particularly useful when upgrading a drum-braked Mini to disc brakes.

Finally, remember that left and right driveshafts are of different length and are not, in normal circumstances, interchangeable.

Modification and upgrading

The driveshaft assemblies on Minis are sufficiently robust for even quite high levels of tune where the car is subjected only to normal road use. Any Mini producing more than around 55bhp should be equipped with front disc brakes (7.5in or 8.4in) and therefore will have the larger disc-braked CV joint at the outer end. Moving to the inner end, although I have never had problems with them, the least desirable set-up at the diff end for the tuner is the rubber coupling, but they were in fact fitted to early Cooper S models. That said, the standard coupling will cope with the power of a tuned road engine, and it will give a very smooth power delivery. If you do not want to convert to pot joints, but feel the need to upgrade the coupling, an easy way to do this is to fit the Quinton Hazell QH5000 joints. These are much tougher than

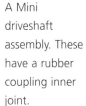

A Mini driveshaft assembly. These have a rubber coupling inner joint.

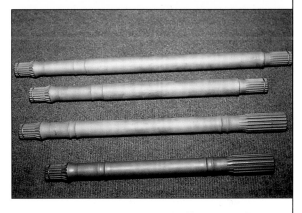

Upgraded driveshafts.

the standard rubber item and effectively take it nearer in design to a Hardy Spicer. With all types of coupling joint, watch the clearance if you are fitting an LCB exhaust manifold.

For a well-tuned 1275 or a 1380, many people prefer to use Hardy Spicers or pot joints, the latter being the cheaper and much more readily available option. The vast majority of Minis being tuned today will be fitted with pot joints anyway and these are absolutely fine for a fast road Mini equipped with a standard diff or with a twin-pin diff.

For competition-level power, many regard the Hardy Spicer arrangement as the best, and the standard 'S' driveshafts are fairly robust – although they are available in upgraded material. The ultimate driveshaft conversion is the Mini Spares Group A set-up. This is intended for serious competition work and is also used by many in sports such as grasstrack racing which can be very punishing to the drivetrain. Designed by Neil Booth of Mini Spares North, the Group A set-up is generally considered to be indestructible.

An inner pot joint.

An upgrade for coupling joints of long standing – the Quinton Hazell QH5000 needle-roller coupling. Many people swear by them, but some folks have criticised them in the past for being harsh.

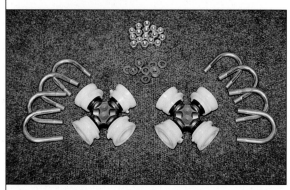

Equal length driveshafts

Jack Knight produces an arrangement which bolts to the side of the differential to enable two equal-length driveshafts to be used. The advantage of the system is that it considerably reduces the effects of torque steer, a problem associated with front-wheel drive and high-powered Minis in particular. Inside the unit the shaft is considerably thicker than the standard driveshaft. It works partly because of this, and partly because the unit is rigidly fixed to the diff. The equal-length kit is available in three versions:

1) To fit a standard pot-joint diff.
2) To fit an LSD with Hardy Spicer joints.
3) To fit an LSD with pot joints, as by far the most commonly used today.

The Jack Knight equal-length driveshaft conversion.

The driver of this wild Mini Rodster demonstrates how to punish drivetrain components. (Picture by Chris Brown; www.miniworld.co.uk)

Hard cornering also places a heavy load on the driveshafts and differential. (Picture by Gerard Brown)

05 the running gear

Right from the launch back in 1959, the Mini has been renowned for its outstanding roadholding. At the time there was no other car – and this included most sports cars – that was able to keep up with a Mini through the bends. Whereas today the roadholding of most modern cars has caught up and in many cases overtaken that of the Mini, very few cars get anywhere near the Mini, even a standard Mini, in terms of driver 'grin factor'. By carrying out a number of relatively simple and straightforward modifications, the already good handling can be dramatically improved, and back when the Mini was new, it wasn't long before people realised this.

The chassis

Lowering, by chopping lumps off the suspension trumpets – usually with a hacksaw – and then the fitting of a set of uprated Armstrong dampers soon became regular practice in the Mini's early days. The great advantage of tweaking Mini suspension was – and still is – that the mods can be carried out in stages. Thanks in the main to aftermarket technical developments, today there is more scope than ever to uprate the handling of a Mini. What is more, there is now a choice between greater levels of ride comfort or stiffer suspension with go-kart cornering ability.

Although great fun, the Mini does not have perfect handling. When pushed hard, the problem with Mini handling is the tendency for the car to understeer, in other words, the faster the car is driven into a bend the more steering lock has to be applied, to the extent that if a bend is approached much too fast the car will simply carry straight on, even when the steering is on full lock. This is a characteristic of most front-wheel-drive cars while most rear-wheel-

drive cars do the opposite and oversteer, so that when powered round a bend the rear of the car will hang out. It is probably true to say that on the whole, a Mini's understeer is more accepted today as the vast majority of everyday cars are front-wheel-drive, whereas in the early days, rear-wheel-drive was the norm. Modifying Mini suspension does go some way towards making the handling more neutral, particularly when front wheel camber is altered either by lowering or by fitting longer bottom suspension arms – or both.

Suspension types

During the years that the Mini was in production, two types of suspension were fitted. Within the two types there were component and specification variations, according to the model or year, but for modification and uprating purposes these variations are largely irrelevant.

Of the two types of system, rubber-cone or 'dry' suspension is by far the most common. It was fitted to the first Minis in 1959, and remained until 1964 when saloon cars were fitted with Hydrolastic or 'wet' suspension. In October 1969, the majority of Minis reverted to dry suspension, with only the Clubman, the 1275GT and Cooper S retaining Hydrolastic. The 'S' was discontinued in 1971, and at the same time the Clubman Saloon and 1275GT went over to 'dry' suspension. This suspension has been fitted to all Minis ever since, and was always fitted to estate and utility Minis. This suspension is actually the less comfortable in terms of ride quality of the two systems, but it is easier to maintain and also to upgrade. There

Lowering a car in the traditional way, by reducing the height of the trumpet.

are a greater number of options and components available for 'dry' suspension, and as the vast majority of Minis on the road are 'dry' – and also as a good few 'wet' cars have been converted to 'dry' – we will concentrate on upgrading this suspension first.

Upgrading 'dry' suspension

Before any suspension modifications are carried out on a Mini there are two basic things to consider. The first consideration is whether the car is going to be lowered. If so, shorter dampers will be required to prevent bottoming out at the front. Any suspension system that continually bottoms out will eventually break its mounting points, which is both expensive to rectify and potentially dangerous. If the dampers are too long for the reduced-height suspension, there will also be too much travel for the shortened trumpets (adjustable or otherwise) at the rear, and too much downward travel can result in the trumpets literally falling out of the rubber spring.

It is perhaps worth pointing out at this time that changing the dampers will not raise or lower the car. Adjustable dampers vary the stiffness of the suspension, while height adjustment is determined by the length of the suspension trumpet which fits between the knuckle joint and the rubber spring.

The second consideration is the diameter and width of the wheels that are going to be fitted. This is important because Minis fitted with 13in wheels cannot be lowered to anything like the same degree as those fitted with 10in or 12in wheels.

The standard 'dry' suspension on a Mini, as with any road car, is a compromise between handling and comfort. In standard form Minis handle well, and in fact, for the design of the car and the length of the wheelbase, they ride fairly comfortably too. This latter comment is best demonstrated by first driving a Mini with lowered and stiffened suspension and then driving a standard Mini! If much of your driving is over bumpy roads, or with a full load on board, too much lowering and stiffening is inadvisable. Later, post-1976 Minis have slightly softer suspension with a rubber-mounted front subframe and larger rubber bushes at the front

of the rear subframe. These later Minis do have an improved ride, but when the front subframe rubber mounts wear or age the handling can start to feel somewhat woolly. This same problem can occur when the suspension is tuned in other areas. There are two possible routes when modifying Mini suspension. The first is to improve handling, which is the route that most owners choose, and the second is to improve comfort – for instance on a latter-day Mini that is used as everyday transport.

Although the first items that should be upgraded on 'dry' Minis are the dampers, because shorter dampers are needed for lowered Minis, we will look at suspension height first.

Lowering the suspension: general points

There really is nothing quite like a Mini with lowered suspension. Lowering has two distinct benefits. First, together with a decent set of wheels any Mini, however standard it is in other respects, will look a great deal faster and sportier when it has been lowered by around 1-1½in. Secondly, the roadholding will be improved because the car stays much flatter during cornering as a result of the considerably reduced body roll: it is still true today that a well set-up lowered Mini will out-corner most things on the road. But by just how much can you safely lower a Mini? The 1970s book *British Leyland Minis* by Marshall and Fraser recommended an 11in measurement from wheel centre to trim as a minimum for a 10in-wheeled Mini at the front – at the rear a slightly greater clearance is usually needed.

In reality, though, there are a number of factors to be taken into consideration before lowering. The first, as previously mentioned, is wheel diameter. If 13in wheels are being fitted, too much lowering is inadvisable, or the tyres will scrape on the wheelarches when going over the smallest bump. Secondly, there is the question of use: if the car regularly carries passengers in the back, again you should avoid going too low or the ride will become uncomfortable, and tyre rubbing will be a problem, even with 10in wheels. The third consideration is the area in which you live.

If it is an urban area the chances are there will be speed humps nearby. In most cars these are not a problem. In a standard Mini they are bad enough, but in a lowered Mini with stiffened suspension they are a nightmare. With the worst of these bumps it will be necessary to slow to 10mph or even less in order to negotiate them without catching the exhaust system. The answer to the original question thus must be that a Mini should be lowered by the maximum amount that is sensible, taking all the above considerations into account. In other words, virtually all cases are individual.

Lowering whilst retaining the main original components and set-up can be achieved in one of two ways: either by the 'traditional' method, of shortening the suspension trumpets, or by fitting alternative, adjustable units. When lowering, make sure the front suspension arms are just clear of the bump stops as the ride will suffer if they are in permanent contact. Watch rear brake pipe clearance, too – this is explained fully in the section on braking. Also bear in mind that altering the ride height will vary the suspension geometry at the front of the car. As the car is raised from standard, positive camber is increased; as it is lowered, negative camber is increased. This is something to bear in mind if negative-camber lower front suspension arms are to be fitted as if the car is both lowered a great deal and fitted with negative arms, too much negative camber can result.

Lowering: the traditional method

The traditional method of lowering a Mini by removing metal from the knuckle joint (narrow) end of the suspension trumpet is fine provided the rules are closely followed. It is a good method which works well, and many of the Minis that I have owned over the years have been lowered in this way. It is ideal for anyone working to a budget as all that is needed is a set of lowered dampers and possibly a set of new knuckle joints. The downside of this method is that there is often a lot of trial and error required to get the height just where you want it, and any

adjustment requires the suspension to be taken apart. If you do choose this way, strictly speaking, the trumpets should be machined on a lathe, but it is possible to cut them with a hacksaw, provided that the mating face for the knuckle joint is absolutely flat. The best answer is to obtain an old set of trumpets and experiment using a hacksaw before having the originals machined to the correct length. If you do this, make sure the rear trumpets come from a late 1970s onwards Mini: the earlier trumpets have a lower spring rate and do not work well with later softer springs – the suspension will be very soft and continually bottom out.

The amount to be removed can vary from side to side in order to get the car to sit level. Lowering a Mini is not an exact science, and the trick is to remove the correct amount of metal. The original BMC/BL Special Tuning Data Sheet states that a maximum of 0.312in (7.9mm) may be removed from both front and rear trumpets. The ratio of metal removed from the trumpet to the amount that the car is lowered is approximately 3:1 at the front and 5:1 at the rear, in other words removal of $\frac{1}{10}$in from the trumpet will lower the car $\frac{3}{10}$in at the front, and $\frac{1}{2}$in at the rear. However, the ratio increases the lower you go, so don't try removing the maximum amount to start with or the car will end up too low. Also remember that to begin with the car will sit higher than it will when the suspension has settled after a few days.

Raising 'dry' suspension

'Dry' suspension can be raised by fitting a washer between the trumpet and the knuckle. There is even a Rover part (21A1845) specifically for this purpose. It is perfectly acceptable to fit a washer to one side of the car to level out lopsidedness, provided that the suspension components are all in good order.

Adjustable-height suspension

The best way today to lower a Mini is without a doubt to fit a set of adjustable trumpets. This way the height is easily adjusted until the optimum height for handling and the conditions is achieved. Also, variations in the ride height from corner to corner, which is something from which nearly all Minis suffer, can be very easily rectified to make the car completely level from side to side. There are several adjustable-height systems on the market, and most are adjusted with a spanner whilst on the car. HiLos and Adjustarides are the original types, the former being invented by Tony Chammings, who went on to produce the spaceframe Gomshall Motor Co Mini racer. Both types of adjustable suspension have a modified spring seat face which slightly increases the spring rate. HiLos, which are available from Mini Spares, are the only homologated types, and are adjustable using either a spanner or a special long hexagonal rod. The latter requires the drilling of holes in the bodywork at the rear of a Mini, and can only be used where there are holes through the rear subframe and rear rubber spring.

Fitting HiLos

Above: Fitting a set of HiLos as supplied by Mini Spares is really quite straightforward. The only special tool required is a rubber-cone spring compressor, and this is needed for the front only. The usual complications are separating components which have been together for years, the main problem areas being at the front knuckle-joint nylon cup, and at the rear separating the rubber spring from the cast-aluminium trumpet and again, the knuckle-joint nylon cup. Accessibility to the latter is very difficult with the radius arm still fitted to the car, and removal takes time and patience.

Front HiLos

Above: With the car parked securely on level ground, remove the top subframe bolt (on later cars) and insert the spring compressor. The threaded section should be screwed into the rubber spring exactly nine turns – any less and there is a danger that the compressor will jump out and damage both car and mechanic. The suspension should then be compressed with the wheel still on the ground as the weight of the car will help to compress the spring. Ensure there is enough room to get a trolley jack under the car – in other words, do not compress too much at this stage.

Left: Then, loosen the wheel nuts, jack the car, remove the wheel and the rebound-stop rubber which is attached under the top suspension arm with a single self-tapping screw. This is not normally rusted as sufficient grease leaks out of the upper suspension arm bearing to prevent corrosion. Extract the original cast-alloy suspension trumpet, levering down on the bottom suspension arm and tie rod to gain enough clearance. The chances are that the trumpet will fall away from the cone – if it does not the suspension is insufficiently compressed. The knuckle will separate leaving the nylon cup in the suspension arm.

Below: Adjust the HiLo so that it is about ¼in or so shorter than the original trumpet. Fit it together with the new knuckle joint. It will fit in easily as it is shorter than the original. Adjust the HiLo as required and refit the damper.

Right: The nylon cup will need to be dug out of the arm using a screwdriver. If you are very lucky it can be extracted in one piece, but 99 per cent come out in tiny pieces.

Right: Fitting HiLos to the rear does not require the use of the cone compressor. The car should be jacked up with the rear wheel removed and the radius arm supported from underneath. The top damper mounting nut must then be undone. Be sure never to press the spanners on to the side panel inside the boot, or an 'outward dent' will appear. The petrol tank on saloon Minis needs to be swung over for access to the nearside top mount – this will need also to be done on the offside if the car is fitted with twin tanks. The operation is easy provided there is no more than a couple of gallons of fuel in the tank at the time, or the weight of the fuel will make the job harder and may also strain the flexible fuel pipe. To be on the safe side, check the fuel pipes for damage and leaks afterwards.

Rear HiLos

Right: With the top of the damper released, the radius arm can be carefully lowered. The lower damper mounting can be undone and the damper removed. It is then possible to remove the rubber spring and the suspension strut. In most cases, they come out joined together, whereas at the front the action of the cone compressor separates them. The spring and strut need to be levered apart – and note that the knuckle is difficult to work on at the rear. The nylon cup still has to be removed in the same way as with the front.

Right: Fit the new knuckle joint to the radius arm, followed by the HiLo unit and spring: the spring will need to be fitted into position before the HiLo. Fit the damper to the lower mount: it will have to be compressed to its shortest position to be fitted, and then extended to full length once in position. A little copper grease on the mounting pins helps to prevent seizure in later years, but it should not be put on the rubber bushes. Use a trolley jack to raise the assembly until the damper can be fitted through the mounting hole in the wheelarch. It is essential to ensure that both the knuckle joint and the HiLo and spring are seating correctly as the assembly is raised. Refit the damper and the tank.

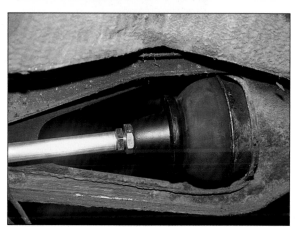

Above and below: The height can now be varied up ...

... and down!

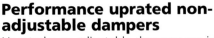

Above: Adjust the unit as required. Once all units have been fitted check the height of the car, and ensure it is sitting level. It is likely that the suspension will settle slightly after the car has been driven. Fine adjustments are normally required to overcome this and obtain the optimum ride height.

Performance uprated non-adjustable dampers

Uprated non-adjustable dampers are ideal for anyone wanting simply to improve the roadholding of their Mini without altering the ride height or having to play around with damper settings to get the ideal balance of stiffness, front to rear. A number of different types are available, starting with Kayaba KYB

Super Gas which are 25 per cent uprated gas units which look the same as the standard oil-filled components. These are ideal where retaining the original look is important. Other types of non-adjustable uprated dampers include KYB Gas a-just, Boge 20 per cent uprated, Gabriel, De Carbon, Bilstein, and G Max – the last-named being excellent-quality budget-priced units developed by Avonbar.

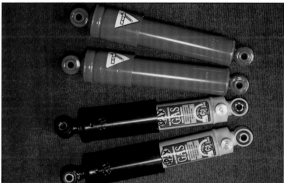

Far Left: G Max non-adjustable performance dampers.

Left: Koni and Spax adjustable front dampers.

A front top damper bracket for lowered Minis is shown on the left with a standard bracket on the right for comparison.

Adjustable dampers

To obtain the ideal handling balance in a Mini, adjustable dampers are the way to go. Designed to be roughly equivalent to the standard damper when they are set at their softest setting, the best-known names in this sector are Koni and Spax.

Konis are built in Holland, and were the original equipment on Sports Pack Minis. They are five-point adjustable and give a good ride/handling balance. They are available for standard-height and lowered Minis. The only real downside is that the dampers have to be removed from the car in order to be adjusted. This is not really a problem at the front, but is less convenient at the rear, particularly on the petrol tank side of saloons. Koni Sport dampers, which are uprated further than the Classic, are also available for standard-ride-height Minis.

Spax are the favourite of many modified Mini owners. They are 14-point adjustable, and have the advantage of being adjustable at the turn of a knurled knob while still on the car. Today, there are some other very good makes to choose from including AVO, which are 20-point adjustable on the car and are fully rebuildable. Both Spax and AVO are available for standard-height and lowered Minis.

Gaz dampers must be the most adjustable of all, with 36 points adjustable on the car, and are of high quality. Gaz are again fully rebuildable.

For Minis lowered to the maximum, modified front damper brackets are available to keep the damper in an upright position. In the photograph above left, a standard bracket is shown on the left for comparison. For rough work a stronger EN8 lower mounting pin is available from Mini Spares.

Adjustment

The actual settings on adjustable dampers are really down to personal choice, and the type of driving and terrain. A general starting point for road-going Minis is to adjust the front to somewhere near the halfway point on the scale, and leave the rears close to their softest setting. Individual cars and different makes of damper will of course vary. Using Spax as an example, try adjusting up four clicks, and then test drive the car. If it is still too soft, go up another four clicks, and so on. When it is felt to be too stiff, click back two stops, and arrive at the final settings from there. Lowered Minis will usually need slightly stiffer settings than those running at standard-ride height. Avoid running the dampers too stiff!

Solid-mounting the subframes

In 1976, in an effort to improve the ride comfort and refinement of the Mini, BL fitted rubber mounts to the front subframe. Before this the front frame was bolted rigidly to the bodyshell. At the same time the front

The rubber subframe mounts must be in good condition.

Front solid alloy mountings from Mini Spares.

Solid rear toeboard mounts for the front subframe.

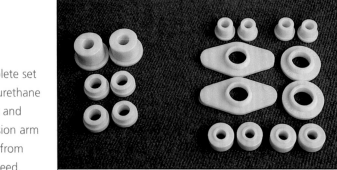

A complete set of polyurethane mounts and suspension arm bushes from Mini Speed.

mountings of the rear subframe were modified and fitted with larger rubbers. The rubber mounts should be replaced if they have become soft, particularly on a modified car, or the benefits of fitting uprated dampers and so on will be spoilt. A modification which is well worth considering on post-1976 Minis is to fit solid or harder front subframe mounting rubbers. It is relatively inexpensive to do, and it will sharpen the handling of the car considerably.

The downside with solid mounts is that noise transmission into the car will be increased and although in my experience this is not to an unacceptable level, there can be some 'wheel balance' vibration felt through the steering wheel. If this is a problem, the amount of vibration can be reduced by solid-mounting only the top and front of the front subframe, and this can be even further reduced by using a solid mount on the upper part of the top mount, and leaving the lower part with the original rubber again, together with original rubber front mounts. This is the system used by KAD and it works well. Solid alloy mounts are available, as are budget hard nylon mounts, the alloy versions probably being the better option in the long term. An alternative to all of this is to fit polyurethane mounts all round which offer some flexibility and therefore reduced noise transmission, but they still stiffen everything up. At the rear the larger rubber mountings and trunnions can be replaced by the earlier type and this will reduce movement and the slightly woolly feel at the rear that the post-1976 rubbers give. I generally find this to be sufficient for road use. Polyurethane upgrade bushes are also available for further stiffening up.

Uprated suspension bushes

Rubber suspension bushes on the lower front suspension arms and tie rods must be renewed if they are at all worn. They can be replaced with upgraded components if any further sharpening of the handling is required: fitting these reduces the tendency for the car to wander under heavy braking. They are available from Mini Spares in varying degrees of hardness.

Negative-camber lower arms and adjustable tie rods

The next step in the quest for better handling is to fit negative-camber lower front suspension arms. This will improve the cornering ability, but may increase tyre wear slightly on the inside. (For anyone who is unsure of the meaning of negative camber, put simply it is when the wheel leans inwards at the top – positive camber is when the wheel leans outwards at the top; in both cases this is with the wheel viewed from the front of the car.)

When they left the factory, Minis usually came with ½–1½° of positive camber. In fact, lowering the car reduces the amount of positive camber at the front, as it alters the position of the lower arm by effectively lengthening it. A Mini lowered to the maximum will have around ½° of negative camber with the standard suspension arms, so if fixed-length negative-camber arms are then fitted it can, in theory, mean that the car ends up with too much negative camber, although this is not often a problem with road-going Minis where ride heights are not normally that low.

The recommended maximum amount of negative camber at the front of a Mini is 1½°, and fixed-length arms are available to give 1½, 2.0°, or 2½° more negative (bearing in mind that on a Mini running at standard height there is positive camber to start with). For absolute accuracy, adjustable bottom arms are available; primarily intended for race use, many owners do all the same use them on road cars.

When negative-camber arms are fitted, longer steering track rod ends must also be fitted, or there will be insufficient thread for safe adjustment of the tracking. Also, a plate ⅛in (3.2mm) thick and 1in by 1½in (25mm x 38mm) should be fitted underneath the rebound platform of the top suspension arm. This should be fixed by drilling and tapping two holes in each suspension arm, and the screws peened over to stop them coming out. This was a recommendation by Special Tuning to prevent excess strain on the driveshafts and any possibility of the steering swivels locking. It is not necessary to do this when the car is lowered and shorter dampers are fitted. It is also possible to fit adjustable tie rods to the front suspension.

Lower suspension-arm bushes. These are upgraded easy-fit bushes from Mini Spares.

Fixed-length negative-camber arms.

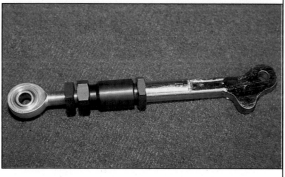

An adjustable bottom arm.

Altering the length of the tie rod changes the caster angle, and affects the degree of self-straightening of the steering. Shortening the tie rod gives more caster, and a greater degree of self-centring of the steering, while lengthening it will give less of both. Most people set the caster angle either to optimise the standard settings or to increase it a little. For road use it is best not to increase the caster angle too much over standard.

If Metro hubs are used (which is not recommended), it is absolutely essential to fit negative-camber bottom arms and adjustable tie rods.

Right: Longer track rod ends for use with negative-camber arms.

Far Right: Adjustable tie rods; these are Mini Speed parts intended primarily for race use. Road bars are similar, but are not rose-jointed.

Right: These are coil springs to replace the rubber cones and are shown with matching height-adjusting trumpets.

Far Rigjht; A Spax coil-over front unit.

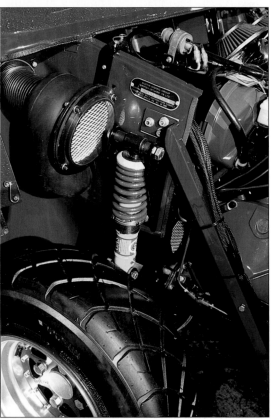

Rear camber brackets

An extremely worthwhile mod at the rear of a Mini in any state of tune, even standard, is to fit adjustable outer brackets on the subframe. These allow the camber to be adjusted, and the wheel alignment to be set to the exact manufacturer's specification – most Minis vary in this area somewhat – or the settings can be altered to suit personal preferences. A significant degree of negative camber, however, is inadvisable at the rear.

Rear radius arms

There is little that can be or needs to be done to the standard rear radius arms fitted to a Mini, but they are extremely heavy. A big weight reduction can be achieved by fitting the excellent alloy radius arms which are available from KAD. The arms can be fitted with drum brakes, in which case light alloy hub flanges can be fitted, or KAD's rear disc conversion can be used – see further details in the brakes section.

Alternative rubber cones

Mini Spares sell three different types of rubber cone spring. Standard springs are available, next up is a stiffer road/rally spring, and hardest of all is the competition spring which is suitable for racing.

Far Left: A conventional rear coil-over which …

Left: … requires body modifications.

Coil-spring cone conversion

An alternative to rubber springs and coil-overs which has come on the British market in recent years – having been available previously in Japan and the USA – is the coil-spring cone conversion. These units are made out of high-quality spring wire to eliminate compression and subsequent reduction in suspension height over time. They can be used with HiLos and other adjustable systems. They give a very stiff ride and are more suitable for competition.

Coil-over kits

Coil-over conversions involve replacement of the Mini rubber spring and trumpet with a damper with a coil spring fitted over it. They fit in place of the standard dampers and are essential when an alloy box section is fitted to replace the rear subframe. They are infinitely adjustable for both height and stiffness. Several different rates of spring are available. Coil-over conversions are manufactured by Gaz, AVO and Spax.

When a conventional coilover set-up is

fitted the rear wheelarch will need turreting, but the Spax kit with an offset pin top mount can be fitted without body mods, although wheel spacers will be required with certain wheels.

Ride-comfort modifications

Now not everyone wants to improve the handling of their Mini; they may instead be after a more comfortable ride. A while back the only way to achieve this would have been to change your 'dry' Mini for one with Hydrolastic suspension. Today, 'dry' suspension can be vastly improved in its ride comfort by fitting Smootha Ride. Developed by Alex Moulton, Smootha Ride is at its very best on a 12in-wheeled Mini, but it can still offer considerable improvement on any model. Fitting the system is no more involved than changing the components for standard items, but it does require the wheel alignment to be set up properly afterwards.

Available from Mini Sport in Padiham, the kit

Right: The full Smootha Ride kit.

Far Right: The Smootha Ride progressive spring is shown here with a standard spring for comparison.

consists of four new progressive springs which are of a different design front and rear. Also included are specially made Adjustarides which give a lower spring rate, new standard Mini dampers, and a pair of adjustable rear camber brackets. Overall the ride really is hugely improved with only a very minor increase in body roll.

Anti-roll bars

Although not that commonly used, anti-roll bars are available for fitting to both the front and rear of the Mini. Fitting anti-roll bars reduces body roll considerably during cornering, by controlling weight transfer. Two types are available, fixed and adjustable, the fixed being suitable for road use and the adjustable for racing.

The road bars are made of ½in steel. If a front bar is fitted it is recommended that it is used together with a rear bar and it is advisable to have the suspension geometry checked and corrected after fitting.

Upgrading Hydrolastic suspension

Hydrolastic suspension is a simple system with

Rear box section

An excellent weight-saving modification at the rear is to dispose of the rear subframe and fit an alloy box section. Designed to allow easy alterations to both camber and tracking, it will accept the standard radius arms. Suitable for road, race or rally, coil-over units will be required in place of the standard trumpet and spring set up, but if offset-pin top-mount coil-overs are used body modifications will not be required. The bar fits to the standard front subframe mountings

few parts. The system comprises a displacer unit at each wheel mounted in the subframe where the rubber spring is normally fitted on a 'dry' car. The displacers, which cannot be dismantled, are pressurised fluid-filled units, which are interconnected front to rear but not side to side. Hydrolastic fluid is made up of a mixture of water, alcohol, and an anti-corrosive agent.

Right: A Mini Spares front anti-roll bar. (Picture by Roger Phillips; www.miniworld. co.uk)

Far Right: An alloy rear box section. (Picture by Tony Butler; www.miniworld. co.uk)

Mini models equipped with Hydrolastic suspension

MkI
All saloon models made between September 1964 and October 1967.

MkII
All 850cc and 998cc Mini saloons and 998cc Coopers made between October 1967 and November 1969, all Cooper S 1,275cc models made between October 1967 and March 1970, and all Wolseley Hornet and Riley Elf models made between September 1964 and October 1966.

MkIII
Mini Clubman Saloon and Mini 1275GT, November 1969 to June 1971; Mini Cooper S MkIII, March 1970 to June 1971; Wolseley Hornet and Riley Elf MkIII, October 1966 to August 1969.

Displacer identification
The original displacers fitted by the factory came in several degrees of stiffness. They were identified by a coloured band at the hose end. Although in most cases the marking will by now have been replaced with rust, the markings were as follows:

Displacer identification		
Type	Pre 1968 cars Marking	Post 1968 cars Marking
Normal		
Front	none	1 orange or green
Rear	none	1 orange or green
Stiff		
Front and rear	1 yellow band	2 orange bands
Hard		
Front	1 red band	1 blue or silver
Rear	2 red bands	2 blue or silver

Suspension pressure and trim height

Hydrolastic Minis tend to ride a lot lower than their dry counterparts unless the suspension is regularly pumped up. Before carrying out any modifications it is worthwhile checking the height and suspension pressures. If you own a 'Hydro' Mini which needs maintenance work carrying out, and you do not have access to a 'Hydro' pump at home, it is perfectly safe to drive at up to 30mph on smooth roads with the suspension de-pressurised . Before you do this, however, check that all the bump stops are still on the car, as they work harder than their 'dry' counterparts, and do have a tendency to break off! The correct standard trim heights for standard Hydrolastic Minis are as follows:

Mini MkI and MkII 848cc, MkII 998cc and Cooper/Cooper S	
Early cars	**263psi (18.49kg cm2)**
Trim height front	13in +/-¼in (330mm +/– 6.35mm)
Trim height rear	13½in +/- ¼in (343 +/– 6.35mm)
Later cars (from Dec 1965)	**282psi (19.74kg cm2)**
Trim height front	12 ⅝in +/– ¼in (320.7 +/– 6.35mm)
Trim height rear	13 ⅛in +/– ¼in (333.4mm +/–6.35mm)
Mini Clubman and 1275GT	
All models	292psi (20.6kg cm²)
Trim height front and rear	13½in +/– ⅜in (343mm +/– 9.5mm)

Trim height – all models

The trim heights on page 113 are with the car unladen, and filled with four gallons of petrol. When a new displacer is fitted the system should be pressurised to 350psi (24.6kg cm²) for early cars, and to 400psi (28.1kg cm²) in the case of later cars, for a period of 30 minutes, before dropping to the recommended pressure.

The rear of a Hydrolastic Mini subframe.

The Hydro uprated bump stop kit. The kit was originally designed by BMC Special Tuning, both to control suspension movement and to eliminate the need to fit harder Cooper S displacers to lesser Minis when they were used in competition.

The front damper kit consists of two dampers, two top brackets, two lower pins, and all nuts and bolts.

Pressures can be adjusted to obtain the correct trim height, and it does not matter if the pressures vary slightly from side to side. The system must be evacuated (which can be done with the pump) before being re pressurised.

Hydrolastic mods

Mini fans generally either love or hate Hydrolastic. On the whole, 'wet' suspension has a less-than-enviable reputation. This is unfair, as 'Hydro' cars do not actually handle badly, and much competition success was achieved with Hydrolastic cars. Having said that, 'Hydro' Minis do need to be calmed down for fast road work. The first thing to do with any 'Hydro' Mini is to fit a larger bump stop kit. This will control most of the pitching and the 'nose-up-under-acceleration' stance which is the most noticeable and famous Hydrolastic feature. With cars made up until early 1968, after fitting the uprated bump stops the next thing to do is to fit a front damper kit. Standard dampers are needed as opposed to uprated ones as there is an internal damping system in the displacers, and fitting uprated dampers will result in the system being over-damped. If further improvement is needed, fit negative-camber lower suspension arms.

With 1968 onwards cars, after the bump stop kit has been fitted you should fit negative camber arms, and then, if needed, fit the damper kit. A rear anti-roll bar helps considerably too. With the above mods, a 'Hydro' Mini can be made to handle very well indeed. If any off-road excursions are intended, the larger bump stop kit must be fitted, otherwise when the car hits a bump at speed all the fluid is displaced to the rear, and if the car then immediately hits another large bump, the displacers have no fluid to cushion the shock, and the chances are that they will be wrecked. Hydrolastic interconnecting pipes have a tendency to rot and leaks will develop. A worthwhile mod is to fit plastic interconnecting pipes: they are easier to fit, and are ideal if you want to run the pipes inside the car.

Lowering and raising Hydrolastic suspension

An adjustable height system for 'wet' cars does not exist. Many 'wet' Minis seem to be low enough in standard form, and much lowering is not really a good idea for road use. But if lowering is required, it can be achieved in the same way as dry suspension is traditionally lowered, by machining metal from the trumpets. Also, the suspension pressures can be reduced slightly to lower the car, but this softens the suspension, and therefore cannot be done to any great extent.

The original BMC Mini Special Tuning literature states that for circuit racing on relatively smooth tracks, a maximum of 0.2in (5.1mm) can be machined from the front struts, and 0.3in (7.6mm) can be machined from the rear. Clearly, less metal should be removed on a road car. The rebound stops under the front upper suspension arms must be packed to prevent excessive suspension travel, and care taken when repressurising to ensure that the knuckles sit correctly.

Once the work has been completed the suspension should be pressurised to 400psi for at least 20 minutes, after which the pressures can be lowered until the car is sitting just clear of the bump stops. As with 'dry' cars, you should not run the car on the bump stops or the ride and handling will be very choppy. The pressure must not be less than 220psi.

The ride height can also be raised by fitting washers up to 0.150in (3.81mm) thick between the knuckle and the strut. Suspension pressure can be increased to a maximum of 300psi, provided the driveshafts remain horizontal.

Converting to 'dry' suspension

Many owners convert to 'dry' suspension. To do this the complete assembled subframes from a 'dry' car, front and rear, are required, as not only are 'dry' subframes different, but the top front suspension arms and the rear radius arms are also not the same. 'Wet' suspension front top arms should not be used with 'dry' suspension as they will make the suspension too stiff. Remember also that Hydrolastic cars have the earlier pre-1976 eight-point-fixing front subframes, so the later rubber-mounted type should not be used. Think carefully before rushing into such a conversion: many would argue that Minis that were built with Hydrolastic suspension should really be kept that way, especially when they are being restored, or future values could be adversely affected.

Wheel bearings

There are no upgrades available for Mini wheel bearings. However it is worth converting the rear of original drum-braked Minis to taper-roller bearings, particularly if spacer brake drums are being fitted. Apart from the bearing kit, no other parts are required for the conversion. Wheel bearings should be checked regularly for play and replaced as soon as there is a problem. Rover Sports Pack Minis in particular have a tendency to go through front wheel bearings quite rapidly.

'Quick' steering racks

The only modification possible to the steering, other than the previously mentioned alterations to the geometry, is to fit a 'quick'-steering rack. Visually the same as a standard rack, the lock-to-lock is reduced from the standard 2.75 turns to two turns. This gives a far more go-kart feel to the car, but steering effort is increased slightly.

Greasing

It is very important to grease regularly the suspension on any Mini. There are three grease nipples, either side at the front: one for each steering swivel and one on the upper suspension arm. At the rear there is one grease nipple on each radius arm. All these points should be greased every 3,000 miles at least. A well greased Mini feels much smoother and quieter and is a lot more pleasing to drive. The technical department at Castrol recommends Castrol LM for both road and racing applications, so it is more than adequate for fast road applications.

Alignment – both suspension types

Although mentioned above in connection with many of the specialised components detailed, when any major work is carried out on the suspension the wheel alignment should be checked and properly set up afterwards by a competent specialist. This applies even when the car is lowered, and is essential when adjustable brackets are fitted to the rear suspension, or negative-camber lower arms and longer track rod ends are fitted to the front. When the ride height of the car is altered it affects the wheel alignment, and once the desired height is obtained the tracking should be re-set.

the brakes

Front Brakes

Including the ERA Turbo, Minis have been fitted with no fewer than seven main different types of brakes throughout the production years. Judged by modern standards the systems vary from being dreadful through to being quite good, but as a general rule the systems became better as time went on. Any Mini which is producing serious power needs a set of brakes to match, and often the best way forward with lesser Minis is to start by fitting Cooper S or later-type front disc brakes. The standard systems and their suitability for tuned Minis are as follows:

Drum brakes – Single-leading-shoe

Fitted up to September 1964 to all non-Cooper Minis. The internal layout of single-leading-shoe front brakes is similar to that of the rear brakes, with one wheel cylinder per wheel. Single-leading-shoe brakes do not work at all well – driving a Mini so equipped today can at times only really be described as frightening. Having said that, they do have one advantage over twin-leading shoes, and that is they are easier to adjust as there is only one adjuster per wheel. These brakes are rare today so it is good to retain them on original cars – provided the car is not used everyday. From a performance point of view, however, they really do need to be changed as soon as possible.

Drum brakes – twin-leading-shoe

Fitted from September 1964 to October 1984 to all non-Cooper Minis. Twin-leading-shoe brakes are a vast improvement, and they were fitted to all non-performance Minis right up until 1984. When the brakes are properly maintained the system with the later master cylinder is acceptable for everyday driving on a Stage 1 '998' or even a '1098'. For real performance driving, however, they still leave a lot to be desired. Before any real performance mods or a 1,275cc engine are considered, braking improvements therefore must be undertaken.

Disc brakes – 7in discs

997cc Cooper
The 997cc Cooper was the first Mini to be fitted with discs and it was a revelation at the time; these original installations are now very rare. Fitting '997' discs is not a conversion even worth considering as an upgrade as the performance is much worse than that of twin-leading-shoe drums. On a dry road, it is impossible to lock the wheels, and in my opinion they are verging on frightening. Leave these to classic original '997s'.

998cc Cooper
The 998cc Cooper used 7in discs but the caliper design was much improved and used larger pads. Performance is a lot better than with the '997' set-up but this is still not a worthwhile upgrade to any Mini except perhaps single-leading-shoe Minis or 997cc Coopers. The '997' caliper can be machined to take '998' pads or alternatively changed for '998' calipers. Both 997cc and 998cc Coopers use the small CV joint from the pre-1984 drum-braked Mini.

Disc brakes – 7.5in discs

Fitted to: Mini Cooper S 970cc, 1,071cc, 1,275cc (1963–71) and to 1275GT (1969–74). From its introduction, the Mini Cooper S was fitted with 7.5in front discs and the same brakes were fitted to the 10in-wheeled 1275GT from introduction in 1969 until 1974. They are good brakes, vastly better than the Cooper's and are still an excellent choice, particularly if 10in wheels are fitted. Parts availability new is excellent, and second-hand sets sometimes appear. At the back, 'S' or late Mini rear-spacer brake drums and longer studs should be fitted, as should Cooper S rear-wheel cylinders – if the latter is not done there is a danger of the rear brakes locking under hard braking.

Disc brakes – 8.4in discs

Fitted to: 1275GT (1974-81); Mini 25 (1984) and all production Minis thereafter. All 8.4in disc assemblies work well, but earlier cars benefit from the addition of a servo. These discs are readily available second-hand with scrapyards, specialist Mini breakers and private sellers all being good sources of supply.

Converting drum-braked Minis to 8.4in discs is identical to the process of converting to 7.5in, except that it is necessary to fit 12in wheels to the car at the same time, as there is insufficient clearance for the caliper under a 10in wheel (KAD produce 10in wheels which will fit over 8.4in discs if alloy calipers are used). As with 7.5in disc assemblies, the rear drums should be swapped for Cooper S/late Mini-type with built-in spacers. With both types of disc there is an increase in track, and this should be borne in mind when deciding upon wheels. With many alloy wheels, wheelarch extensions will be required.

Disc brakes – Turbo-vented discs

Fitted to: ERA Mini Turbo. The ERA Turbo is the only 'production' Mini ever to have been fitted with vented discs and four-piston calipers. The discs and calipers were taken from the Metro but fitted to Mini hubs. They retain the Metro's twin flexible hoses.

Far Left: These are 997cc Cooper brakes. Those of a 998cc Cooper look the same externally.

Left: Cooper S 7.5in brakes.

Far Left: 8.4in disc brakes.

Left: ERA Turbo brakes.

A second-hand set of 8.4in brake discs.

Right: To fit the assemblies the front end must be securely raised on axle stands with the front wheels removed. The first job is to remove the nuts and break the taper joints on the steering swivels and track rod ends using a ball-joint splitter.

Above: Unless the Mini is pre-1973 and with rubber driveshaft couplings (in which case they can simply be undone), the plunging joints need to be split. If the engine is in situ, leaving the diff-end sections in the diff will avoid the need to drain the engine oil. Splitting the joints is simple once the securing straps for the rubber boots have been cut. Place old newspaper on the floor to catch any oil which might spill out of the couplings.

Left: The flexible hoses need to be changed for the disc brake variety. The worst part is gaining access to the inner end of the flexible brake hoses. Both sides are difficult to reach unless the power unit has been removed from the car, as it has been here. The brake pipe, or union (depending upon the side), needs to be removed, and a socket used with an extension bar to undo the nut securing the flexible hose, while using an open-ended spanner on the underside. Keep the serrated washer that fits between the nut and the subframe and have a container ready to prevent brake fluid leaking onto the floor.

Conversions to discs

If disc assemblies are purchased second-hand, a careful inspection of all the components is necessary, replacing parts where needed. Even if the discs and pads are satisfactory, a new set of decent-quality pads is a good idea – pads for 8.4in discs are not expensive. Use a new rubber boot and new grease for the inner driveshaft coupling, and consider replacing the steering swivels if there is any play present.

The new disc/drive assembly can then be fitted into position. If the engine is in situ, the driveshafts will need to be connected during this process; on a pre-1973 Mini, the original driveshafts will need to be fitted into the disc brake outer CV joints, and a new rubber boot fitted.

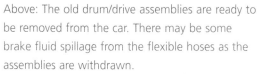

Above: The old drum/drive assemblies are ready to be removed from the car. There may be some brake fluid spillage from the flexible hoses as the assemblies are withdrawn.

Disc upgrades

The most important thing to consider first, when upgrading discs, is the diameter. This goes to a large extent hand-in-hand with the chosen wheel diameter. Once that decision has been made, the next consideration is the type of discs. There are many to choose from, including solid, solid slotted, solid drilled, vented, vented and drilled, and finally those that are vented, slotted and drilled. Virtually all types are available in all diameters, and all will fit the standard Mini disc brake type of hub. Some will require different calipers (those of a different diameter or that are vented), while with others the standard calipers can be retained. Disc-braked Minis have over the years used three types of drive flange: 997/998cc Cooper (which

The track-rod ends can be connected up and everything tightened to the correct torque. If the engine is not in the car, the swivel joints should not be tightened until after it has been refitted as the joints must be disconnected to allow the driveshafts to be fitted.

Left: New flexible hoses are the last part to be fitted. Braided hoses are being used here and new copper washers must always be used. The hoses are connected to the caliper first and then to the car, as the subframe end can be tightened in any position and the hose will not be twisted. The brake pipes are then reconnected on the subframe in the engine compartment. The system has to be bled thoroughly all round using the sequence described in the Haynes Service & Repair Manual for your particular Mini. An Eezibleed kit will help. Finally, the front wheel alignment should be checked and adjusted.

Far Right: The disc conversion can also be carried out using all new components. This is a Cooper S installation.

also used the smaller drum-brake type of CV joint and must be changed when discs are upgraded); 7.5in Cooper S, and 8.4in late 1275GT/late Mini type. It is the 8.4in flange which is required with the great majority of uprated discs and calipers. Whatever the size of wheels, it is best to fit the largest brakes possible under them. With most 12in and 13in wheels this is 8.4in and with most 10in wheels it is 7.9in. With some 10in diameter wheels – particularly Mamba and some original magnesium Minilite wheels – slightly smaller 7.75in diameter discs will be required. The exception to all of this is the KAD 10in alloy which will fit over 8.4in discs and alloy calipers.

Calipers
There is a large range of calipers to choose from, ranging from standard 'S', 8.4in Mini, and Metro four-pots, through to a variety of light alloy four-pot and six-pot calipers.

Vented and solid discs.

Vented and drilled grooved discs with pads.

Four-pot and six-pot alloy calipers

With a set of four-pot calipers and suitable discs on the front of a Mini, braking performance is much improved. The calipers are very light, they are easy to fit, and in the case of the billet alloy variety they look exceptionally good too – especially when they are on view through the spokes of an alloy wheel. There is a large range from which to choose. Most alloy four-pots are available for fitment to 7.5in, 7.75in, 7.9in and 8.4in discs, whether solid or vented. Probably the best known are KAD; the original KAD four-pots were sand-cast, the latest type are CNC-machined from HE30 (6082) extruded billets which improves the caliper body stiffness – an important point on very fast Minis. The pistons are anodised aluminium and are fitted with dust seals. Good alloy calipers are also available from Mini Spares, Mini Speed and Mini Sport – among others.

When fitting alloy calipers it is important to check the fit on the mounting area of the hub before attempting to bolt them on. All KAD calipers fit perfectly and go straight on, but with some other types of alloy caliper this is not the case and the hub has to be relieved to allow the mounting holes in the caliper to line up with those on the hub. This is not an easy operation with the hub mounted on the car.

Another point to note with 10in wheels, alloy calipers and 7.9in discs is the clearance between the wheel and the caliper. With many types of alloy wheel there is not enough room to fix wheel balance weights, and therefore they must be stuck to the rim of the wheel and taped over with tank tape to prevent them from flying off. Some alloy calipers will need additional machining for certain types of alloy wheel. It is best to check fitment with the caliper supplier before purchase. For instance, Mini Sport calipers will need machining for 5 x 10 Minilites.

KAD's special big disc conversion for 13in-wheeled Minis.

KAD calipers: six-pot left, four-pot right.

KAD four-pot and 7.9in vented disc.

Right: Mini Sport four-pot and 7.9in solid disc.

Far Right: Areas to be relieved to allow fitment of some types of four-pot.

Right: The machining needed on Mini Sport alloy calipers for 5 x 10 Minilites.

Far Right: When there is insufficient clearance between the wheel and the caliper the balance weights need to be fitted to the edge of the rim and taped over.

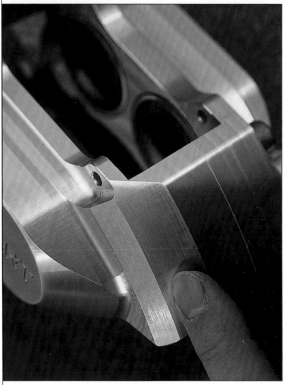

Fitting vented discs and calipers

Vented discs give a useful improvement over solid discs as they will cool more efficiently. The discs used are Metro discs (turned down to reduce the diameter where applicable), and some minor modification is needed to both the hub and disc to enable them to be fitted. This is because the width of the disc from the inner pad face through to the drive flange mounting face is greater on vented discs. The extra width is internal when fitted on the car and therefore there is no increase in track. Because of this, the discs need to be machined internally to prevent fouling the dust seal on the hub upright. The thickness of the part of the disc which bolts to the drive flange should be 0.660in when modified. The discs supplied by some Mini specialists are ready-machined. New, different flange mounting bolts are supplied with vented discs.

Steering arm modification
Again, because of the extra width, ventilated discs run too close to the steering arms. The arms need to be modified by removing the minimum amount to obtain clearance. This is easily carried out with an angle grinder and is best done with the hub assembly off the car.

Drive-flange modification
Vented discs need to have 8.4in drive flanges. The stud holes on the 8.4in flange must be bored or drilled accurately to 10mm diameter to enable fitment to the Metro disc.

Far left: The area to be machined on vented discs.

Far Left: The clearance problem area.

Left: A hub with a modified steering arm.

Left: Mounting holes requiring to be enlarged on an 8.4in drive flange.

Fitting 8.4in vented Metro brakes

There is some confusion regarding the fitting of Metro front brakes to Minis. In fact, a good set of brakes can be obtained very cheaply for a tuned Mini by fitting the 8.4in vented four-piston caliper disc brakes from later Metros. These are components fitted to all Metros from 1984 onwards, and to all Metro Turbos. The earlier Metro brakes do not have vented discs. Metro vented discs and calipers must be fitted to Mini hubs. The vented discs will fit Mini hubs if they are machined – (see the above section on vented discs and alloy calipers) – and so will the calipers provided that ERA caliper bolts are used – these being available from Mini specialists. A brake hose two-into-one kit, which is also available from most specialists, is also required. This set-up is close to that of the ERA Mini Turbo.

The reason, incidentally, for using Mini hubs is that Metro hubs are of a different design and they alter the front geometry of a Mini quite considerably. If Metro hubs were used, negative-camber bottom arms would have to be fitted at the same time to restore the camber to standard Mini specification. Metro hubs also greatly reduce the castor angle as well, resulting in little or no self-centring of the steering, and on a highly tuned Mini the torque steer would create a car that is quite simply dangerous to drive. The problem would be made even worse when using 13in wheels. Fitting adjustable tie rods would help but they need to be adjusted close to maximum to effect a cure. The problem is avoided by using Mini hubs.

If you use Metro calipers then you must use 12in or 13in wheels, as 10in wheels are too small to clear them. Never yourself try to grind away part of the caliper to obtain clearance for 10in wheels as this can be dangerous. Some specialists do offer this service, but they are well practised in it and can pressure-test the calipers afterwards. If you do want to fit 10 inch wheels, fit special calipers available from several specialists. Metro drive flanges can be used, but it will be necessary to machine the lugs off the front of the flange.

A set of Metro brakes straight off an MG Metro.

Disc pads

Good-quality disc pads are essential if the maximum stopping power is to be achieved from disc brakes. Very cheap pads should be avoided – they are best avoided anyway, but certainly they have no place on a performance-modified car. There are a number of types of pad available for the Mini; depending upon the type of caliper used (excluding 997/998cc Cooper brakes), they will be one of three basic types, namely Cooper S, Mini 8.4in, or Lockheed Metro Type A. Most of the well-known makes are good, the type fitted being down to personal preference. Notable pads are Pagid fast-road pads, EBC Kevlar pads and Red competition pads. In fact, EBC make a range of pads including the excellent Greenstuff Fast Road and Blackstuff OE standard replacement pads. Some people fit carbon metallic pads, but really these are only suitable for competition use: brake discs wear out very quickly and alloy wheels can deteriorate on account of the dust produced.

Top-quality pads: left is for the Cooper S and right is an 8.4in Metro for four-pot calipers. The wear sensor wiring is removed for Mini fitment.

Braided hoses

A special hose kit obtainable from most Mini specialists is required to convert from the Metro twin-flexible-hose system when fitting Metro four-piston calipers to a Mini. The kit is not required for the specially produced alloy four-piston and six-piston calipers detailed on page 121.

Braided hoses are also available to replace the four standard flexibles. They are stronger and less prone to damage, and also look very nice; the only downside is that they cannot be clamped to prevent fluid loss if work is being carried out on the brake hydraulic system.

Rear brakes
Upgrading rear brakes

The standard rear brake set-up is common to all Minis. Wheel cylinder size varies and backplates vary slightly from model to model, while S and 1275GT/late Mini are fitted with a spacer drum. Some 998cc Coopers used a drum with a smaller, built-in spacer for a while – these are now very rare. With disc brakes at the front it is generally best to use the latest type (8.4in). If rear wheel locking is a problem experimentation with different cylinders may be needed.

Drum brakes can be upgraded by fitting the cast alloy 'Minifin' type of drums. Original Minifins were available in a standard size and as Super Minifins with a built-in ¾in spacer to replace the rear drum on a Cooper S. Today, Superfins are available which are similar to the Super Minifin, and also KAD finned alloy drums which have a slightly wider built-in 1in spacer. Cast in LM25TF alloy, they use plasma-spray technology for the friction area, and they are reconditionable if wear occurs through use of hard competition linings. They look good, save weight and improve cooling.

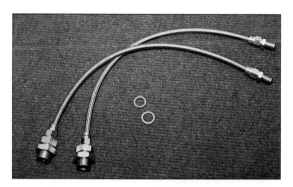

Far Left, top: Braided hoses.

Far Left, middle: A standard 'S'/late Mini rear spacer drum.

Far Left, bottom: A KAD finned alloy drum.

Left: A KAD rear disc conversion.

Further up the scale, the ultimate rear brake set up must be the KAD rear disc conversion, which is now available for road cars and comes complete with built-in handbrake.

Upgrading drums front and rear

In the old days it was common practice to upgrade drum brakes, largely because a disc conversion was both incredibly expensive and the parts not so readily available. The usual upgrade was to fit Ferodo AM4-lined shoes to the front, leave the rears standard and, if funds ran to it, to fit standard (non-spacer) Minifin drums all round. Unfortunately this is no longer possible as Ferodo AM4 lining material has not been available for many years. To upgrade single-leading-shoe Minis, which are not being kept as original classics, it is best to convert to twin-leading shoes. Twin-leading brakes can still be fitted with Minifin drums, although the non-spacer variety is only available second-hand.

Spacer drums (see under Rear brakes) can be fitted to both front and rear, and Cooper S offset wheels can be used. Upgraded shoes which are suitable for road use are not available so it is best to fit EBC brake shoes all round, part numbers 5145 (front), and 5146 (rear). The 5146 rear shoes will also fit the front of single-leading-shoe Minis. Strictly speaking these are not upgraded shoes but top-quality standard items that enable the drums to work at maximum efficiency.

Regular cleaning and dust removal, and also regular adjustment, is absolutely essential with all drum brakes. A set of drum brakes with a late master-cylinder, set up as above, will provide adequate stopping power for a 1,098cc or Stage 1 998cc Mini.

Handbrake mods

There is little that needs to be or can be done to a Mini handbrake to improve the performance. It is still possible to fit the fly-off handbrake conversion that was popular in the 1960s and which is still used on some competition Minis today. It is ideal for a quick getaway, but check that you are happy with the operation before fitting. Underneath the car, KAD handbrake quadrants can be fitted to the rear radius arms to replace the standard steel items. They look good and are ideal for concours

cars, but they are also lighter and less prone to seizure than the solid-steel standard variety.

Master cylinders

When fitting bigger brakes to a Mini, it is best to use the late-type front-to-rear split master cylinder, or failing that, a Cooper S one on older, single-circuit Minis – if you can find one. Avoid using the diagonal-split master cylinder – there are too many problems involved with these.

Servos

Fitting a servo to a pre-1989 Mini which is not already so equipped is a popular and worthwhile mod, but it will not improve the stopping power of the braking system. What it will do is to reduce pedal effort by providing a boost. This gives the impression to the driver that the brakes are more efficient, and it makes the car much more pleasurable and less tiring to drive. With Cooper S 7.5in discs a servo is more or less essential, as without one, pedal effort will be unacceptably high. Although 8.4in discs work well without a servo, fitting one will make a good set of brakes feel a lot better.

The above applies to discs fitted with standard cast-iron calipers: if four-piston calipers are fitted the need for a servo, whether to 7.5in or 8.4in brake set-ups, is reduced, but is all the same, a good idea. Servos can of course be fitted to drum brakes too. When fitting a servo, an inlet manifold adapter is required, and you will find that most aftermarket and twin-carburettor manifolds are drilled and tapped, and fitted with a blanking plug. Servos should be mounted with the air control valve below the axis of the servo, and with the unit pointing upwards at the slave cylinder end.

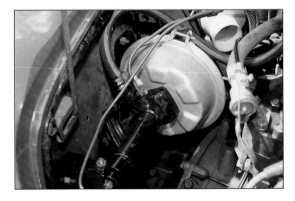

A problem which can occur when changes are made to the braking system is the rear wheels locking prematurely under heavy braking. An adjustable brake bias valve can be fitted to enable the front-to-rear bias to be adjusted. The valve can be mounted inside the car to allow quick adjustment. Although primarily intended for competition cars, there are some instances with highly modified Minis when this could be useful on a road car. Unfortunately, at the time of writing, the limiting valve from which the adjustable valve is made has just gone out of production. Hopefully, it will be remanufactured. In the meantime, if bias adjustment is required it is a case of searching for a second-hand example.

Rear brake pipe clearance on lowered cars

On lowered Minis it is important to watch the clearance of the rear brake pipe on the top of the radius arm and on the bodywork between the subframe and the wheelarch. The offending section is the union of the flexible hose and metal brake pipe, and if it hits the body on full bump, it will soon break. If contact does occur, the knock can clearly be felt through the car. If it is found to be a problem the easiest remedy is to fit the Aeroquip type of steel-braided flexible hoses for the run from the wheel cylinder to the union at the subframe, securing the hose to the radius arm in a safe, non-chafing route. Fouling is in fact more of a problem with drum-braked Minis fitted with early-type lower-rate rear suspension trumpets and 4½ x 10 or 5 x 10 wheels – particularly if they are fitted with 145-section tyres. Today, with larger diameter wheels and even with wider 165/70 tyres on 10in wheels – especially when 'S' spacer drums are fitted – the chances are that the tyre will rub on the underside of the wheelarch lip before this happens. Nevertheless it is still very important to check. Hydrolastic Minis are not affected, as the brake pipe is routed underneath the radius arm.

The late-1989 model year onwards Mini servo is attached to the master cylinder and is a neat fitment. Braided hoses are available so the servo does not need to be disconnected when the engine is removed – it can simply be positioned to one side. When fitting this servo to earlier cars where a 1,275cc engine has been installed, a late-type engine breather is required. It is also necessary to fit the latest type of servo master cylinder and pedal box.

I always use DOT4 brake fluid in my Minis and change it at the recommended two-year period. Many people prefer silicon fluid as they maintain it gives a firmer pedal. Silicon fluid does not absorb moisture as does conventional fluid, and therefore it lasts longer. It is manufactured by Automec of Buckingham who also produce non-rusting copper brake pipe sets – which, incidentally, I have used and found to be very good. When changing to silicon fluid, the whole system should be flushed through with silicon fluid by bleeding the braking system in the normal way before finally filling. The silicon fluid is purple in colour, so it is very easy to see when clean fluid is flowing through. It is very important to ensure that all the old fluid is out of the system before refilling.

Check the clearance here, at full bump.

Safety

All braking components must be maintained in tip-top condition on any car, but it becomes more important than ever on a tuned vehicle. Major work to the brakes and suspension areas should be carried out by a qualified person. When any work is undertaken on the hydraulics, the system must be bled through thoroughly afterwards to ensure there is no air present. Brake fluid should be changed every two years. Follow the bedding-in instructions for the brake pads carefully, and remember that great care should be taken with new pads and linings as they do not reach maximum efficiency until they are fully bedded in – which takes a few hundred miles of running.

wheels and tyres

Of all the modifications that can possibly be carried out to a Mini, the most popular must surely be to upgrade the wheels and tyres. Nice wheels make a car stand out from the crowd more than anything else, and fitting them is one of the most pleasing modifications that it is possible to make.

First, let us take a look at what was fitted as standard, as not all the standard-equipment wheels have been bad. They have varied somewhat over the years, from the time when the first Minis were fitted with 3½in-wide wheels and 5.20 x 10 crossply tyres. The road-holding compared with other cars of the time was outstanding, but by modern standards driving a crossply-shod Mini at speed is an experience, shall we say, that is best left to very practiced drivers. Radial tyres were not fitted as standard on Minis until 1973 – and that was on all models except the 850 which had to wait until 1976. Radials made a huge improvement to the handling, even on standard-width wheels.

Steel wheels fitted on the first production Minis were made of material 0.080in thick. These early wheels were notorious for breaking around the centres, particularly in competition conditions. As a result of this the steel was increased to a thickness of 0.120in, which largely cured the problem. When the Cooper S was introduced, 4½in wide wheels were an option. These wheels would only fit Minis with 'S' discs and rear spacer drums, and so reverse-rim Cooper S wheels, which had a different offset allowing them to be fitted to standard Minis and Coopers without the need for spacers, soon became available. These were the most popular wide wheels of the time, in much the same way as Minilite-style wheels are today. Standard 5.20 x 10 crossply or 145 x 10 radials could be fitted to both types of 4½in wheels. On the competition front, the works-backed Cooper racing Minis were fitted with magnesium rose-petal alloy wheels, and the works rally Minis with 4.5 x 10 magnesium Minilites. The first popular alloy wheels for road cars were the Dunlop Formula D and the Cosmic, and they were the thing to have on your Mini in the early to mid 1970s.

The first alloy wheels ever to be fitted to a Mini as standard were the Exacton 5 x 10 wheels fitted to the Mini 1100 Special in 1979. They were also fitted to the 1983 limited edition Mini Sprite and were available on the Mini Mayfair as an option from 1982 until 1984. Twelve-inch steel wheels had first appeared on the 1275GT in 1974, and were equipped with either conventional tyres or optionally with Dunlop Denovo run-flat tyres eliminating the need for a spare wheel. Later on, in 1977, Denovos were fitted as standard to the 1275GT. Denovos were also an option on the Mini Clubman saloon and estate, the offset of the wheel being different for the drum brakes.

This size wheel was fitted to the Mini 25 and standardised across the Mini range in 1984. Twelve-inch alloy wheels similar to those of the MG Metro Turbo were an option on the Mayfair from 1984 and were fitted as standard to the Ritz and Chelsea special editions in 1985 and 1986 respectively. In 1989, the Mini 30 was launched, with the now-familiar Minilite-style 12in wheels. Thereafter, the Rover 'Minilite' was fitted to most of the better-specification 12in-wheeled Minis right up until the end of production.

Then came the 13in wheel, which was first introduced in the UK on the LAMM Cabriolet. This size wheel, but of a different style, was fitted to the Sports Pack Minis from 1997 and, largely as a result of this, converting to these wheels is an extremely popular modification today.

Upgrading wheels

Wheel trims
Back in the 1970s it was popular to fit wheel trims that were supposed to make standard steel wheels look like alloys. The best-known of these was the Savage 500 and they really were quite appalling. Occasionally, wheel trims are available in accessory shops today, although most are intended for larger diameter wheels and not for Mini fitment. All these trims are awful and have no place on a properly modified Mini. The only wheel trims that should be considered are the original chrome or stainless steel hubcaps for 10in wheels and the various plastic trims produced by the factory, which are good for original concours cars.

Steel wheels
In the 1960s and '70s virtually all modified Minis ran on 10in wheels. A few people fitted Hillman Imp or Vauxhall Viva 12in wheels, but in the main the standard upgrade for a road-going Mini was to fit 4½in-wide, reverse-rim S wheels. Reverse-rims were available from Special Tuning in Abingdon and were listed in the ST tuning booklet under part number C-AHT182 with a statement in block capitals that no other non-standard wheels were approved! When fitted with a decent set of radials, 4½in reverse-rims looked very good in their day, particularly as most Minis then were fitted with skinny crossplies. Some companies produced 5in and wider steels, and a number specialised in low-priced wide wheels which were produced by cutting standard Mini wheels in two and welding in a steel band to increase the width. Properly welded, these wheels were reasonably safe and were even permitted in certain types of competition, but there were also some dodgy people producing wheels which

Far Left: The right wheels really enhance the look of a Mini.

Left: Original, 4½in reverse-rim steel wheels.

Right: Minilites are available in 10in, 12in and 13in diameters and a variety of widths and colours.

Far Right: Minilites were fitted to many of the works Minis, and no works replica is complete without them.

Right: Classic Rose Petal alloys as fitted to the Cooper Car Co works racing Minis. These excellent wheels are 4½ x 10 and are available in a variety of offsets, mainly to suit racing regulations. They are still cast from the original moulds by Vortz Racing Cars.

Far Right: The excellent MB racing wheels are rare and are a good way to make a Mini stand out. They are available in 10in and 13in diameters, these being of different designs.

could break up under heavy cornering – with disastrous results. For those who were after something a little different, Weller Wheels produced a white-spoked steel wheel, which was available into the 1990s. Today, there are no new wide steel wheels available for Minis, but plenty can be found second-hand and when bead-blasted and repainted, a set of Dunlop 4½in reverse-rims provide an excellent period look. Nearly everyone today though fits alloy wheels on serious performance Minis.

Alloy wheels
Fitting a set of alloy wheels is the best way to create instantly a 'modified' Mini. Unless radical body modifications are carried out it is the wheels which most affect the overall appearance of the car, and to a large extent, determine the style. There is a fair range of alloy wheels available for Minis. Some of the famous names from the past such as Minilite are readily available while Mamba and Revolution are still produced new although availability does tend to fluctuate. The prices of the different types of wheel vary too:

there are a number of budget alloys around, and these are fine if that is what you want. As with anything, quality costs – budget wheels may look attractive when first bolted on, but it could well be a different story after the winter. Alloys are very much a matter of personal taste, and for optimum looks alloy wheels must be matched to the style of the car. My personal favourites are genuine Minilites; today these are produced in aluminium alloy rather than the magnesium alloy of the originals (although the ultra-light magnesium wheels are available at a price), and are smoother looking and much more resistant to corrosion as a result. Although there is an opinion held by some that 'everyone fits Minilites', a genuine set, as opposed to copies, cannot be beaten for looks – and they were after all fitted to the works rally cars. There are a number of Minilite-copy wheels available, which are basically similar in design. Examples are Minilight, GB, and of course the Rover Cooper 12in alloys. Other excellent-looking and high-quality wheels include MB Racing, Revolution, Mamba, Superlite, Ultralite, Image, and KAD.

Far Left: Revolution wheels are good for road and competition use.

Left: Certain types of alloy wheels take standard wheel nuts, and the better ones are fitted with inserts, as on this Superlite wheel. Cheaper copies often do not have inserts.

A 10in alloy; this is a genuine Minilite 5 x 10 shod with a Yokohama A008 tyre.

Deciding on a diameter

10in
Pros: This is the classic wheel diameter for a Mini and it is the opinion of most enthusiasts that for out-and-out handling on the road 10in wheels have the edge. There is a wide choice of wheels both new and second-hand: 4½ x 10 and some 5 x 10 wheels will fit under the arches without the need for wheelarch extensions, while 6 x 10s give the car a racier look. The suspension can be lowered by the maximum amount permissible for road use.
Cons: None really, but 10in wheels look better as a general rule when the Mini has been lowered.

12in
Pros: Again, a wide choice of new and second-hand wheels available. Handling is still good with 12in wheels and most alloys will fit straight on to post-1984 Minis without any modifications, but 6 x 12s need body mods. The suspension can be lowered, but not quite as much as with 10in wheels.
Cons: Again, none really, but they do look better on the whole when fitted to later Minis. Apart from some standard BL/Rover steels and some early 1970s Minilites, all 12in wheels need wheelarch extensions.

The Rover Cooper 5 x 12 Minilite-style alloy.

13in
Pros: The right 13in wheels do look good. Rover Sports Pack alloys and arch extensions make all Minis look like late-1990s models.
Cons: The wheels are very heavy and increase bearing and steering joint wear dramatically.

The Rover Sports Pack 6 x 13 alloy.

Rare wheels are sometimes available from specialist Mini breakers and autojumbles.

Bodywork surgery is required to fit them. If fitted to earlier Minis, 13in wheels could adversely affect future values. Handling is not as good as with tens and twelves, and upgraded suspension, preferably including solid subframe mountings, is needed. The suspension cannot be lowered much or the wheels will foul the arches on every bump.

Buying used alloy wheels

Rare wheels are sometimes available from specialist Mini breakers and autojumbles at Mini shows, and occasionally they even turn up in scrapyards. More recent alloys are readily available second-hand at a substantial saving on the new price. Buying used can be a risky business however, unless you know the history of the wheels, especially with old magnesium ones. The golden rule is that whenever buying used alloys, particularly if they are of unknown origin, is to have them crack tested by a reputable engineering shop before fitting them to the car or having them refurbished. Most alloys can be refurbished by competent companies, including original, genuine Minilite magnesium wheels that are in sound condition – these can be refurbished by Minilite themselves.

Dunlop alloys look good on period modified Minis.

Insets and offsets

It is important when buying alloy wheels to choose ones with the correct offset for the model Mini concerned. Provided they are intended for Minis, most 12in and 13in wheels will fit straight on to a disc-braked Mini without the need for any modification or spacers, but it is always best to confirm this with the wheel supplier before parting with any money. Twelve-inch and 13in wheels will not fit straight on to drum-braked Minis – spacers, or to do the job properly, a disc conversion, will be required. Ten-inch wheels are slightly different in that they are designed with the correct offset for drum-braked (or 997/998cc Cooper disc-braked) Minis, while others are specifically designed for those fitted with 'S' discs or similar.

Changing wheel diameter

Going up – 10in to 12in
Going from 10in to 12in wheels is simple if the Mini is already equipped with 7.5in disc brakes. On drum-braked Minis, 12in wheels can be fitted using spacers, but converting to 8.4in discs is much better and safer. At the rear, spacers are needed for Minis without 'S' or late Mini drums – or ideally you should convert to 'S' drums. The longer wheel studs from a late-model Mini are also needed. While 5 x 12 alloys will fit without any bodywork modifications, 6 x 12 will need some cutting of the bodywork at the front, similar to that required when fitting 13in wheels.

Going up – 12in to 13in
In terms of brake and suspension there are no problems in fitting 13in wheels to cars originally equipped with 12in wheels. It is particularly important, all the same, to ensure that the suspension is in first-class condition, and the reduced-turning-circle Sports Pack steering rack should be fitted to prevent the front wheels rubbing the rear of the wheelarches on full lock. Bodywork modifications are needed to the front wings and front panel, which has to be cut away to provide clearance for the tyres, and wide wheelarch extensions are required. If standard steel 12in wheels are being replaced with 13in alloys, the dampers must also be uprated if this has not already been done. Minis fitted with 13in wheels feel a little 'over tyred', and from a

This is a Cooper S offset 5 x 10 wheel, which would foul the rear suspension on a drum-braked Mini.

The 5 x 10 wheel with drum-brake offset. It would still fit a Cooper S, but would protrude further out from the bodywork, requiring wheelarch extensions.

6in-wide Minilites have a different offset; the built-in 'spacer' will fit standard drum-braked Minis and cars with Cooper S brakes, but wheelarch extensions will be required.

handling point of view it is definitely better to stay with 10in or 12in rims. Solid top and front mountings on the front subframe do help though. Big wheels and tyres also absorb performance – the Sports Pack Mini was quoted as 6mph slower, and 0.6 of a second slower in 0–60mph acceleration than the 12in-wheeled Mini.

14in wheels
The advice from most Mini specialists regarding fitting 14in-diameter wheels is simple – don't! It is much better to stick to 10in or 12in, or 13in if

you want something larger. However, if you really must have 'fourteens', the procedure for fitting is much the same at the front as for fitting 13in wheels, but more so – in other words, the front wing and front panel need to be cut away to clear the wheels. A reduced-turning-circle steering rack will also be necessary, and even with this, you will need to check for clearance. At the rear, the radius arms need to be modified, as do the outer brackets, to give clearance to the tyre. Tyre-wise, something such as 195/45 x 14 is along the right lines – basically you want as low a profile tyre as possible.

Going down – 12in to 10in
The problem with this conversion is that the caliper on the 8.4in disc brakes is too large to allow fitment of 10in wheels. The conventional way around the problem is to convert to 7.5 in Cooper S discs and calipers. The simplest way, though, is to fit four-pot alloy calipers to the 8.4in disc assembly. The discs themselves must first be machined to 7.75 or 7.9 inches in diameter – depending upon the calipers and wheels to be fitted. Several specialists sell

ready-machined 7.9in discs, both solid and vented. Modifications to the drive flange and steering arm are required when fitting vented discs – for details, see the brakes chapter.

How wide?
Alloy wheels for Minis are available in widths ranging from 4½in through to 7in and wider. How wide it is possible to go for road use is determined as much as anything else by the availability of suitable tyres; 5 x 10, 5 x 12 and 6 x 13 are the 'normal' width alloy wheels. Regarding going further, as a general rule the widest usable width, particularly when the car is in regular use, is 6in for 10in and 12in wheels, and 7in for 13in wheels where 175 section tyres are available. Fitting wheels this wide will give the car a more aggressive look, and will fill wheelarch extensions nicely. It is of course possible to go very wide, and for instance, to fit 7.5 x 10 wheels, but the 165/70 x 10 tyre is then well stretched over the rim, and this is unlikely to do anything to enhance the handling.

Modifications required to fit 13in wheels

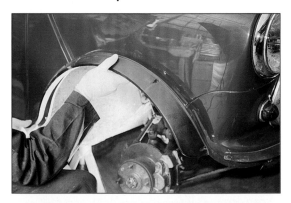

First, the wheel and front bumper must be removed. The rivets holding the standard plastic Mini arches to the car (if it is 1984 onwards) have to be drilled out carefully to avoid slipping and damaging the paintwork and it is a good idea to cover the paint with stiff cardboard and masking tape to lessen this risk.

From forward of the top of the arch on the front wing, the finisher lip needs to be flattened to allow part of the wing to be cut away. The best way to do this is with a hammer and dolly; although it can be done with a set of adjustable grips, the finished result will not be as neat or professional looking. The flattening-down of the lip must continue to below the bumper mounting flange.

The area of metal to be removed can be indicated with a felt-tip marker pen. The picture shows the amount of metal that has to be removed and modified – the line going through the rivet hole for the front lower wheelarch mounting. If there is any doubt, it is always a good idea to fit a wheel to confirm that there is clearance. Remember that when the car is jacked up clearance will be different and allowance should be made for this. The join between the wing and front panel should be hacksawed through at the weld, to remove the lips which form the panel-joining faces. Sharp metal edges are now exposed, so care is needed. This work was carried out by Minispeed, who do this job on a regular basis – if you are working on the car at home, a pair of welder's gauntlets will help prevent any injury.

The section of the front wing and front panel can now be carefully cut away, approximately half-an-inch below the line marked on the car.

The reason for leaving that half inch is that the edge of the wing must now be bent back up to continue the original lip. This is best done gradually with a pair of adjustable grips. Although completely hidden under the wheelarch extension, the newly created lip must be panel beaten with a hammer and dolly to make a nice smooth continuation all round. The edge is then smoothed off with an angle-grinder to straighten the edge and remove any sharpness. After this the area should be primed and painted to prevent rusting. It a good idea to trial-fit the arch and wheels before final painting, and test drive the car just in case any further minor corrective surgery is required.

Fitting the arch. Wood & Pickett wheelarches are being used here by Minispeed as they will cover 13in wheels. Arches such as the Rover Sport Pack type look really good with 13in wheels. The process must of course be repeated on the other side of the car, and the front bumper refitted. The front end treatment is then completed.

The rear end is much more straightforward; all that is required is to drill the rivets on the wheelarch extension, remove the arch, treat any rust that may be present, and fit the new arch. The 13in wheel should then fit straight on.

The finished job certainly makes the car look good. It is essential to have the tracking checked and adjusted after fitting a new steering rack and before fitting the larger wheels.

Wheelarch extensions
With most alloy wheels, wheelarch extensions have to be fitted to Minis not already so equipped. To keep everything legal and to pass the MoT the tread of the tyre should not be visible outside the wheelarch when viewed from above. Wheelarch extensions are fully covered in the Bodywork section.

Wheel spacers

Certain types of wheel and tyre combination will require the use of wheel spacers. Spacers increase the loading on wheel bearings, and for this reason, whenever spacers are used it is important to keep them as narrow as possible while still achieving the necessary clearance. Interestingly, on this point, the original *Special Tuning* booklet made clear that BMC/BL did not approve of the fitting of spacers of more than ⅛in (3.2mm) width for any reason. Fitting spacers to the front of a Mini alters the suspension geometry. At the rear, this is not the case and Cooper S and late-type Mini rear brake drums have a built-in ¾in spacer. If discs are fitted to the front of a Mini it is acceptable to use a separate, ¾in spacer if an S drum is not available, and I use this system successfully on the rear of one of my Minis, which is fitted with standard Minifin rear drums.

When wheel spacers are needed, solid-type spacers with longer replacement studs fitted to the flange should be used. As mentioned above, spacers are not really a good idea on the front of a Mini. If you want to fit 'S' offset wheels and retain drum brakes, then fit 'S' rear drums front and rear with the appropriate studs and check the front wheel bearings regularly. Also, never use spacers or spacer drums with reverse-rim 10in wheels.

Wide spacers (normally 1½in wide) with screw-on stud extenders were very popular in the 1970s. In most cases these were fitted to 850cc Minis with standard 3½in wheels to give the car a racier look, as wide wheels and alloys were more expensive and harder to come by in those days. This type of spacer should not be used as they are not particularly safe – especially with today's wider and larger-diameter wheels and grippier tyres. They are normally banned in competition.

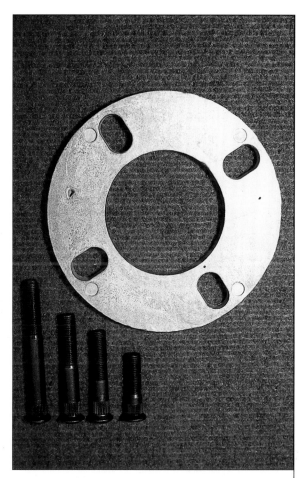

Solid wheel spacers.

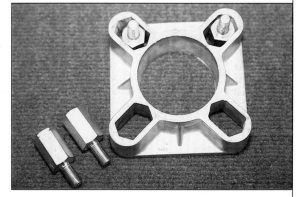

1¼in wide spacers with screw-on stud extenders – don't be tempted.

Tyres

Fitting wider alloy wheels to a Mini is one thing, but to obtain the most benefit from them it is necessary to fit some decent tyres. These should be of the correct width for the wheel, – it is no good for instance trying to stretch a 145 x 10 tyre over a 6 x 10 rim!

In the 1960s, the only superior road tyres suitable for Minis were 145 x 10 radials, if you needed anything wider, racing tyres were the only way to go. Everything changed in the early 1970s with the introduction of the Dunlop Formula 70 165/70 x 10 'Graunchy Gripper'. These made an absolutely massive difference to the handling, and I will never forget the moment one Christmas Eve when I replaced the standard wheels and Dunlop SP4 tyres on my first

Mini with a set of Cosmic Mark 4 alloys shod with Formula 70s. The car really did feel as though it were on rails. Grip was fantastic, but the wear rate could be, too, on an enthusiastically driven Mini – 1,500 road miles on a front set is my record! Sadly, at the time of writing Formula 70s are not available; however, the moulds are still in existence and hopefully these classic tyres will at some point in the future be manufactured again.

Which tyres?

Sizes available:

Wheel	Tyre
3½ x 10	145 x 10
4½ x 10	145 x 10, 165/70 x 10
4¾ x 10	145 x 10, 165/70 x 10
5 x 10	165/70 x 10
6 x 10	165/70 x 10
4½ x 12	145/70 x 12
5 x 12	145/70 x 12, 165/60 x 12, 165/55 x 12
5½ x 12	165/60 x 12, 165/55 x 12
6 x 12	165/60 x 12, 165/55 x 12
5 x 13	175/50 x 13
6 x 13	175/50 x 13
7 x 13	175/50 x 13

Budget tyres

Many Mini specialists offer wheel and tyre combinations at a cheaper package price. Often, there is a choice between a well-known brand of tyres and budget tyres, the latter reducing the package price further. Whether you are buying new wheels and tyres or simply replacing worn tyres, don't be tempted to go for budget tyres unless it is absolutely unavoidable, or if the car is only to be used as a local runaround. Price-wise they may seem tempting, but in general such tyres will not last as long as more expensive tyres, and will often not grip the road as well – particularly in wet or slippery conditions. Balance can also be a problem: some very cheap tyres are so far out of true that the wheel and tyre cannot be brought into balance.

Top-quality tyres

A nice set of wheels is incomplete without a decent set of tyres. Good tyres make a huge difference to the handling and ride of a Mini, and also to the amount of road noise generated. Tyre choice should be decided by quality and grip, followed by appearance. Although all the tyres listed are good, the Yokohama range for 10in, 12in and 13in wheels are the favourite of many enthusiasts. Excellent tyres for the Mini are made by the several companies whose products are listed opposite. The Yokohama range, as mentioned, is certainly a popular choice for a great many Mini owners. Other favoured tyres are those made by Dunlop and Falken.

Yokohama	
Tyre	*Size*
A008	165/70 x 10, 175/50 x 13
A032	165/70 x 10
A510	165/60 x 12
A539	165/60 x 12, 175/50 x 13
A048R	165/55 x 12

Dunlop	
Tyre	*Size*
SP2000	175/50 x 13
SP3000	175/50 x 13

Falken	
Tyre	*Size*
Falken	165/70 x 10
Falken	165/60 x 12

Further good tyres are made by Pirelli (standard 145/70 x 12), Bridgestone (175/50 x 13), and Avon (165/70 x 10) – the Avon is primarily a race tyre with very stiff sidewalls, but one which is used by some on the road. Which tyres you choose to fit is a question of personal taste. Tyres from Yokohama and Falken with conventional tread patterns look good and provide excellent handling in both wet and dry conditions while tread patterns such as the Yokohama A032 look superb, but generally perform better in the dry than they do in the wet.

Tread patterns

Far Left: A Yokohama A539 tyre.

Left: A Falken tyre.

A Yokohama A032 tyre.

06 the body and interior

Unless you buy a Mini which has been properly and/or professionally restored in the recent past, the chances are that some panels will need to be replaced either immediately or at some point in the not-too-distant future. Structural soundness is of paramount importance on all Minis – not just modified ones, although extra performance does put more stresses into the body, so priority must always be given to these areas.

Body restoration and repair

Restorations fall into two main categories: ground-up, with the car completely stripped, and a running restoration when repairs are carried out gradually while the vehicle is kept on the road. Unless you are planning to undertake a complete restoration, it is best to buy a Mini which is as structurally sound as possible as a starting point.

The key to long-lasting repairs is not to weld patches over rusty areas – this is not restoration anyway, it is bodging – and one of the worst examples of this is the fitment of oversills. These are much wider than the original sills and replace the whole of the sill and the angled section of the floor. They are designed to be fitted over the existing sill, which means the old metal continues rusting and causes corrosion to spread very quickly into the new metal. This type of sill should only ever really be considered as a last resort to keep a banger of a Mini going for another year. If you must fit this type of sill, at least remove all remains of the rusty original sill first. The correct way to repair sills and floors is to use proper repair panels, such as those manufactured by M Machine, and to fit genuine sill panels. Other rusty areas, such as wheel-arches, should either be replaced completely or the rusty areas cut out and new sections, properly cut-to-shape, seam-welded into place.

The other panels which are likely to require replacement on many older Minis are the rear valance, the front wings, the front panel, and the A-panels. Both the rear valance and the wings on their own are fairly straightforward, but when the front panel is replaced the subframe must be left in situ to ensure perfect alignment. Minis with rubber-mounted

subframes should be supported to ensure that there is no movement when the original panels are removed: aligning the wings and front panel takes a fair amount of care and time if a good result is to be obtained, and those Mini seams really do need to look right . . .

Fitting A-panels to MkIII onwards Minis is relatively straightforward, so long as there is not too much repair work to be done behind them; using a door skinning tool is the best way of folding the door aperture edge correctly. MkI, MkII and commercial A-panels are more complex: there is an inner and an outer panel, and normally both should be replaced.

The rear subframe is also a straightforward replacement, provided the bolts in the end of the sills come undone reasonably easily and there is no structural rust in the mounting areas. Minis are often advertised for sale very cheaply when in need of a rear subframe, and if they meet the aforementioned criteria, they are often very good buys. Always use a genuine Heritage frame – they fit!

Panel availability

Just about everything in the way of panels is available for restoring a Mini. A large number of panels are available from Heritage – and, most that are not are reproduced by M Machine. Buying good-quality panels is vital when carrying out bodywork repairs: it is false economy in many cases to buy anything other than the genuine parts or top-quality M Machine reproductions. All panels will need fettling for a good fit, with some cheap panels requiring ten times as much work, and then still not fitting as well in the end. You have been warned.

Body filler

Any refurbishment of the bodywork will almost certainly require the use of some body filler. This

Front wing replacement, in this case to replace a poorly fitted non-standard panel. The wing was actually removed by hand to this stage!

The new wing and A-panel welded in place.

Right: Sills should be checked regularly, and replaced if necessary – with the correct type. This is a MkIII sill which will require replacement soon. Replacing sooner rather than later often avoids the need for major repairs to the floor section.

Far Right: If everything else is sound, subframe replacement is fairly straightforward.

tends to be frowned upon by some people, as has a reputation for being a bodge-method of repair. True, it can be used for bodge repairs, but when it is used for what it is intended – and that is to restore the correct contour to areas of bodywork that have been repaired or have minor dents – there is nothing at all wrong with it. It does not fall out unless the areas to which it is applied are not properly prepared. Most of the best Minis have filler under the paint; in fact, it is probably true to say that the better the Mini the greater are the chances that more filler was used in the preparation. Filler has no strength and should never be used to repair structural areas, which should be welded. Depending upon where the repair is, a thin skim of filler can be used to make the repair perfect afterwards. There is one further point worth mentioning: if cellulose or acrylic single-pack paint is being applied, filler should be left for 24 hours before being primed, rubbed down, and then left for a further 24 hours before the finish colour coat is applied. If it is not, a definite outline of the filler will be visible in the paint finish, as a result of sinkage a few days later – however good it looked when the paint was first applied.

Reshelling
New bodyshells

Brand-new Mini bodyshells are manufactured at the British Motor Heritage facility at Witney, Oxfordshire. Built entirely from the original tooling, the shells are assembled on state-of-the-art jigs, and therefore alignment should be better than original. They are available through the Heritage Approved Specialists network either as a bare shell or a shell complete with bonnet, boot lid and doors.

Under UK law, vehicles which have been substantially rebuilt have to be examined by a Vehicle Registration Office to be assessed as to whether they can retain the original registration number. It will all depend upon whether the majority of components come from the original vehicle. The major assemblies are given a numerical value and the car must have a minimum score of eight points to retain the reg number. Points are allocated as follows:

Chassis or both subframes/bodyshell (if original or brand-new)	5
Suspension	2
Axles	2
Transmission	2
Steering assembly	1

Brand-new bodyshells, if of original type, qualify for five points.

Second-hand bodyshells

Second-hand shells can be used for rebuilding Minis in the UK, but upon inspection by the VRO they will automatically qualify for a Q registration.

The materials and equipment needed for body repairs.

Sometimes a
new shell is the
only way . . .

. . . luckily, they
are now
available again
from BMH.

Painting

A new or fully restored bodyshell needs to be painted well or the job will be ruined. Finding a good paint shop can be time consuming, but it will be worth it in the end. Very cheap paint jobs should be avoided – but, on the other hand, very expensive jobs are not necessarily always the best. Checking previous work done by a specialist, and then looking at work in progress, is the most sensible way forward. Many bodyshops are a bit dusty and scruffy, but this should not put you off, as it is the standard of work that is important.

Two-pack paint is by far the best, but it should not be sprayed at home, for health and safety reasons, as it is very toxic. For home spraying, cellulose paint is the only possibility. It is certainly feasible to get very good results this way, as I have done on more than one of my own Minis. For a really good finish, though, the body should preferably be stripped of all old paint.

It is also possible to respray a car using aerosols – provided they are of the type mixed by a paint factor, and not off-the-shelf items from an accessory shop. Aerosols are a good way for a budget paint job, but any method of painting at home will require a great deal of work in both preparation and in rubbing down between coats and finishing with cutting compounds. It is essential to ensure proper ventilation, to wear a proper mask, and keep children, pets (and neighbours!) well out of the way.

Rust prevention

There are several products available for helping to inhibit rusting in box sections such as the sills. In my many years of experience trying to prevent Minis from rusting, the best of these products, I have found, is Dinitrol. This is backed up by it being the product that proved to be best in a long-term test carried out a few years ago by *Practical Classics* magazine. Dinitrol is used by major manufacturers such as Volvo, Nissan and Boeing, which might help convince you.

All box sections, and particularly the sills, need to be injected every few years, and more frequently if the car is used regularly. Dinitrol can also be applied to the underside, and is especially useful around the heelboard, the subframe mountings, the subframe itself, and the under-wing areas. It should be sprayed everywhere where moisture and dirt can accumulate. If rust is already present, Dinitrol RC800 Rust Converter is very good. Generally, I do not believe in rust converters, but this one really does seem to work: after three years' use, including through the winter, heavily surface-rusted areas on one of my Minis are still rust free.

The underside of a Mini should be inspected regularly, and any damaged or missing seam-sealer renewed. Under-wing shields are available for the front wings of both Clubman and traditional-fronted Minis, and they are well worth fitting to any Mini in regular use.

When restoring items such as suspension parts, it is best to have them bead-blasted if this is possible. I always spray them afterwards with a couple of coats of 09113 Weld Thru zinc primer made by 3M, and finish with two coats of chassis black. This looks good and is very durable.

Stripping, ready for repainting.

One I did earlier: I sprayed this Mini at home using cellulose paint and a hired spraygun.

Brightwork

Renewing rusty or tarnished brightwork will make a massive improvement to any Mini. The latest-type stainless genuine bumpers are more rounded at the ends than the earlier types, but this is hardly noticeable – and so likely to be a problem only on very original or concours Minis. Cheaper, non-genuine bumpers are available, many of which are chrome-plated. Some fit better than others, but none fit as well as the genuine bumpers, and in some cases it is necessary to enlarge the holes in the bodyshell to get the bumper to fit at all. Similar comments apply to radiator grilles: some non-genuine ones fit very badly, in my experience. When going the non-genuine route, buy from a reputable source or the chrome could well be a bright shade of orange after a few weeks of winter.

When rear overriders are fitted to a late car with a rear fog warning lamp, the lamp must be moved to a new position to clear the over-rider. Special brackets are available for this, suitable for both right-hand-drive and left-hand-drive cars.

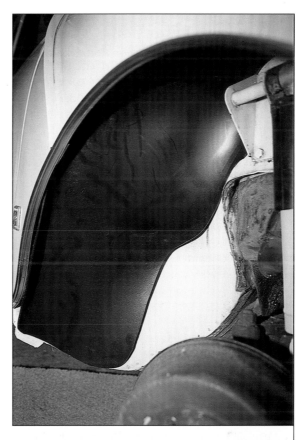

Under-wing shields are a good way to help prevent further rusting.

Good brightwork will set off any Mini.

body modifications

Wheelarch extensions

The most likely bodywork modification to be made to any Mini is to add or to change wheelarch extensions. The original early Minis did not have any wheelarch extensions. The first production Minis to be fitted with wheelarch extensions were the Italian-built Innocentis, and the first UK-produced Mini to be so equipped was the Mini 1100 Special which was made in 1979 to celebrate 20 years of Mini production. After this, early arch-fitted Minis were the Mini Sprite limited edition and the Mini Mayfair when equipped with the optional 5 x 10 Exacton alloys. The Mini 25 was the next, when it came out with 12in wheels, and all 12in and 13in-wheeled Minis produced thereafter were equipped with extended arches. The Mini 1275GT was never fitted with wheelarch extensions, even when it went over to 12in wheels in 1974.

When should you fit arch extensions? By law, wheelarch extensions must be fitted if the tread of the tyre is visible when the car is viewed from above. Also, if the side of your Mini is being liberally coated with dirt every time it rains this is another reason for fitting arches. What should never be done is to fit wheelarch extensions to a Mini with standard 3⅛in wide, 10in steel wheels – simply because it looks absolutely awful.

To look right, wheelarch extensions should be wide enough to do the job that they are required to do, with a small overhang, and no more. As a general rule, provided the correct-offset wheels are used for the Mini in question, arches will be required with any wheels wider than 4½in. Sometimes it is just about possible to get away with 5in wide wheels, but this is pushing it and it does also depend somewhat upon the actual width of the tread of the tyre fitted.

The first consideration, therefore, is wheel diameter and width. Once this has been decided, the width of the wheelarches can be determined. There are many variations in the design and width of wheelarch extension available. Group 2 and Group 5 arches are available with a lip for fitting wheelarch/sill trim, so if this is important these are the type to fit.

Group 5 arches are also available without the lip. Both types of arch have the fixing screws on show – not necessarily a bad thing, as the original BMC works arches were like this. If you do not like exposed screwheads, then you could always fill them and paint the arches either to match the car, or in a contrasting colour. Many people leave them in black, which is the colour in which most arches are supplied. Some arches come with a rubber sealing strip to be fitted between the body and the arch. This does make the fit neater, but for a truly original look, at least on works-type arches, it should be left out.

Other popular types of arch include the Wood & Pickett type, which fit from underneath and are very tidy with no screws visible. Sports Pack arches, which are available in both genuine and cheaper reproduction form, are the same in this respect, although unlike the Wood & Pickett they do require the bodywork to be drilled. Finally, when the body is drilled for arch fixing make sure to rustproof the area thoroughly.

Whatever type of arches you decide upon, do buy good quality – I have seen some where the fit is so bad that it would have been easier to mould some new arches from scratch rather than try to correct them to fit. That said, most arches, particularly if they are glass-fibre, will need some adaptation to make them fit really well. It is worth spending some time doing this, as it makes the difference between a very good-looking Mini and an average, or even below average, example.

Flip fronts

In days gone by, many Minis were fitted with a glass-fibre front end to cure rust in the front wings and front panel. Today, flip fronts, as they have become known, appear on some of the smartest Minis around, and are often fitted to absolute perfection. There are several ways of flip-fronting a Mini, the first being a one-piece glass-fibre front, the second a two-piece glass-fibre front retaining a separate bonnet – this type also being available in carbon-fibre – and the third being to make up a steel, two-piece front end. If the work is being carried out

Well-fitted arches look good. The easiest to fit are Mini Special arches.

Left: The Mini 30 and RSP Cooper had their Mini Special arches colour-coded.

Far left: Group 2 wheelarches are the classic originals and many companies supply them, but I have found those produced by Somerford Mini Specialists to be the best all-round for quality, looks and fit.

at home the latter is often the best way as it is much easier to obtain a good fit – steel can be bent slightly to the correct contour whereas glass-fibre cannot.

Steel flip fronts are best constructed using genuine front wings, as the fit is superior, although a good-quality aftermarket front panel is perfectly acceptable. If you are going the glass-fibre route, do buy good quality: all grp fronts require work to make them fit well, but a cheap front will require a huge amount of work and still not fit well.

These arches will cover up to 6in wide wheels in some cases and are my own favourites for 10in and 12in wheels.

Group 5 wheelarches, without the trim facility.

How to fit a flip front

Front end panel removal is very straightforward
and is done with an air hacksaw if available,
and if not, with an angle grinder or a
sharp metal chisel. In all cases, suitable
protective gloves and goggles should be worn.
All trim, electrical wiring, lighting and the
bonnet together with the front subframe
mounting bolts/tear-drop mountings on post-
1976 Minis must be removed first. If the
windscreen is fitted to the car it should be
covered, especially if an angle grinder is being
used, or the glass could be permanently
peppered.

Far Left: A close-
up of the body-
to-arch sealing
strip.

Left: With 13in
wheels, Sports
Pack arches do
look good.

A superbly fitted
flip front.

A one-piece traditional Mini glass-fibre front end.

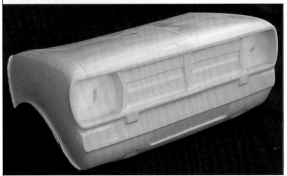

Clubman front ends are also available.

Steel panels made up to form a two-piece removable front end. With any two-piece set-up, either a steel or glass-fibre bonnet can be used.

decent results are to be obtained, because unless steel panels are being used, there will be a fair bit of trimming and tweaking to obtain a really good fit. It is perfectly possible to do this at home, provided you have the necessary tools and bodyworking skills, but even so, considerable patience and care are definite requirements. Before a new glass-fibre front can be fitted there is some preparation needed to the front itself, such as cutting holes to the right size and in the correct position for the headlamps, indicator lamps and in most cases, the radiator grille. The easiest way to do this is to make templates and mark the panels before cutting. Also, a fastening system at the rear will need to be sorted out. Small plates must be made up from sheet steel and welded to the A-panel. The rear section also keeps the glass-fibre panels in line when they are in the closed position – this is particularly necessary with this type of front as alignment is not always what it should be. At this point a decision must be made regarding wheel diameter if this has not already been done, as if 13in wheels are being fitted the closure plate must be mounted higher up on the A-panel to allow for any cutting away that may be required. In such cases the new front end will also need modifying accordingly.

In the heyday of the glass-fibre front all Minis had solid mounted subframes and no-one worried about any strengthening. Today, all Minis with removable fronts need bracing bars fitted in order to pass the UK MoT test. Most people fit road brace bars which bolt to the inner wing and front subframe. Hinges to allow the front to tip forward are bolted to the lower front panel and to the front subframe.

A variety of fastening systems are available including the large and very ugly rubber type which could be seen on nearly every glass-fibre-fronted Mini a few years back. Most people use Dzus fasteners today, as they make a very neatly finished job.

None of the glass-fibre or carbon fibre fronts come with a bumper lip attached. The metal lip can be removed from the original front panel and re-used, or new non-genuine lips are available.

The outer front panels should all be removed and in virtually all cases, the forward section of the inner wings will need to be removed too. These are cut straight down in front of the damper mounting.

Once the panels are off, the cleaning-up process can start. This is normally done using an angle grinder. Everything remaining needs to be tidied, as much more will be on show afterwards than with a conventional front-end. This includes the edge of the A-panel.

Fitting a flip front is a complicated job if

Body kits

One way of giving a Mini a very different look is to fit a bodykit. Aftermarket front spoilers became popular in the 1970s for most cars of the time, and were available for Minis, but a front spoiler on its own does not really look right on a Mini. As part of a complete bodykit it is a different story, and this is surely confirmed by the factory-approved ERA Turbo Mini and the LAMM and Rover Mini cabriolets, all of which sported complete bodykits. Original LAMM and ERA bodykits were very expensive, but today there are a number of copies available from different manufacturers as well as different bodykit designs.

Before fitting a bodykit, there are two very important things to remember. First, the body of the Mini to which the kit is to be fitted must be in first-class structural condition. Most kits cover structural metal such as the sills, but they should never, under any circumstances, be used to cover rust. The more responsible manufacturers will refuse to sell kits to people when they know this is the intended course of action. The second point to bear in mind is that virtually all body kits have been designed around 13in wheels.

The vast majority of kits are manufactured from grp. They rarely, if ever, fit straight on to the car without some fettling and modification, not least because Mini bodyshells vary somewhat and this variation is often increased when restoration and repair work has been carried out. Before a kit is fitted, therefore, structural repairs must have been carried out, to a high standard, and the panels to which it fits should be stripped back to bare metal. The kit can then be fitted with any trimming and alteration carried out at this stage. The panels in the kit are best fixed on mechanically using nuts and bolts and then bonded in place. Glass-fibre is best used here, as filler tends to be too brittle, and major companies in this line, such as Autofashion in Norwich, use their own special bonding material. With many kits it is a good idea to cut away the rear wheelarches and re-weld the inner arch to the outer side panel higher up. This will permit a greater degree of lowering with 13in wheels.

The beautifully constructed fastening area on the A-panel of Nicky Knight's Clubman.

The hinge area on a steel flip-fronted Mini.

Different kits require a greater or lesser amount of work to get them to fit. The ERA replica kits are complicated, while the LAMM replica and the more modern Majic, which was designed to fit around Sports Pack arches, are comparatively easy. The Majic is the most popular bodykit today.

The ERA Mini Turbo – the first production Mini with a body kit.

A Clubman with full bodykit and modified bonnet.

Rear spoilers are often fitted with bodykits and several designs are now available including Majic, Kudos and Minicos.

Cabriolets

Almost from the beginning, various companies and individuals have been creating convertible Minis. Probably the best known early conversions were those produced by Crayford, who became well-known through the Heinz 57 competition Wolseley Hornets. In 1991, Rover launched a limited-edition cabriolet of their own in conjunction with Rover dealer LAMM Autohaus of Germany, who had been producing high-quality conversions to Minis for some time. A total of 75 LAMM cabriolets were made. Following the success of the LAMM, the Rover Mini Cabriolet was launched in 1992. This time, the body engineering was developed by Rover Special Products in conjunction with Karmann. The Rover is constructed very differently, with the strengthening mainly being on the inside, as opposed to the LAMM, where it is on the underside. Both systems were very effective, and result in a very strong shell which gives little scuttle shake. The Rover Cabriolet uses a third sill which fits over the existing inner sill creating an additional box section, and narrowing the floor area internally. Together with a strengthened seat crossmember this is the main shell strengthening, but in addition the A-pillars and rear seatpan area are also reinforced. All this adds 154lb to the weight of a standard Rover Mini Cooper 1.3i which gives an idea of the amount of work involved in producing a Mini cabriolet – it is not just a case of cutting off the roof!

Nowadays there are a number of companies carrying out convertible conversions and also offering DIY kits. Before you buy, the company needs to be checked for its quality of workmanship – look at cars in progress and finished examples if possible. There are some

A genuine Rover Cabriolet.

There are many possibilities when it comes to cabriolets.

Deseaming can be left to bumper flanges only.

good conversions; but unfortunately there are bad ones too. To do the job yourself means being a very competent welder, and very brave – as it is, after all, a very big thing to cut off the roof.

Deseaming

Deseaming a Mini is the removal of the external gutter uprights and often the roof guttering as well. It is a job which needs to be done very well or the finished result will look terrible. The reasons for deseaming are cosmetic, but removal of the seams reduces the frontal area of a Mini by around 40 square inches, so the car will be more streamlined as a result.

Deseaming is a job which must be carried out by a competent welder. Small areas of seam should be removed at a time – around 6in intervals is the normally recommended amount – and the areas welded before moving on to removing the next 6in section. In this way the welder will be used twice per seam to weld the alternate 6in sections. Once the welding is completed the weld must be tapped in and ground before being finished with body filler. Because of the compound curves, someone very experienced in the art of filling should carry this out – especially if a dark colour is being used, as any rippling or imperfections will stand out a mile. The front bumper mounting lip can be removed without welding, although filling will still be necessary. The rear bumper lip will need to be removed using a similar deseaming method as with the gutters.

Chopping

The whole idea of roof-chopping a Mini probably started with the Mini Sprint in 1967. The bodyshell was lowered by removing one and a half inches of metal from the roof pillars and a similar amount from the panelwork below the waistline. There was an attempt at a revival of production of Sprint shells in the late 1980s which looked good but never sold well. A number of chopped Minis have appeared since, some done only in the roof pillars, some with complete glass-fibre bodies. Carried out properly, the Mini Sprint looks

Here, the front gutter uprights have been deseamed.

Rear gutter upright and roof deseaming.

Right: Here, a home-made radiator grille has been fitted.

Far right: In this case, a Clubman Estate has been modified with a saloon Mini numberplate light and a square numberplate. A Mini can be every bit as individual as its owner.

The bootlid has been extensively modified on this Mini to give a much more rounded look.

good – if you like that sort of thing. Minis with a roof-chop alone on the whole do not look as good. From a DIY point of view this type of mod is again only for someone with a great deal of experience, not least because when you remove metal from the roof pillars and lower the roof the remaining parts of the pillars do not line up. Removing

height from the rest of the panelwork is even more complex.

Other body mods
There are so many ways to present a Mini. Mods can vary from different grilles to two-seaters to three-wheeler Minis. Front and rear end changes are also very popular.

the interior

The interior of my original Mini, which is currently undergoing restoration. Period features include a Rokee dash and Billover seats. The centre console is from a Mini 1100 Special.

If anything, there are more possibilities with the interior of a Mini than there are with the exterior. There are so many styles and so many parts available – and that is before any parts are specially made or adapted from other cars. Most people start with a leather-rim steering wheel, a lowered column (when an airbag is not fitted), and a set of seat adjuster brackets. Then they just keep going from there . . .

Steering wheels

Fitting a better steering wheel is one of the best modifications that can be made to a Mini, particularly to 1970s and early '80s Minis which were equipped with the 'bus twirler', or even worse, the later Allegro-style padded steering wheel. Unless you are building a classic modified Mini and wish to retain originality, in order to drive any distance in comfort you will really have to change the steering wheel. Fitting a leather-rimmed wheel was the first 'real' mod I ever carried out on my first Mini and I will never forget the huge improvement it made.

My favourite steering wheel, the Moto-Lita MkIV 13in with leather rim.

Very small steering wheels increase the steering effort considerably.

There are many types of wheel available, and as a general rule the more expensive wheels are best, but there are some budget-priced wheels in the Mountney range which are very acceptable, both from a feel and appearance point of view. My personal favourite is the Moto-Lita 13in leather rim, which looks good in a Mini of any vintage and is supremely comfortable to hold. Moto-Lita will even recondition them – one of mine was bought from a scrapyard for £6 and repolished and recovered in new leather, making it indistinguishable from new, so they really are a wheel for life. Wood-rimmed wheels look very good on classic Minis from the 1960s and also on later, 1990s cars. Minis with a more modern theme look good with steering wheels such as the Momo.

Take care when buying second-hand steering wheels: if you buy a classic Les Leston wheel, for example, make sure that the centre boss comes with it and that it is for a Mini. If you are buying new, avoid very cheap vinyl-rimmed wheels, as they feel horrible after a few miles, and remember that very small wheels reduce car control and increase steering effort. To make the most of a steering wheel upgrade it is usually necessary to adjust the rake of the steering column using the bracket which is available from most specialists.

Seat adjuster brackets

If your Mini has standard seats then a set of seat adjuster brackets will make driving

Lowering the steering column

Lowering the column is achieved simply by fitting an adjuster bracket between the column and the bracket on the lower dash rail. It is very important to loosen the steering rack to enable it to turn freely to its new position.

To fit an adjuster, remove the front carpet, and tape back the soundproofing material with tank tape. The four nuts – two each side – on the steering rack U-bolts, need to be loosened. Minis with a steering lock have a shear bolt fitted at dash level on the column which must be undone and removed from the column bracket. If the bolt has not been sheared, care needs to be taken not to shear it, but if it has been, then it can be undone by filing two flats and undoing with a Mole grip, a new bolt being fitted during reassembly.

The column will need to be supported while the lowering bracket is fitted into place, and on Minis from the MkII onwards, the job will look much neater if the wiring is routed through the lowering bracket rather than left on the outside. The correct column angle can only be reached by sitting in the driver's seat and experimenting – as a general rule, the smaller the diameter of the steering wheel the more lowering will be required. Avoid lowering the column to the maximum as a lot of sideways movement can be felt even when the bolts are fully tightened – around halfway on the adjustment scale is ideal for most people. The column must be held in position while the bracket bolts are tightened, after which the rack U-bolt nuts must be re-tightened. At the same time check the steering-column clamp bolt at the base of the column. This is particularly important when a new steering wheel or bushes have been fitted.

It is not safe to lower the steering column on airbag-equipped Minis because the angle of airbag operation will be altered.

Far Left: A
steering-column
adjuster bracket.

Left: Loosening
the steering rack
U-bolt nuts that
are under the
carpet.

much more comfortable. The brackets work
best on pre-1990s narrow standard seats, as
the later, larger seats foul the rear storage
pockets even on the furthest-back standard
setting.

Seats

Standard Mini seats have never had a
reputation for being very comfortable. There
was a gradual improvement over the years,
and later models generally had better seats.
The first improvement came in November 1965
when Cooper models could be specified with
reclining seats. In October 1975 the seat
frames for all Minis were redesigned to include
an anti-tip mechanism, and in Clubman models
the seats reclined. It was not until July 1977
that the Mini 1000 was fitted with rake-
adjusting seats as standard equipment and
even then, 850 and City models retained fixed-
back seats.

In the last years of production, seats based
on the Metro design were fitted and were
considerably more comfortable than the earlier
types. Fast Minis need better seats, and when it
comes to upgrading Mini seats there are
basically three options.

Upgraded standard seats

One way of improving Mini seating is to fit the
seats (and preferably the trim as well) from a
later Mini. The seats should really be in keeping
with the model of Mini – 1990s Cooper trim
would look wrong in a MkI, for example. The
next step up is to fit a set of Newton
Commercial seats, these having been designed

The column
adjuster in
position.

Seat-adjuster
brackets.

Newton
Commercial
upgraded
standard Mini
seats.

around the Mayfair reclining frame. These are
extremely comfortable and look good in MkII
onwards Minis, although for seriously modified
Minis the driving position tends to be on the
high side.

Scrapyard seats from other cars
Seats from Fords, Vauxhalls, Hondas and the
like will all fit into a Mini and many are
available from breakers for very reasonable
sums of money.

Many people fit MG Metro seats into Minis.
Most non-Mini seats will need brackets
making to enable them to be fixed securely
into the car. Metro seat-fitting brackets are
available from Mini Speed.

Specialist seats
Choosing replacement seats is a serious
business, and not a task which should be
hurried. The most important thing is not to
be influenced purely by cosmetic appeal.
The primary consideration is safety, both from

the point of view of offering comfort,
good visibility and access to all the controls
and also providing protection in the
event of an accident. An example of this
is the correct positioning of headrests
to help prevent whiplash injuries in a
rear-end shunt.

There are a large number of aftermarket
specialist seats on the market, and some are
more suitable than others for Minis, usually
because of their size. When looking at
new seats, sit in them and try them, check
the construction, and satisfy yourself that the
seat is right for the type of use you have
planned. Seat requirements for most
types of competition are different from those
for road use. On the race track, a tightly
fitting wraparound bucket seat will be
exactly what is needed to hold the driver in
place during extreme cornering, but being
in the same seat after a 200-mile motorway
drive on a hot day could prove
uncomfortable. Reclining seats are usually

These Metro
GTa seats have
been retrimmed.
Retrimming
non-Mini seats is
generally not
economic unless
you particularly
want a certain
design, and in
many cases it
would be
cheaper to fit
specialist
aftermarket
seats.

better for long distance motoring, and it will be easier to find the ideal driving position because of the rake adjustment. Although not so important on a road car, weight is another consideration: competition seats weigh in at around 11–13lb, recliners are up in the 28½–31lb region.

Many owners will need access to the rear seats. This not only means getting into the back of the car easily, but also getting out again quickly in an emergency. Bear this in mind when choosing seats – if going the non-Mini route, fit seats from a two-door car and thus with a tip-forward action. The same applies to specialist seats, where recliners or small bucket seats will be needed.

Specialist seats have been around for a long time, with names such as Billover, Terry Hunter, Huntmaster and Restall being familiar to long-term Mini enthusiasts. The main seat producers today are Cobra, Raceland, Sparco, Corbeau and Newton Commercial. Most manufacture seats in a range of different materials and colour options, and in some cases it is possible to buy rear seats and door-panels and side-panels to match.

Different seats suit different people. I have tried a great many in different Minis, and my personal favourite non-recliner road seat is the Cobra Clubman, which is both reasonably priced and supremely comfortable, and also features a four-point harness facility. As with most of the Cobra range, it is available in a variety of colours and trim options. The best recliner for a Mini in my opinion, is the Cobra Le Mans, which was fitted to the Mini Cabriolet as original equipment. Again, it is exceptionally comfortable, and it is good-looking and has a tilt-forward facility for improved rear-seat access. Raceland seats are also very good, and are available in fixed-back and reclining versions.

Seat subframes
There are two main types of specialist Mini seat subframe. Later Minis need the type with the anti-tip mechanism which works with the catch bar fitted as standard on the rear floorpan.

The other type of subframe does not have an anti-tip system, but has the advantage of being adjustable for height at the rear. Specialist competition seats nearly always need to have modified or made-up mountings.

Door panels and rear seats
When new front seats are fitted, the chances are that the panels on the door-panels and side-panels will need replacing, too, and the same is likely with the back seat. Even if the colour matches, the new seats will make everything else look tatty. As mentioned earlier, a few of the seat manufacturers produce matching panels and rears – the biggest range being offered by Newton Commercial, who can supply a full range of original replacement and upgrade trim for Minis. The quality and fit is in my experience excellent, and one of my own Minis is fully retrimmed in their materials, with another in the pipeline. Among other things, Newton also make dashboard vinyl,headlinings and soundproofing mats for under the bonnet.

Seat belts – front
All but the very earliest Minis are fitted with front seat-belt anchorage points and later cars have inertia reels fitted inside the rear pockets. Wearing a seat belt doubles the chance of surviving a road crash, so if the existing belts in your Mini are at all worn, torn or frayed you will need to renew them – and do not buy second-hand seat belts! Belts are designed to elongate by up to 15 per cent during an impact to absorb some of the shock and further help prevent injury to the wearer. The elongation is irreversible, and if involved in a second accident, the belt may still restrain the wearer, but there will be no impact absorption properties, which may result in crush-injuries to the wearer.

Full-harness belts are available for both road and competition use. Both types are made to the same quality and are of equal strength, but the competition (FIA) belt has a wider shoulder strap. Three-point and four-point mounting harnesses are available with the four-point better for post-1982 Minis as a result of the position of the rear seat-belt

mountings. Full-harness belts need eye-bolts which screw into the standard mounting points on the car. The rear mountings of a full-harness belt mean that the rear seat is no longer usable.

Seat belts – rear

Rear lap seat belts were fitted as standard to Minis from October 1986, and mountings to enable their fitment were incorporated in the saloon bodyshell from 1982. Fitting a set of rear belts to a Mini not so equipped, and where rear passengers are carried, is an essential modification.

Minis with provision for rear seat belts can be quickly identified by looking in the boot for the reinforcing plates and captive nuts. On earlier cars, belts can be fitted by drilling holes in the rear seat panel in the same places as later Minis, and welding plates to the shell behind the holes, to reinforce the area. The most difficult part is the upper belt mounting, which must be fitted to the parcel shelf as the

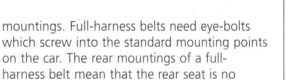

C-post is single skin. It is only possible to do this provided that there are no large speaker holes or any other mods to the parcel shelf metalwork. Bracing plates must be fitted, and these should be angled so that they bear against the underside of the parcel shelf and the seat back panel and are welded to both panels. The steel plating used should be of sufficient thickness and have rounded corners in order to provide the required reinforcement. This information was provided by seat belt manufacturers Securon, who point out that nothing can be guaranteed in the event of an accident where mounting points have been fabricated, but it is better to have belts fitted than not. It is possible to fit either static or inertia-reel belts to Minis of this age, and in the case of the latter the reel is mounted on the parcel shelf. Static belts are both easier and neater to fit.

It is also possible to fit rear belts to Mini Estates. The mounting points need to be carefully chosen to ensure sufficient strength, and plates should be welded to the back of the mounting area. The upper mounting is probably best located on the rear wheelarch, and again either static or inertia reel belts can be used.

Carpets

Not every modified Mini will be fitted with carpets. For an out-and-out fully stripped race-car look, painted floors and mats are popular. This is fine where noise levels are not a problem, but most Minis will have carpet, and a poor set lets the interior down badly. Many specialists sell replacement carpets, with the price along with the quality varying enormously. As with most things, you get what you pay for – and very cheap often means a poor fit and fast wear. Good-quality carpets that fit and are good for Minis of all ages are made by Newton Commercial and are readily available from Mini specialists.

Pedals

Up until May 1976, Minis had very small pedals. From then, larger pedals based on those fitted to the Austin Allegro were used. It is not really worth swapping to the larger

pedals unless you are fitting a later-type brake master cylinder with built-in servo, in which case a different late-type pedal box is required.

One thing that is worth doing is to fit a larger accelerator pad. These have been popular since the 1960s when they made heel-and-toe operation easier on rally cars. Modified accelerator pads – either the Speedwell-type original or the later Rover Sports Pack lookalike – are available from most specialists, and are easily fitted. The brake and clutch pedals can either be fitted with new standard pedal rubbers or alloy race-type pads.

Dashboards and instruments

Until the later years, Mini dashboards were rather basic. The earliest central speedo-only dash continued to be fitted well into the 1980s on basic Minis.

The three-dial cluster with a central speedo and flanking oil and temperature gauges is the most classic dash of all, and kits are available to convert later Minis. The only real problem with this type of dashboard is fitting extra instruments, although it is possible to buy a small 80mm rev counter and pod to mount on the parcel shelf in front of the driver. The three-dial central dash can be made more luxurious by fitting a Rokee wooden dashboard, this being available in a number of different finishes. Extra instruments can be mounted in the glovebox area on the driver's side. Still with this type of dash, rally cars and rally-lookalike Minis can have a works-style supplementory dash panel mounted on both sides of the dash to house extra instruments and switches.

Later Minis all have the dials in front of the driver. This began in 1969 with the Mini Clubman, which had two dials, and the 1275GT had the benefit of a rev counter in its three-dial dash – the first UK Mini to have this feature as standard. This type of dash can also be improved with a wood dashboard kit, and extra instruments can be mounted in the centre. Many of the very last Minis were equipped with a wooden dash as standard. It is a very popular mod to update any Mini by

A works-style Mini interior showing the dashboard with additional instrumentation and switches.

fitting this type of dash, and many different aftermarket styles are available in a variety of colours and finishes including wood, painted, carbon-fibre and stainless-steel. The range just seems to go on increasing; you can even have your own design airbrushed by A Dash of Colour.

Beyond this, virtually anything is possible for a confident DIYer – home designs, good and bad, have been around for years. Centre consoles are useful for electric-window switches and can also be used to house a stereo – although the latter is not ideal, because of the position of the heater. Extra instruments do not really work in a centre console, as they are too far away from the driver's line of vision.

Finishing touches

It is the small items which put the edge on a really smart interior. A high-quality gear knob is a good example and there is a huge range

available in leather, wood, alloy, and carbon-fibre. The type to fit will depend upon individual choice and the style of the rest of the interior. In the past, it was popular to fit an extension to the gear lever, usually chrome-plated. This works well with a 'magic wand' change when sports seats are fitted, but is not necessary and is in fact a hindrance on a remote change.

A smart set of door furniture is another excellent finishing touch. Cooper-style drilled-alloy items are very popular and these are also available in carbon-fibre, which also looks good. An alternative is the classic chrome set which works well on older or more luxuriously equipped Minis. Wooden cappings for the doors and the rear quarters are also an attractive feature when matched to the dashboard.

Rollbars and rollcages

A rollcage is excellent in helping to create a

A totally different but effective approach – an alloy dash.

The wooden dashboard and door cappings in a Mini cabriolet.

race-style or *Italian Job* look for your Mini, while if you intend to hill-climb the car or use it in some form of competition at the weekend it is probably an essential requirement. Many people feel safer with a rollcage; after all, the Mini is a small car and a roll cage does in theory provide a safety cell. In practice, on the road this is not always true. Whereas a cage will provide a rigid frame for the passenger compartment in the event of an accident or roll over, it is also introduces a very large amount of metal tubing on which to hit your head. In competition cars a crash helmet is worn, which guards against head injuries of this nature.

The above is not an anti-rollcage statement, it is just trying to explain why your insurance company is likely to take a very dim view of your newly fitted rollcage. Insurance companies also want to know exactly what the car is to be used for when a cage is fitted. By all means fit a cage if you want one, as they do look good, but do check with the insurance company first, and remember also, that access to the car, and rear seat use, are very restricted when a cage is fitted.

Boot boards and liners

The boot is usually left to last when a Mini is being improved. Don't forget it, though, as a tidy boot interior does complete a modified Mini, whether it is simply repainted and kept minimalist or luxuriously appointed. The traditional boot improvement is to fit a Cooper-type carpeted boot board. These are available to fit single-tank and twin-tank Minis. With some kits the board is supplied on its own, while with others the fittings come, too. Various other options are available to cover the fuel tanks and for those who use their Mini for more practical purposes a plastic boot liner is the answer. These fit most single-tank saloon Minis.

The centre console in Kay Drury's Mini, with electric-window switches.

Cooper-style alloy door furniture.

The full rollcage in a road/competition Mini.

converting to MkI

A later shell which has been given the MkI treatment and looks very effective. This is actually a re-shelled MkI, but the same principles apply.

Late in 1967, the MkII Mini was introduced. The MkII looked very much more modern and gave the Mini a new lease of life. The result was that everyone wanted to update their MkI and make it look like a MkII and many a MkI Mini could be seen with a MkII grille fitted – in many cases without the bonnet bar, as the mounting lip was not present on the MkI bonnet. Some owners made up brackets to hold the bonnet bar, and some went even further and modified the rear panel to accept MkII rear lights. This type of mod was particularly popular in the 1970s; but today it would be severely frowned upon because first it would destroy the originality of rare, early Minis, and secondly, the MkI look is very much in fashion. For the foreseeable future, as real MkI Minis become more scarce, it is very likely to remain that way.

Although the basic shape of all traditional saloon Minis is the same, there are many differences between the bodyshell of the MkI and the MkIV onwards, the latter being the most likely today to be given the MkI treatment. It is actually not difficult to create the MkI look, and it is possible to go virtually all of the way to create a close replica, but the further in you go the more complicated it becomes. The majority of MkI lookalikes are converted at the front and rear only, yet still look very much the part. The various stages of MkI conversion are as follows.

Radiator grilles

The radiator grille is the most popular part of a MkI conversion, and many enthusiasts fit one of these and leave it at that. There were in fact, between 1959 and October 1967, seven different MkI grille designs. This excludes the 'built in' van and pick-up grille and aftermarket grilles such as the Benelite. The different versions were: Austin 'wavy', Morris painted, Morris chromed, Austin Super, Morris Super, Austin Cooper and Morris Cooper. Today, there are three designs of grille available new: the Austin 'wavy', the Austin Cooper and the Morris Cooper. Regarding the others, the Super grilles are so rare that the number remaining is probably in single figures, while the Morris is reasonably obtainable second-hand (chrome and painted are the same pressing) and can easily be rechromed if you are after a non-Cooper look. The majority of MkI conversions, though, are fitted with a Cooper grille.

Fitting a MkI grille is not difficult: you fit the moustache trim, followed by the grille. Minor re-painting will be needed to fill the odd hole, and to cover the scratch marks near the indicators which are nearly always present where the MkII grille rubs. On twin-point shells the MkI grille does not fully cover the apertures at the bottom of the front panel.

It is not possible, however, to fit a MkI

This Mini is fitted with a MkI Morris Cooper grille, handlebar bumpers and, for some reason, a MkI Austin Cooper S badge.

bonnet to later Minis as the hinges are different, so on the later bonnet it is necessary to remove the bonnet lip which is redundant with a MkI grille. The welds must be ground away or drilled through with a spot weld remover, and the paintwork made good afterwards.

The moustache end pieces finish the job properly. They are fixed on using clips which are available in reproduction form.

Bumpers and overriders

Three bumper designs were fitted to the MkI Mini. These were: bumper only (no overriders), bumpers with overriders, and bumpers with overriders and 'handlebars'. All types are still available in stainless steel. The most popular on a lookalike is the overrider-with-handlebar design, as fitted to the Cooper and Cooper S. With all designs the bumpers are the same, but 'handlebar' bumpers have holes for the handlebar mounting. It is possible to drill other Mini bumpers to fit handlebars which are of different-length front and rear to allow the bootlid to open.

All Mini saloon bumpers will fit any Mini, Clubman front excepted, but overriders do not

fit some non-genuine bumpers very well. At the rear the foglight (where present) will need to be moved when overriders are fitted, and the best way to do this on right-hand-drive Minis is to use the left-hand drive bracket, and vice-versa. This moves the foglight slightly nearer to the middle of the car and allows clearance for the overrider.

Rear lights

The rear panel of MkII onwards shells has rectangular apertures for the larger rear lights. Both types of the later rear lamp (with and without reversing lamps) will fit the aperture, but MkI lights will not. However, metal plates are manufactured specially to allow conversion. These plates require welding into position and finishing with filler or lead, and the rear panel spraying afterwards.

Roof

If you are building a MkI lookalike from scratch and the body is being repainted, it is worth considering fitting drip-rails down either side of the roof-gutters. These were fitted to MkI, II and III Minis and make the conversion look more authentic. Roof-gutter drip rails are manufactured by M Machine in Darlington.

The rear handlebar bumper – in this case on a genuine MkI.

A pair of MkI rear light conversion plates.

number plate light and replace it with a MkI/MkII item – preferably mounted on a MkI/MkII hinged, rear numberplate surround – although attaching the numberplate and light directly on the bootlid will give a 1960s racer look. A set of MkI badges, most of which are available in reproduction form, will complete the exterior.

Doors

MkI doors are available new from Heritage, but they will not fit a MkIII onwards shell. The aperture is a different shape and the MkIII door is taller. The only way really to make a MkI/II door fit a MkIII onwards shell properly would be to fit the complete body side from the earlier type, which is a massive job, assuming you can find the parts. It is therefore not worth considering – if you are going to these lengths it would make more sense to restore an original MkI shell. For the really keen it is possible to fit MkI hinges to a MkIII door, but again it is a very involved job, with inner A-panel strengthener sections having to be fitted to the inside of the MkIII A-panel. Thus, most people forget about the hinges and simply convert the rest of the car.

Bootlid

The same MkI external design of bootlid appeared on the MkII, but those on the MkIII and onwards are a different shape below the numberplate. Second-hand MkI/MkII examples can be found, but they are rarely in good condition and are expensive. It is also possible to buy new, remanufactured MkI bootlid skins which fit later lids and even complete bootlids, but again these are very expensive. A cheaper alternative is to remove the MkIII onwards

The MkI and
MkII rear
numberplate
and light set-up.

A MkIV Mini
door converted
to MkI hinges.
The front lower
corner of the
door has been
reshaped.

A radius-arm nipple shroud.

The MkI instrument cluster.

The wood-rim Moto-Lita steering wheel is perfect for the period look.

Wheels

Although wheels are fully covered in a separate section, they also deserve a mention here. While many people fit 12in and 13in wheels to modified MkI lookalikes, for the really authentic MkI look it is essential to fit 10in wheels. Period steel wheels or appropriate alloys such as Minilite, Revolution, Mamba or Cooper-pattern rose petals tend to look best.

Wheelarches

Many a good MkI conversion is spoilt by fitting Mini Special or late 12in-wheelarch extensions. Although these arches can look good on a latter-day Cooper for instance, they are completely out of period on a car intended to resemble a MkI. If you want narrow arches the best ones to fit are Group 2 works arches, while for wider wheels, go for the Group 5 style.

Interior and dashboard

If you are buying a Mini with the intention of creating a MkI lookalike including the interior, the best type to buy is a model with a central speedometer. Mini Citys were made well into the 1980s with a single, central speedo, and these are easily converted to the three-clock dash by buying the relevant parts from a breaker. Later Minis, with the instruments in front of the driver, can also be converted to the three central dials, as special kits with the wiring included are available. The padded Clubman-style top dash rail, where fitted, can be removed and the original metal top rail covered in vinyl in the manner of the Coopers. Suitable vinyl is available from trim specialists, while the escutcheons which fit around the de-mister vents can be purchased from most Mini specialists. The bottom padded dash rail and switchgear are best left alone, as converting to MkI toggle switches is not going to be easy. The steering wheel can be changed for something period such as a Moto-Lita, and the seats can be period bucket seats or some of the appropriate upgrades that are available from Newton Commercial. Original MkI seats are not very comfortable, in any case, on a long run. Later cars will also need to retain the anti-tip mechanism which was fitted from the late 1970s onwards.

For the Cooper S look, stainless-steel window-frame finishers are available to fit to MkIII doors – the original MkI finishers will not fit.

Nipple shrouds

Radius-arm nipple shrouds were fitted at the end of the sills to all MkI Minis. They are obtainable from specialists and easily fitted to later shells, provided that they have not been repaired with several layers of oversill.

useful enhancements

There are so many things that can be done to a Mini that it would be impossible to cover them all. Every Mini can be as individual as its owner, even when similar mods and accessories have been fitted. This section gives a rundown of some ideas.

Cooper stripes

Cooper racing Minis in the 1960s had two white bonnet stripes. In 1990, the RSP Cooper was fitted with similar stripes, endorsed with a John Cooper signature, and since then it has become

fashionable to have stripes on the bonnet. Self-adhesive stripes are available from Mini specialists in white or black, and are easily applied; care is needed to ensure no air bubbles are trapped. An alternative and more permanent method is to spray-paint the stripes. Bonnet stripes are a must on a 1990s Cooper-lookalike Mini.

Nudge bars

Nudge bars became popular in the 1970s. Made by people such Wood & Pickett, they are still available today and you either love them or hate them. I am not a fan, but they are suitable for a certain type of Mini, and do perform a useful function if the car is parked in the street as they offer protection to the bumpers and lights.

Mirrors

Wing mirrors were popular on earlier Minis and are still available today in reproduction form. Since the mid-1970s it has become usual to fit door mirrors – they are less dangerous to pedestrians and are much easier to keep

Cooper bonnet stripes – these are original John Cooper signature stripes.

Rear Wood & Pickett nudge bars.

A clear front indicator lens.

A clear rear lens.

doors, but there is not normally sufficient adjustment for them to work properly. That said, a racing mirror on a fully adjustable base is made by Tex (who also produce the 1970s chrome mirrors and kits) and this is the type to use if you want racing mirrors on the doors. Door mirrors do not really look right on MkI and MkII Minis – an overtaking mirror fitted to the driver's side is probably the best way around this if originality is important. Moving inside the car, the interior mirror on Minis before the twin-point injection model can be replaced with a chrome-plated item. Available from many specialists, this looks much better than the standard fitment.

Clear-light lenses

For an up-to-date look, clear-light lenses and coloured bulbs can be fitted. These are usually available as car sets and as a general rule tend to look better on later Minis.

Quick-release bonnet hinges

Quick-release bonnet hinges for the speedy, complete removal of the bonnet are available for Mini MkIIIs and onwards. These are good when regular tuning is needed, and also for concours events when you want to show off the engine.

Bonnet straps

For a competition look – and also to keep the bonnet shut if the locking mechanism has been removed – ST-type tan leather bonnet straps are available. They fit to the front of the bonnet, attaching to the radiator grille, and do look very good indeed on the right car. Where the bonnet has been converted to lift-off and quick-release hinges are not used, bonnet pins are needed to hold the bonnet at the rear. It is necessary to fit – and preferably to weld – a triangular section between the wing gutter and the bulkhead when pins are fitted.

Grille buttons

Grille buttons became popular in the 1960s and '70s. They are excellent in that they enable the grille to be removed very quickly to gain access to the distributor and oil filter, amongst other things. They are thus very useful on competition

properly adjusted. The chrome 1970s/80s mirrors make a big improvement to later Minis which have plastic-backed units. The original chrome door mirrors were fitted slightly further back than the plastic type, but there is a kit available to fit chrome mirrors using the plastic mirror mounting holes.

Original racing 'bullet' mirrors were intended for wing fitting. Some people fit them to the cars, and all Minis without electronic ignition, but require holes to be drilled in the front panel and grille. The buttons look good, but they are not ideal from a security point of view, and rather undo the gains made if you have fitted an interior bonnet release!

Interior bonnet release

Various types of bonnet lock have been sold over the years, the best original type probably being the hinge-down locking plate. Today, the best bonnet lock is an interior bonnet release as fitted to the later production Minis. It is easy to fit, adds an extra element of security – and also allows a radiator grille without the bonnet release aperture to be fitted, for a neater and cleaner look. Many MkIII grilles and some MkI designs are available without the release aperture.

Filler caps

Unless you are intending to create an MGF-type recessed fuel filler, then an upgrade to the standard filler cap will enhance the rear styling. Since the 1980s all Minis have been fitted with a locking filler cap. The standard stainless locking cap actually is not too bad, especially when polished up, and these are a good upgrade for an earlier car with a painted fuel filler. Over the course of time there have been some rather nasty locking caps around, but thankfully the range available today is good. Probably the most popular are the Monza and Aston style, in both locking and non-locking form, and in alloy or chrome. All look exceptionally good. An Aston cap is also available to fit the Mini filler neck and house the standard Rover locking cap inside. Although this is good idea, the cap does look a little on the large side. Whatever you do, do not fit the chrome reproduction 'original' cap, as it is a very poor copy and looks nothing like the original.

Additional petrol tank

A worthwhile addition to any Mini, but especially one with a big engine, is a right-hand fuel tank, as this will virtually double the car's fuel capacity. Tanks are available for both carburettor and fuel-injection Minis. Fitting to an injection car is more

Front grille fixing buttons.

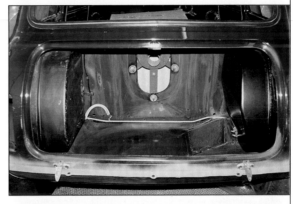

Fitting a right-hand tank.

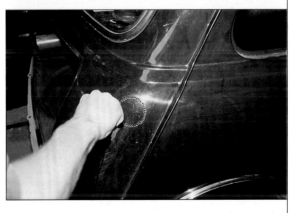

The worst bit, cutting that hole.

involved and may best be left to someone with specialist knowledge. Fitting to a carburettor Mini, however, is straightforward, the worst bit being cutting the hole in the body for the filler cap. The main problem is that Minis are not totally symmetrical from side to side and so absolutely exact measurements cannot be taken from the position of the left-hand filler. I always cut the hole smaller than required and then enlarge as necessary when the tank has been trial fitted, just to be on the safe side. In actual

Emma Priest's Mini with a Webasto electric sunroof.

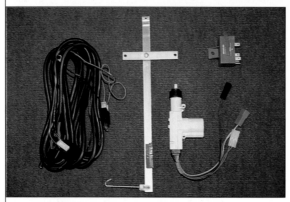

The central-locking kit for one door.

fact, there is some leeway, but it is still a nerve-wracking job.

If you want just the look of a right-hand tank the cheat's way is to fit a dummy filler neck. These are very convincing, easy to fit and of course do not prevent you fitting a right-hand tank at a later stage. Just make sure that no-one is looking when you open the boot!

Sunroof

Back in the 1960s and '70s, a fabric folding sunroof was just about the ultimate mod to

have installed on your Mini. The original, manually operated Webasto folding sunroof for Minis is no longer made, although new old stock can usually be located for anyone wanting to fit one of these roofs to an early Mini and thus keep it strictly in period. For later Minis, or when 'period' is not important (including the estate and van but not the pick-up), a new design, full-length electrically operated Wesbasto sunroof is available.

It is possible to DIY fit a sunroof, but cutting the hole in the roof of the car requires enormous bravery, and as a general rule is something that is best left to the experts who have all the necessary templates and cutting equipment to do the job properly. There are a number of approved Webasto fitting centres throughout the country.

Central locking

A worthwhile luxury for a latter-day Mini is central locking. Conversions are only available for MkIII cars onwards which have internal door hinges. The doors are locked centrally, but the boot remains manual. Minis that benefit most from this type of conversion are later cars, particularly those that are used regularly or as everyday transport.

Electric windows

Electric windows are another very useful enhancement that can be fitted to MkIII and onwards Minis. Late-type doors with built-in side-impact bars will still accept electric windows, but fitting is harder because of restricted accessibility. Even on earlier cars the job requires some specialist tools for use in inaccessible areas, and setting up electric windows calls for a great deal of patience. Anyone with any doubts should leave this one to the experts. The window switches are best mounted in a centre console as there is not a lot of room anywhere else.

Soundproofing

If you drive a modified Mini a great deal, particularly at constant speeds on dual carriageways and motorways, the interior noise even on later cars with improved soundproofing can become tiresome. Tweaks such as a single-box exhaust and a K&N filter can suddenly become less pleasing, and a soundproofing kit can make the car very much more pleasurable to drive. The Minis that will most benefit are those made between 1976 and 1980 as they have virtually no soundproofing at all. Most kits are made from double-needled jute felt, and although they will not make you feel that you are driving a Rolls-Royce – you will still hear the engine – the boom that occurs in most Minis around the 70mph mark is very significantly reduced.

Before fitting soundproofing, check for water leaks, and for any potential points of water entry. Floor rust should be treated, and the drain hole bungs checked for correct sealing, and replaced if necessary.

To fit the kit it is necessary to strip the interior, and although it is not absolutely essential to remove the front seats, it is much easier if you do. For Minis with dark-coloured cloth upholstery, it is certainly worthwhile to do this as fibres from the jute felt stick to the material and they are not particularly easy to remove.

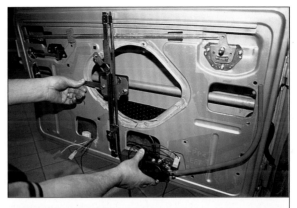

Fitting an electric-window kit.

A soundproofing kit.

Glass fibre Mini trailer built by P&L Minis.

Trailers

The boot on all Mini saloons is small to say the least. If you are touring or just going on holiday and if there is more than just a driver and passenger on board, a roof rack may be needed. If more capacity is required then the answer is a trailer. Real Mini trailers can be made from the rear end of a scrap Mini and when painted to match the towing car, and fitted with the same type of wheels, they do look very good indeed. If you do not fancy

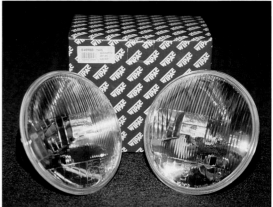

Right: A Mini towbar.

Far Right, top: A front towing eye.

Bottom: A Wipac halogen headlamp conversion.

cutting up a Mini shell, P&L Minis make excellent glass-fibre Mini-shaped trailers which look equally good.

Towbar

If you are intending to buy or make a trailer you will need a towbar. Bars are available from towing specialists and also sometimes appear second-hand. Under UK law, strictly you should not fit a towbar to a Mini made after 1 August 1998, because neither the towbar nor the car has type approval for towing. This has nothing whatsoever to do with the structural integrity of the Mini or the towbar, or the ability of either to do the job, and is purely the result of an EC regulation.

Towing eyes

Towing eyes as fitted to the works Minis can be fitted to the front of the car, replacing the subframe mounting bolts. Towing eyes which bolt to the rear can also be purchased, from Mini Mail. Both are also useful when securing a Mini onto a trailer.

Halogen headlamps

Standard Mini headlamps leave a lot to be desired. Halogen headlamp conversions are well worth fitting, and make a huge difference to night-time driving. Lucas or Wipac kits are the best, but budget kits are also available.

Additional lighting

Many later model Minis had additional driving or fog lamps, and in some cases four extra lights were fitted. Many different types are available as aftermarket fitments: and if some of your driving is down dark country roads, this is an essential mod. If two extra lamps are being fitted radiator grilles are available with holes for flush-mounting the lamps.

Rear wash/wipe

The Mini rear window becomes dirty, particularly when the car is being driven fast in the wet. Most modern hatchbacks have a rear wash/wipe, and kits are available for Minis from some specialists.

Additional driving lamps.

Far Left: A rear screen wash/wipe.

Left: A Mini Shop dashboard clock.

Dashboard clock

If you are accustomed to driving a modern car, you will probably miss having a clock on the dashboard. This is easily resolved if you have a Mini with a Clubman-type dash top rail, as there is a clock designed to fit the space normally occupied by the ashtray; this is available from The Mini Shop.

Alarm

With a lot of performance parts and accessories in and on a Mini it is best to fit an alarm to ensure that the car does not fall into the wrong hands. A number of alarms are on the market; fitting is a specialist job and is often best entrusted to an appropriate company.

six of the best

All models and all ages of Mini lend themselves well to modification. Modification is a very personal thing, and needless to say, modified Minis can come in all shapes and styles. Deciding on which type of modification to go for can be difficult. To give an idea as to what can be done, six modified Minis are featured here, each very different in character. As far as bodywork is concerned, some are virtually standard, while others are radically modified. The same applies to the mechanical side, and one of the Minis here uses completely standard 1275GT mechanics, but more than makes up for this with a highly modified bodyshell. The others range from a turbocharged Mini through a superb concours example to a full race-spec Miglia-engined car, as well as two very different commercials.

Mini pick-up

*(Pictures by Anthony Butler;
www.miniworld.co.uk)*

Mini pick-ups lend themselves particularly well
to modification. This example has been
extensively restored with the bodywork left
virtually standard apart from the fitting of a
Cooper radiator grille. The genuine 4½in Minilite
alloy wheels fit under the body without the
need for wheelarch extensions. The approach is
very neat and works exceptionally well.
Mechanical modifications are plentiful and
include a bored and stroked 1,430cc engine by
Southam Mini Centre. The result is very pleasing
– a fast and well-sorted car.

Key features

Engine: 1,430cc. Stroked Metro Turbo cross-drilled, wedged-crank. Omega pistons. Kent 296 camshaft. Vernier timing gears. Mini Sport Stage 5 head. 13-row oil cooler. Twin 1½in SU carburettors with K&N cone-type filters. Facet Red Top fuel pump. Modified Cooper S distributor. Lumenition Magnetronic ignition. Lucas Sports coil. Four-core radiator with Metro Turbo electric 16-blade fan. Maniflow large-bore LCB. 3in stainless single-box exhaust system.

Transmission: Four-speed straight-cut close-ratio gears. Straight-cut transfer gears. Twin cross-pin-differential with 3.1:1 final drive. AP 'orange' plate clutch.

Brakes: Front: Cooper S 7.5in discs with AP racing four-piston calipers and EBC Kevlar pads. Rear: 'S' drums with EBC shoes. No servo.

Suspension: Dry rubber-cone. HiLos and Spax adjustables all round. Adjustable tie rods and negative-camber bottom arms at front; negative-camber brackets at rear.

Wheels and tyres: 4½ x 10 Minilite alloys with 165/70 x 10 Yokohama A008 tyres.

Interior: Black Clubman low-back bucket seats. Grey carpets. Smiths magnolia three-dial instrumentation with 130mph speedo and Smiths magnolia rev counter. Downton steering wheel. Sony 10-disc autochanger. Fire extinguisher. Map-reading light.

Exterior: Standard Mini pick-up bodyshell; front panel modified for radiator grille and surround. Stainless-steel 'bullet' door mirrors.

Mini 1293 Turbo

(Pictures by Chris Brown; www.miniworld.co.uk)

Turbocharging a Mini is an involved conversion that should not be entered into lightly. This car is particularly worthy of note, as not only is it immaculately turned out, but it features a home-made twin-point injection system and mappable Emerald ECU with a modified turbo

and intercooler. Fully road legal, it is closer to a
competition Mini in its approach, with a rollcage
and an unfussy partially stripped interior.

Key features

Engine: 1,293cc Metro Turbo block. Cross-
drilled, wedged, bladed, ni-tempered crank.
Turbo rods. Omega low-compression pistons.
Avonbar turbo camshaft. Kent timing gears.
Titan 1.5:1 ratio-roller rockers. Home-made
twin-point injection system. Modified Metro
turbocharger. Custom-built intercooler. Emerald
engine management system.

Transmission: Four-speed Jack Knight straight-
cut close-ratio gears. Straight-cut transfer gears.
Quaife LSD 3.6:1 final drive. AP 'orange' plate
clutch.

Brakes: Front: Cooper S 7.5in discs with Mini
Spares four-piston calipers and EBC Green Stuff
pads. Rear: Super Minifin drums with standard
shoes, adjustable bias.

Suspension: Dry rubber-cone. HiLos and Spax adjustables all round. Adjustable tie rods and fixed negative-camber bottom arms at front; negative-camber brackets at rear. Nylon suspension bushes.

Wheels and tyres: 6 x 10 Minilite alloys with 165/70 x 10 Yokohama A008 tyres.

Interior: Sparco bucket seats. Full harnesses. Chequerplate flooring. OMP steering

wheel. Sparco pedals. Rev counter and boost gauge. Engine management system mounted inside.

Exterior: Reshelled, sprayed Applejack Green. Group 2 wheelarches. Drilled, vented bonnet. Bonnet straps.

Mini 1380 eight-port

(Pictures by Anthony Butler; www.miniworld.co.uk)

Concours builds take a huge amount of time and effort. This Arden eight-port-engined Mini is just about the ultimate. The power unit is built up from an original ex-works BMC Special Tuning engine. The MkI bodyshell has been superbly restored and improved, top quality components having been used throughout. Performance is outstanding too.

Minis of this standard do not come cheap, and this is by far the most expensive-to-build car described here.

Key features

Engine: 1,380cc Metro Turbo block. Billet crank. Mini Spares pistons. Eight-port camshaft. Vernier timing gears. BMC ex-works eight-port head. Titan 1.5:1 roller-rockers. Twin Weber 45DCOE carburettors. 13-row oil cooler. Mini Spares two-core radiator. Silicon hoses. Kenlowe race-spec fan. Ultra-light steel flywheel and backplate. BMC tubular exhaust manifold. Play Mini race-spec stainless exhaust system. Facet Silver Top fuel pump.

Transmission: Paddle clutch. BMC works four-speed straight-cut close-ratio gears. 1:1 straight-cut transfer gears. Centre oil pick-up. Twin cross-pin differential with 3.7:1 final drive. Works universal joints and driveshafts. Modified works remote-shift.

Brakes: Front: modified Metro Turbo vented discs with Mini Sport four-piston calipers and Ferodo pads. Rear: Super Minifin drums with Ferodo shoes. Cooper S master cylinder.

Suspension: Dry rubber-cone. HiLos and Spax adjustables all round. Adjustable tie rods and

negative-camber bottom arms at front. Quickshift steering rack. Alloy subframe mounts and negative-camber brackets at rear.

Wheels and tyres: 6 x 10 custom made Minilite style split-rim alloys with 165/70 x 10 Yokohama A032 tyres.

Interior: Retrim in two-tone Cooper Grey. Low-back bucket seats. Custom-made

walnut-veneer dash and centre console. Smiths magnolia three-dial instrumentation with rev counter, clock and voltmeter. Moto-Lita steering wheel. Rollcentre colour-matched rollcage. Willans three-point harnesses.

Exterior: MkI Mini completely rebuilt with new wings, front panel, inner and outer sills. Custom-made glass-fibre bonnet to clear

carburettors. Mini Special wheelarches. Dark blue custom pearl mica paint. New and rechromed bright-work. Twin fuel tanks.

Mini Roadster

(Pictures by Chris Brown; www.miniworld.co.uk)

This Mini has had its bodywork modified extensively, with much strengthening added to the floor and sill areas to compensate for the removal of the roof. The mechanicals, principally a standard 1275GT engine and braking system, have been considerably upgraded from the car's original Mini 1000 set-up. Professionally built, the end result is superb, making it one of the most outstanding Minis around.

Key features

Engine: Standard 1275GT. HIF44 carburettor. K&N air filter. Standard points ignition. Play Mini stainless-steel exhaust system.

Transmission: Four-speed standard manual gearbox.

Brakes: Front: 8.4in discs. Rear: Standard drums.

Suspension: Dry rubber-cone. HiLos and Spax adjustables all round. Adjustable tie rods and negative-camber bottom arms at front; negative-camber brackets at rear.

Wheels and tyres: Superlite 5 x 13 alloys, 165/60 x 13 Goodyear tyres.

Interior: MDF dashboard with additional instruments. Anodised door furniture. Astra GTE front seats. Cut-down rear seat. Six-point bespoke rollcage. No carpets.

Exterior: 1972 Mini 1000 bodyshell with roof removed. Extensive internal strengthening. Deseamed. External door handles removed. Numberplate recess removed from bootlid. Glass-fibre bonnet. Group 2 wheelarches. 6in Perspex front screen and side windows. Motorcycle wing mirrors.

Mini Sprint

*(Pictures by Anthony Butler;
www.miniworld.co.uk)*

Overall this is the most modified Mini featured. Body mods are extensive, as the Mini Sprint conversion involves removing metal from below the waistline and from the roof pillars to lower the entire shell. It is not a straightforward conversion and one like this should only be undertaken by the very experienced. Mechanical mods are extensive too, the engine and transmission being close to full-race spec.

Key features

Engine: 1,380cc Metro Turbo block. Miglia-spec crank and rods. Omega pistons. Billet 296 scatter cam. Miglia full-race head. Titan 1.5:1 roller-rockers. 45DCOE carburettor. 13-row oil cooler. Facet Red Top fuel pump. Modified Metro distributor. Lumenition electronic ignition. Lucas Sports coil. Farndon steel flywheel and steel backplate. Maniflow large-bore LCB. 2in twin-box exhaust system.

Transmission: Four-speed straight-cut close-ratio gears. Timken straight-cut 1:1 transfer gears. Centre oil pick-up. Twin cross-pin differential with 3.9:1 final drive. Paddle clutch. KAD Quickstick gearchange.

Brakes: Front: Cooper S 7.5in discs with EBC Green Stuff Kevlar pads. Rear: Super Minifin drums with AP shoes. Cooper S master cylinder. Fly-off handbrake.

Suspension: Dry rubber-cone. HiLos and Spax adjustables all round. Adjustable tie rods and rose-jointed 1.5° negative-camber bottom arms at front. Adjustable camber brackets at rear.

Wheels and tyres: 6 x 10 Spectrum alloys with 165/70 x 10 Yokohama A032 tyres.

Interior: Custom speedo binnacle. Smiths tacho. Speedwell seats trimmed in light grey vinyl. Mountney steering wheel. Newton Commercial carpets. Three-point race harnesses.

Exterior: 1960 Morris Mini MkI bodyshell fully restored with new wings, front panel, inner and outer sills, front floors, rear valance, doorskins, 'one door step' (upper section of the sill), rear-wing lowers and boot floor. Minisprint modifications: 1½in cut from below waistline, 2in from roof pillars, front and rear screens raked by extra 10°. Partly deseamed. Custom-made glass. Somerford Group 2 wheelarches. Halogen headlamps. Seam-welded subframes. Island Blue with black roof.

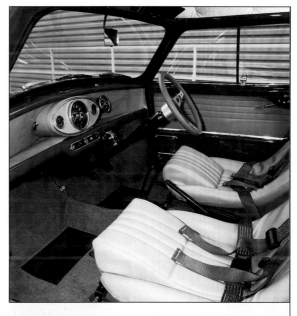

Mini van

(Pictures by Anthony Butler;
www.miniworld.co.uk)

Like the Mini pick-up, the van is becoming rarer and therefore very sought after. Today, although many Mini vans are restored to their original standard condition, they have always been modified, and this trend continues. The style of this one is very extrovert with 13in wheels and wide wheelarch extensions – bodywise, it is the opposite of the pick-up at the beginning of this section as it is extensively modified. Mechanically, the car is well sorted too, with a 1,380cc Bill Richards engine.

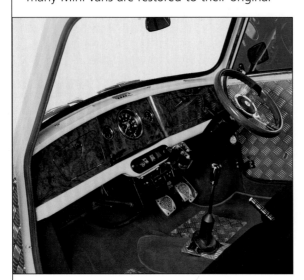

Key features

Engine: 1,380cc. 7cc dished Mega pistons. Metro Turbo conrods. Steel centre main strap. Piper 285 camshaft. 12G940 11-stud head. Twin 1.5in SU carburettors. K&N filters. Electronic ignition. Steel flywheel. Two-core radiator. LCB exhaust manifold, Play Mini stainless exhaust system

Transmission: Rally clutch plate. 'Orange' diaphragm. A-Plus gearbox. Centre oil pick-up. Twin-pin-differential with 3.6:1 final drive.

Brakes: 8.4in front discs. Standard, late Mini rear drums. Aeroquip hoses.

Suspension: Dry rubber-cone. HiLos and Spax lowered adjustable dampers. Negative-camber bottom arms and adjustable tie bars at front; negative-camber brackets at rear.

Wheels and tyres: 7 x 13 Superlite alloy wheels; 175/50 x 13 Dunlop SP2000 tyres.

Interior: Corbeau Forza seats. Full harness seatbelts. Wooden steering wheel. Alloy chequerplate interior door panels. Somerford carpets. Tinted glass.

Exterior: Van bodywork with front spoiler and wheelarch extensions: Group 5 front, Sports Pack rear. Fiat Yellow.

appendix I

The Mini, year-by-year

During its time in production, a great deal of work went into the Mini, both to maintain its appeal to the car-buying public and also to enable it to meet ever-tightening regulations, both for safety and emissions. Although the basic shape remained the same, there are in fact very few parts, either body or mechanical, that are interchangeable between a 1959 Mini and one of the last Minis made in the year 2000. The list below details most of the technical changes and model introductions that have taken place since 1959. Some very minor changes have been left out as they are not really relevant to this book, and it is possible that one or two details may not have been included from 1994 onwards, because information covering the last few years of production does not seem to have been recorded very thoroughly.

Technical history – 1959 to date

1957	March	Leonard Lord commissions a small BMC car, code-named ADO15.
1958	July	Issigonis told to have Mini in production 'within 12 months'.
1959	Summer	Final prototype testing at Chalgrove, Oxfordshire.
1959	August	Austin Seven and Morris Mini Minor launched. Available in basic and DeLuxe versions. Both fitted with 848cc engine.
1960	January	Austin and Morris Mini van introduced, with 848cc engine.
1960	April	Driveshaft splines changed from square section to involute.
1960	September	Austin Mini Countryman and Morris Mini Traveller introduced, with ornamental wood framing to the rear.
1961	January	Austin and Morris Mini pick-up introduced, with 848cc engine.
1961	May	Cast aluminium suspension trumpets introduced.
1961	September	Austin Super Seven and Morris Mini Super introduced, fitted with the yet-to-be-announced Mini Cooper interior trim and paint finishes. Central oval instrument binnacle with oil pressure and water temperature gauges and key-start ignition. Stronger steel wheels fitted.
1961	October	16-blade fan fitted to reduce engine noise. Morris radiator grille chromed instead of painted. Austin and Morris Coopers introduced. Similar to Super saloons, but with 997cc twin-carburettor engines, 7in front disc brakes, and remote gearchange.
1961	October	Riley Elf and Wolseley Hornet announced. Larger boot, luxurious seats and wood veneer dashboard/ instrument panel; 848cc engine.
1962	January	Austin Seven models renamed Austin Mini.
1962	August	Revised bonnet prop and rest bracket.
1962	October	Baulk-ring synchromesh on upper three forward ratios progressively introduced. Windscreen washers, interior light and overriders made standard on van and pick-up. DeLuxe and Super DeLuxe models replaced by Super DeLuxe. All-steel Countryman and Traveller available at lower price. Anti-chafing rubber strips fitted to metal fuel pipe.
1962	November	Riley Elf and Wolseley Hornet MkII introduced. Twin-leading-shoe front drum brakes, 998cc engine with 'magic wand' gear lever.
1963	January	Plastic strip fitted to rear seat pan leading edge. Three-piece stainless-steel wheelarch trims replaced by single-piece plastic chromed strip.
1963	February	Improved door-sealing rubbers.
1963	March	Mini Cooper S introduced, with 1,071cc engine, 7½in servo-assisted front disc brakes and ventilated steel wheels. Improved calipers fitted to brakes of 997cc Mini Cooper. Redesigned fresh-air heater.
1963	May	Chrome sliding window catches replaced with black plastic catches.
1964	January	Cooper 997cc engine replaced with 998cc unit.
1964	February	Wiper arc reduced from 130° to 120° to prevent fouling of windscreen rubber.
1964	March	1,275cc and 970cc engines available on Cooper S models. SP41 radial tyres standard fit on all Cooper and Cooper S models.
1964	July	998cc Cooper given lower pressure

		setting on rear brake anti-lock valve.
1964	August	Mini Moke introduced. Utility body with fabric roof and 848cc engine.
1964	September	Improved gearboxes with B-series teeth and new forks with improved contact area. Diaphragm-spring clutch introduced. Hydrolastic suspension fitted to all saloon models. Twin-leading-shoe front brakes fitted to non-Cooper Minis, and cutaway-skirt front panel fitted to all models. Positive crankcase ventilation for all Cooper S models. Door courtesy lamp switches introduced.
1964	October	New driveshaft coupling with larger bonding area.
1964	November	Three-position adjustment brackets fitted to driver's seat.
1965	January	970cc Cooper S engine discontinued. 998cc Cooper radiator uprated from 13 to 16 gills per inch. Gradual introduction of scroll-type oil seal on primary gear.
1965	October	Automatic gearbox option introduced. Auto models have larger HS4 SU carburettor.
1965	November	Reclining seat option introduced on Cooper and Cooper S models.
1966	January	Safety bosses fitted to door handles. Smoother-action clutch. Twin petrol tanks and oil cooler standard on Cooper S.
1966	April	New steel/rubber lower front suspension arm bush. Cooper S models fitted with higher-rate Hydrolastic units, taper-roller rear wheel bearings and Hardy Spicer universal joint inboard driveshaft couplings. Boot and door hinge gaskets made more waterproof.
1966	May	Hydrolastic units modified to prevent squeaking.
1966	September	Cross-drilled crankshaft introduced on Cooper S. Improved engine mountings fitted.
1966	October	MkIII versions of Riley Elf and Wolseley Hornet introduced. Concealed door hinges and wind-up windows, fresh-air vents, and remote gearchange.
1966	December	Double-skinned boot lid.
1967	October	MkII introduced. Saloons with larger rear window and front grille, new badging and interior trim. Model range consists of 850 standard and Super DeLuxe saloons, 1000 Super DeLuxe saloon and estate (with or without wood trim). 1000 models have remote
		gear change and optional automatic transmission. Gradual introduction of all-synchromesh gearbox on Cooper S. Plastic cooling fan fitted. Riley Elf and Wolseley Hornet given restyled seats and multi-purpose stalk on steering column. Automatic now optional. 998cc engine option on van and pick-up.
1968	February	Spare-wheel retaining bracket deleted. Cooper models have SP41 tyres replaced by SP68.
1968	June	Cable-type internal door release replaced by handles.
1968	July	Redesigned rear quarterlight frames.
1968	September	All-synchromesh gearbox introduced throughout range
1968	October	Moke production in Britain ceases. Redesigned lockable heater and choke knobs introduced.
1969	April	Heated rear window option on saloon models.
1969	June	Redesigned, crushable sun visors.
1969	August	Riley Elf and Wolseley Hornet discontinued. Plastic-cased heater unit.
1969	October	MkIII saloons introduced, re-badged Mini 850 and Mini 1000 (marque names dropped). Concealed door hinges, wind-up windows and suspension changed back to rubber cone. Negative earth electrics and mechanical fuel pump. Morris Mini Traveller and Austin Mini Countryman discontinued. Van and pick-up are badged 'Mini'. Mini Clubman saloon and 1275GT introduced, both with Hydrolastic suspension. 1275GT fitted with 1,275cc single-carburettor engine, Cooper S with 7½in front disc brakes and Rostyle wheels. Mini Clubman Estate introduced. Early MkIII cars fitted with four-vent sills, then changed to six-vent type. Cooper S MkII continues in production.
1969	November	Austin/Morris Mini Cooper 998cc discontinued.
1970	March	Mini Cooper S MkIII introduced. MkIII bodyshell, with Hydrolastic suspension.
1970	October	Ignition shield fitted. Steering lock fitted.
1970	December	1275GT final drive ratio changed from 3.65:1 to 3.44:1.
1971	June	Improved driveshaft boot for longer life. Rubber-cone suspension introduced on Clubman Saloon and 1275GT.
1971	July	Mini Cooper S MkIII discontinued.
1972	February	Improved synchromesh.

1972	April	Split-type needle roller bearings fitted to idler gears.
1972	December	Alternator becomes standard.
1973	January	Phased introduction of rod-change gearbox.
1973	February	Radial-ply tyres standard, except on 850.
1973	April	New driveshafts with plunging inboard joints.
1973	June	Improved door check pivot fitted.
1973	August	Single door mirror replaces wing mirrors on Clubman Estate.
1973	October	Distributor suitable for low-octane fuel discontinued on Mini 850.
1974	January	Automatic gearbox option restricted to home market.
1974	February	Inertia-reel seat belts fitted as standard.
1974	April	Heater now standard on Mini 850.
1974	May	Air intake system with temperature control introduced on 1275GT. All models except 1275GT receive HS4 carburettor, revised manifold and ignition timing. Twin-silencer exhaust system fitted.
1974	June	12in wheels and larger, 8.4in disc brakes (without servo) fitted as standard to 1275GT; also, larger, 7.5-gallon fuel tank. Laminated windscreen optional.
1974	July	Passenger sunvisor fitted as standard to 850.
1974	August	Dunlop Denovo run-flat tyres available as an option on 1275GT.
1975	October	88° thermostat fitted. New seat frames (reclining on Clubman, estate and 1275GT); anti-tip catches and new trim (cloth on all Clubman models). 1,098cc engine fitted to manual-transmission Clubman saloon and estate. Seat-belt anchorages moved to rear pockets. Mini 1000 'Stripey' limited edition. Reclining, orange-striped cloth seats, Safari carpets, two chrome door mirrors, coachline along waist. Available in Brooklands Green and Glacier White.
1976	May	Twin-stalk controls, heated rear window, radial-ply tyres on 850, and hazard warning lights made standard equipment. Rubber-mounted front subframe and revised mountings to the rear. Lower-rate rubber springs, new ignition lock, moulded carpets,

		larger, Allegro-style pedals. Face-level ventilation standard on Mini 1000. Clubman models have new-style black grille with two polished horizontal bars. Models known as the MkIV Mini.
1977	July	Mini 1000 improved with two-tone striped nylon trim, rake-adjusting front seats, front door pockets, dipping rear-view mirrors, and built-in Innocenti-style reversing lights. Mini Clubman given new wheeltrims, leather-bound steering wheel, locking fuel cap, and tinted glass in addition. Clubman Estate has stick-on stripes instead of imitation wood.
1977	August	Matt-black radiator grille (850/1000), vanity mirror, and revised steering wheel. Denovo tyres standard on 1275GT.
1978	December	'Mini 95' gross weight badge fitted to van and pick-up.
1979	July	Mini City announced. Basic trim with single-dial centre binnacle, houndstooth check seat facings, and no heated rear window. Black bumpers and wheelarch trim. Mini 850 Super DeLuxe introduced, trimmed as Mini 1000.
1979	October	Mini 1000 given coachline, and redesignated Mini 1000 Super.
1979	August	Mini 1100 Special limited edition launched to celebrate 20 years of the Mini. Silver or Rose metallic paint, shaded body stripes, 5 x 10 Exacton alloy wheels with 165/70 x 10 tyres, Innocenti wheelarch extensions, Clubman-style bumpers, twin door mirrors, tinted glass and vinyl roof. Interior features 1275GT instruments, centre console, clock and tartan check trim.
1979	October	Black door mirrors and gutter trim.
1979	November	L pack introduced for 850 van. Standard on 998cc van, but not available on pick-up; comprises carpet, cloth seats, passenger sun visor, and improved sound insulation.
1980	February	7½-gallon fuel tank fitted to saloons.
1980	May	New soundproofing fitted to all models.
1980	August	Production of Mini 850 ends. Mini Clubman Saloon and Estate and 1275GT discontinued.
1980	September	Mini 1000 City introduced, trim as per 850 City.

1980	October	Mini 1000 Super replaced by Mini 1000HL. Clubman instruments, tinted glass, larger door pockets, four-spoke steering wheel, Metro interior door furniture and gearlever knob. Mini 1000HL estate replaces Clubman 1100 estate.
1980	November	850 pick-up discontinued.
1982	February	Estate bodyshell ceases production.
1982	April	Mini City renamed Mini City E. Higher final drive ratio, and higher compression ratio. City decals on doors and boot, stripes deleted. 1000HL and Estate has same mechanical modifications, and redesignated 1000HLE and 1000HLE Estate. All models fitted with matt black bumpers.
1982	September	1000HLE saloon and estate discontinued. Mini Mayfair saloon launched. Improved cloth trim and carpets, head restraints, tinted glass and radio. City E includes heated rear window, passenger sun visor, reversing lamps.
1982	December	Van and pick-up discontinued.
1983	October	Mini Sprite limited edition introduced – 2,500 made. Cinnabar Red or Primula with black side stripes and Sprite logo. Twin door mirrors, 'Mini Special' alloy wheels, 165/70 x 10 tyres, wheelarch extensions, 1275GT instruments, head restraints and black vinyl and herringbone cloth trim.
1984	July	Mini 25 Anniversary model. Limited edition of 5,000 cars of which 1,500 exported. Silver with grey and red coachline. Luxurious Flint Grey velvet interior trim with rev counter, stereo and twin speakers. Tinted glass and twin door mirrors.
1984	October	12in wheels with 8.4in disc brakes and 'Mini Special' wheelarch extensions on both City and Mayfair. Upholstery upgraded.
1985	January	Mini Ritz limited edition. Silver Leaf metallic, Ritz decals, Nimbus Grey bumpers and grille. Alloy wheels. Multi-coloured velvet panelled interior trim. 2,000 cars for UK, 1,725 for export.
1985	September	Colour-coded dashboard, door handles, and seat belts. Exterior trim (bumpers, grille etc.) finished in grey.
1985	November	City E given face-level ventilation, four-spoke steering wheel, trimmed rear

		wheelarches and new City decals on rear quarter panels. Mayfair receives three-spoke steering wheel, rev-counter, carpet inserts on dashboard and rear parcel shelf. New seat trim, door trim and wheeltrims. Side repeater indicators fitted to front wings on both models.
1986	February	Mini Chelsea limited edition. Targa Red, alloys, Osprey Grey interior trim with red piping. 1,500 made.
1986	May	Mini Piccadilly limited edition. Cashmere Gold, chrome bumpers, steel wheels with wheel trims. Bitter Chocolate, Coffee and Claret interior trim. 2,500 made.
1986	October	Rear lap seat belts standard.
1987	January	Mini Park Lane limited edition. Black paintwork with chrome bumpers and grille surround and full wheeltrims. Interior trimmed in beige/dark velvet. 4,000 made of which 2,400 exported.
1987	June	Mini Advantage limited edition. Diamond White with white wheeltrims, 'Advantage' decals and side flashes. Flint Grey and Jade Green upholstery. 4,675 made of which 2,175 exported. 'Austin Rover' badge on grille replaced with 'Mini' badge.
1988	January	Mini Red Hot and Jet Black limited editions launched. Finished in red or black according to model, with chrome bumpers and full wheeltrims. Black velour interior with red piping. 6,000 made of which 4,000 exported.
1988	June	Mini Designer limited edition. Black or White Diamond, with Nimbus Grey fittings. Interior finished in Mary Quant striped fabric. 2,000 made.
1988	August	City E renamed City, and fitted with different instruments, three-spoke steering wheel, and front head restraints. Mayfair fitted with radio cassette as standard, new interior trim, wheeltrims and badging.
1988	October	Brake servo standard.
1989	January	Mini Racing, Flame, Rose, and Sky limited editions. Racing and Flame painted in British Racing Green or Flame Red respectively. Sky and Rose in white with blue and pink roofs respectively. Crayons fabric interior trim. Full-width white wheeltrims. Racing and Flame 2,000 made, Sky and Rose 1,000 made.

1989	Early	Engines compatible with 95 octane unleaded fuel.
1989	May	998cc John Cooper conversion available from John Cooper Garages and Rover Dealers.
1989	June	Mini Thirty limited edition anniversary model. Pearlescent Cherry Red or black paint with chrome fittings, Minilite-style alloy wheels, black leather and lightning trim. 3,000 made for UK, including 200 automatics. Catalytic converter available as option.
1990	February	Mini Racing Green, Flame Red and Checkmate limited editions. Racing Green and Flame Red as previous year's Racing and Flame, but with Minilite-style alloy wheels. Checkmate same spec, but black with white roof. 2,500 made.
1990	June	Mini Studio 2 limited edition. Black, Nordic Grey or Storm Blue, with chrome grille, full-width wheeltrims and Doeskin fabric trim. 2,000 made.
1990	July	Rover Special Products Mini Cooper limited edition. Flame Red, British Racing Green or black, all with white roof. 1,275cc carburettor engine with oil cooler, half-leather trim, Minilite-style alloy wheels, and white bonnet stripes with John Cooper signature. 1,000 made.
1991	February	Mini Neon limited edition. Nordic Blue with chrome fittings and chevron velour trim. 1,500 made.
1991	March	'Mainstream' Rover Cooper. Fabric trim, 1,275cc engine without oil cooler. Paint as RSP, plus white, Quicksilver and Storm Grey, all with black roofs, also available. Cooper S conversion available through John Cooper Garages.
1991	June	Limited edition LAMM Cabriolet announced. Cooper engine, Mayfair trim, body-styling kit, and 13-inch Revolution alloy wheels. 75 made.
1991	October	Mini Cooper 1.3i replaces carburettor model. 1,275cc single-point fuel-injected engine with closed-loop catalyst. Driving lamps and plain bonnet stripes matching roof colour. Winged 'Mini Cooper' badges. Redesigned front subframe to move engine forwards.
1991	November	Full-width wheeltrims, chrome bumpers, and harlequin cloth trim for City. Mayfair receives chrome grille, body-coloured door mirrors and numberplate-lamp housing. Improved R652 stereo. New chrome 'Mayfair' boot badge. Steering wheel and interior fitments in black on both models.
1992	March	Cooper Si conversion available from John Cooper.
1992	May	City and 998cc Mayfair replaced by Mini Sprite 1.3 and Mini Mayfair 1.3. Both powered by 1.3 carburettor engine.
1992	June	Mini British Open Classic limited edition launched. Metallic British Racing Green with full-length electric sunroof. Chrome fittings and Minilite-style wheels. 1.3 carburettor engine; Stone Beige leather and Countryman tweed upholstery. 1,000 made.
1992	October	Mini Italian Job limited edition. Flame Red, British Racing Green, Diamond White or Electric Blue paint, with white alloys, black bumpers and black tweed upholstery. 1,750 made of which 1,000 for UK and 750 for Italy.
1992	November	Alarm immobiliser and internal bonnet release with modified grille. VIN number etched on windscreen.
1993	February	Cooper, Mayfair and Sprite receive new seats; VIN now etched on both front and rear screens. Sprite fitted with passenger door mirror, front door pockets, boot mat and new trim. Alarm and walnut-veneered dashboard on Cooper and Mayfair. Leather trim and optional alloy wheels with locking wheel nuts on Mayfair.
1993	June	Mini Rio limited edition. Black, pearlescent Caribbean Blue, or metallic Polynesian Turquoise paint, wheeltrims, black and bright green interior trim. 750 made.
1993	July	Rover Mini Cabriolet introduced. 1.3i Cooper engine, bodykit with 12in alloys, different hood system from LAMM Cabriolet.
1993	October	Mini Tahiti limited edition. Pearlescent Tahiti Blue paint and Minilite-style wheels. Interior trimmed in black with blue and black inserts. 500 made.
1994	January	Monte Carlo Anniversary decal pack available at no extra cost on new Coopers from Rover dealers.
1994	May	Mini 35 Anniversary limited edition. Pearlescent Nevada Red, metallic

Arizona Blue, or White Diamond paint. Chrome grille, basic Jamboree interior trim. Automatic transmission and alloy wheels optional. 1,000 made.

1994 July — Mini Cooper Monte Carlo limited edition. Black or Flame Red with white roof. Gunmetal alloy wheels, two extra fog lamps. Interior in red with cream cloth centre panels; wood dashboard with cream dials. 200 made.

1995 May — Mini Sidewalk limited edition. White Diamond, Charcoal metallic or Kingfisher Blue. Wheeltrims and blue tartan trim. 1,000 made.

1996 April — Mini Equinox limited edition. Pearlescent Amaranth Purple, Charcoal metallic, or Platinum Silver metallic. Chrome bumpers and grille. Interior with sun, moon and stars theme.

1996 May — Mini Cooper 35th anniversary limited edition. Almond Green with white roof. Gunmetal alloy wheels, and two extra fog lamps. Interior trimmed in Porcelain Green leather. 200 made.

1996 October — Mini Cooper 1.3i and Mini 1.3i twin-point injection models. Redesigned cylinder block with distributor housing deleted, front-mounted radiator, larger, 65amp alternator, 2.76:1 final drive. Improved safety with driver's airbag, side-impact bars and seat belt pre-tensioners. Improved sound deadening and one-piece carpet. Large range of accessories available to personalise the car in 'period' style. Sports Option Pack available including 13in wheels, large wheelarch extensions, Koni dampers and extra driving lamps.

1998 April — Paul Smith limited edition. Available in Paul Smith Blue with Charcoal alloy wheels and unique badging. Body-colour dashboard and black leather seat facings and Citrus Green colour in glovebox, engine compartment and boot. 300 made.

1999 April — Mini 40 limited edition. Mulberry Red pearlescent, Old English White or Island Blue. Sports Pack 13in wheels and wheelarch extensions, special badges, two driving lamps and chrome GB badge. Interior fitted with turned alloy dashboard, leather-trimmed seats and CD player.

2000 April — Mini Finale limited edition, in one of three retro guises. Mini Classic Se7en, in Solar Red, Old English White or black, with chrome bumpers and grille. 'Premium' alloy wheels, and superior sound system with ICT speakers and optional CD player. Tartan red leather with cream cloth centre panels. Body-colour dashboard. Mini Classic Cooper, in Solar Red, British Racing Green, black, or Tahiti Blue with chrome bumpers and grille, Minilite-style alloy wheels, stereo radio/cassette, black half-leather trim, body-colour dashboard, drilled accelerator pedal. Mini Classic Sport, in Solar Red, British Racing Green, Anthracite, or Tahiti Blue with chrome bumpers and grille, full Sports Pack, two driving lamps, two fog lamps, and large chrome tailpipe finisher. Nickel Silver and black leather trim, black leather steering wheel, optional electric canvas sunroof and CD player. Alloy interior door furniture and dashboard.

2000 September — Final production run of limited edition Mini Classic Cooper Sport 500, in Solar Red, British Racing Green, Anthracite, or Tahiti Blue. Chrome bumpers and grille, full Sports Pack, two driving lamps, two fog lamps, large chrome tailpipe finisher. Nickel Silver and black leather trim, black leather steering wheel, optional electric canvas sunroof, and CD player. Alloy interior door furniture and dashboard.

2000 October — Production ceases. A total of 5,387,862 Minis have been made during 41 years of production.

2002 August — Mini bodyshells back in production at British Motor Heritage, Witney, using the original tooling.

At the time of writing, a total of 117,504 Mini saloons and estates, and 1,771 vans and pick-ups, were recorded by the DVLC as being on the road in Great Britain. (*Source SMMT 1 August 2002*)

appendix II

Recommended suppliers

The following addresses, telephone numbers and internet details were believed correct at the time of going to press. However, as these are subject to change, no guarantee can be given for their continued accuracy.

This is not a complete list of Mini specialists, but includes those whose products and services which have particular relevance to this book.

Aldon Automotive, Breener Industrial Estate, Station Drive, Brierley Hill, West Midlands DY5 3JZ. Tel: 01384 572553 Fax: 01384 480418

Autoline (Dinitrol), Eagle House, Redstone Industrial Estate, Boston, Lincolnshire PE21 8EA. Tel: 01205 354500

Automec, 36 Ballmoor, Buckingham MK18 1RT. Tel: 01280 822818

Avonbar Racing, Avcon House, Bullocks Farm, Bullocks Lane, Takeley, Essex CM22 6TA. Tel: 01279 873428 Fax: 01279 873427 Website: www.avonbar.com

A to Z Car Centre, Wingfield, Mill Lane, Sutton St James, Nr Spalding, Lincolnshire PE12 0EJ. Tel/Fax: 01945 440394

Peter Baldwin Rolling Road Engine Tuning, Wilsher Garages Ltd, 18 Cambridge Road, Wimpole, Cambridgeshire SG8 5QE. Tel: 01223 207217 Fax: 01223 207996

British Motor Heritage Limited, Range Road, Witney, Oxfordshire OX29 0YB. Website: www.bmh-ltd.com

Burlen Fuel Systems, Spitfire House, Castle Road, Salisbury, Wiltshire SP1 3SA. Tel: 01722 412500 Fax: 01722 334221 Email: info@burlen.co.uk Website: www.burlen.co.uk

Carburation & Injection Tuning Ltd, Rolling Road Tuning, Unit 2, 36 Sutton Road, Coxside, Plymouth, Devon PL4 0JE. Tel: 01752 256262

Cobra Superform Limited, Units D1 and D2, Halesfield 23, Telford, Shropshire TF7 4NY. Tel: 01952 684020 Website: www.cobraseats.com

John Cooper Works, North Lane, East Preston, West Sussex BN16 1BN. Tel: 01903 784784 Fax: 01903 787722 Email: works@johncooper.co.uk Website: www.johncooper.co.uk

Dash of Colour, The Workshop, 40 Mill Lane, Gosberton, Spalding, Lincolnshire PE11 4NN. Tel: 01775 841078 Email: adashofcolour@aol.com Website: www.dashofcolour.co.uk

Federal Mogul Aftermarket UK Ltd, Greyhound Drive, off Legrams Lane, Bradford, West Yorkshire BD7 1NQ. (Customer Service Department) Tel: 01274 723481

Green Cotton Air Filters, Auto Inparts Ltd, Unit L2, Cherrycourt Way Industrial Estate, Stanbridge Road, Leighton Buzzard, Bedfordshire LU7 4UH. Tel: 01525 382713

Induction Technology Group Ltd, Unit 5 Fairfield Court, Seven Stars Industrial Estate, Whitley, Coventry, West Midlands CV3 4LJ. Tel: 02476 305386

Kent Auto Developments Ltd, Brooker Farm, Newchurch, Romney Marsh, Kent TN29 0DT. Tel: 01303 874082 Fax: 01303 872451 Email: sales@kad-uk.com

Kent Performance Camshafts, Units 1–4 Military Road, Shorncliffe Industrial Estate, Folkestone, Kent, CT20 3SP. Tel: 01303 248666 Email: kentcams@btinternet.com

K&N Filters (Europe) Ltd, John Street, Warrington, Cheshire WA2 7UB. Tel: 01925 636950

Maniflow, Mitchell Road, Churchfields Industrial Estate, Salisbury, Wiltshire SP2 7PY. Tel: 01722 335378

MED, Unit 6, 238 Tithe Street, Leicester LE5 4BN. Tel: 0116 246 1641

Midland Mini Centre, 317 Highfield Road, Hall Green, Birmingham B28 0BX. Tel: 0121 777 1961 Fax: 0121 702 2329

Mini Classics, The Barn, Bawtry Road, Blyth, Nr Worksop, Nottinghamshire S81 8HG. Tel: 01909 591065

ML Motorsport, New Stables Farm, Rushmore Hill, Knockholt, Kent TN14 7NS. Tel: 01959 533130 Website: www.mlmotorsport.com

Mini Mail, Springbank Farm, Kilcot, Gloucestershire GL18 1NG. Tel: 07000 850 1275/01989 720111 Fax: 01989 720777

The Mini Shop, 385 Hertford Road, Enfield, Middlesex EN3 5PP. Tel: 0208 805 8085 Fax: 0208 805 8075

Mini Spares Centre, Cranbourne Industrial Estate, Cranbourne Road, Potters Bar, Hertfordshire EN6 3JN. Tel: 01707 607700 Fax: 01707 656786 Email: spares@minispares.com

Mini Spares Midlands, 991 Wolverhampton Road, Oldbury, West Midlands B69 4RJ. Tel: 0121 544 0011 Fax: 0121 544 0022

Mini Spares North, Unit 6, Freemans Way, Harrogate Business Park, Harrogate, North Yorkshire HG3 1DH. Tel: 01483 881800 Fax: 01428 881801

Mini Spares South, 3 Crane Street, Cranborne, Dorset BH21 5QD. Tel: 01725 517999 Fax: 01725 517878

Mini Speed, Units 4 and 5, Abbot Close, Oyster Lane, Byfleet, Surrey KT14 7JN. Tel: 01932 400567 Fax: 01932 400565 Email: sales@minispeed.co.uk

Mini Sport Ltd, Thompson Street, Padiham, Lancashire BB12 7AP. Tel: 01282 778731

Min-Its, R/O 2192 Stratford Road, Hockley Heath, Solihull, West Midlands B94 6NU. Tel: 01564 783045

M&M's, Unit 5b, Bank Quay Trading Estate, Slutchers Lane, Warrington, Cheshire. Tel: 01925 444303 Website: www.mini-metro.co.uk

Moss Europe Ltd, Hampton Farm Industrial Estate, Hanworth, Middlesex TW13 6DB, Tel: 020 8867 2020 Fax: 020 8867 2030 Website: www.moss-europe.co.uk

Moto-Lita, Thruxton Circuit, Nr Andover, Hampshire SP11 8PW. Tel: 01264 772811

Newton Commercial, Eastlands Industrial Estate, Leiston, Suffolk IP16 4LL. Tel: 01728 832880 Fax: 01728 832881 Email newtoncomm@anglianet.co.uk Website: www.newtoncomm.co.uk

Owen Developments Building S28, Rectory Lane Trading Estate, Kingston Bagpuize, Oxford OX13 5AS. Tel: 01865 821062 Fax: 01865 821076

F. J. Payne & Son Ltd, Oakfield Road, Eynsham, Oxfordshire. Tel: 01865 882299

Piper Cams, 2 St John's Court, Ashford Business Park, Sevington, Ashford, Kent TN24 0SJ. Tel: 01233 500200 Fax: 01233 500300

Pipercross Performance Air Filters, Units 4-6, Tenter Road, Moulton Park Industrial Estate, Northampton NN3 6PZ. Tel: 01604 494945

P&L Minis, 34 High Street, Thurnscoe, Rotherham. Tel: 01709 889922 Website: www.plmini.com

R. T. Quaife Engineering Ltd, Vestry Road, Otford, Sevenoaks, Kent TN14 5EL. Tel: 01732 741144 Fax: 01732 741555 Website: www.quaife.co.uk

Bill Richards Racing, Unit 24, Ellingham Industrial Estate, Ashford, Kent TN23 6JZ. Tel: 01233 624336 Website: www.billrichardsracing.com

Securon Ltd, The Hill, Winchmore Hill, Amersham,

Buckinghamshire HP7 0NZ. Tel: 01494 434455

Slark Race Engineering, Unit 2a, Bunas Park, Hollom Down Road, Lopcombe, Salisbury, Wiltshire SB5 12BP. Tel: 01264 781403

Somerford Mini Specialists, Unit 1, Broadfield Farm, Great Somerford, Nr Chippenham, Wiltshire SN15 5EL. Tel: 01249 721421

Southam Mini & Metro Centre, Unit 16, Warwick House Industrial Park, Banbury Road, Southam, Warwickshire. Tel: 01926 815681

Southern Carburettors and Injection, Unit 6, Nelson Trading Estate, Morden Road, Wimbledon, London SW19 3BL. Tel: 0208 540 2723 Fax: 0208 540 0857

Spamspeed Motorsport, Unit C2, Backfield Farm Business Park, Wotton Road, Iron Acton, Bristol BS17 1XD. Tel: 01454 228946

Speedy Cables, Instruments Division, Abercrave, Swansea, West Glamorgan SA9 1SQ. Tel: 01639 732213; Cables Division, Unit 14, Merchant Drive, Hertford SG13 7AZ. Tel: 01992 581600

Swifttune, Longs Corner Farm, Bethersden, Ashford, Kent TN26 3HD. Tel: 01233 850843

Tech Del Ltd (Minilite Wheels), Unit 4A, Roughmoor Industrial Estate, Williton, Taunton, Somerset TA4 4RF. Tel: 01984 631033

Vortz Racing Cars, The Old Works, Braishfield, Romsey, Hampshire SO51 0QB. Tel/Fax: 01794 368344

Rob Walker Performance Engineering, Unit 4, Greystones Business Units, Burford Road, Chipping Norton, Oxfordshire OX7 5XL. Tel: 01608 645666 Fax: 01608 644593 Website: www.robwalkerengineering.com

Webasto Hollandia UK Ltd, Unit 8D, Stockton Close, Minworth Industrial Estate, Sutton Coldfield, Birmingham B76 1DH. Tel: 0121 313 1222 Website: www.webastohollandia.com

Wizards of Nos, TMC Group Ltd, Rands Lane, Armthorpe, Doncaster, South Yorkshire DN3 3ER. Tel: 01302 834343 Website: www.noswizard.com

Wood & Pickett Ltd, Unit 14, Faygate Business Centre, Faygate, Horsham, West Sussex RH12 4DN. Tel: 01293 852100 Fax: 01293 852110 Website: www.woodandpickett.com

Yardy Products (UK) Ltd, Unit 2 Fieldside Farm, Quainton, Nr. Aylesbury, Buckinghamshire HP22 4DQ. Tel: 01296 655840 Email: John@yardyprod.sagehost.co.uk

other books from Haynes Publishing

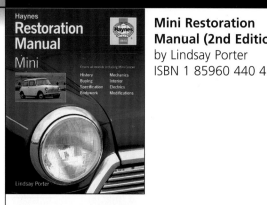

Mini Restoration Manual (2nd Edition)
by Lindsay Porter
ISBN 1 85960 440 4

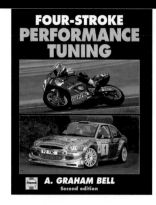

Four-Stroke Performance Tuning (2nd Edition)
by A. Graham Bell
ISBN 1 85960 435 8

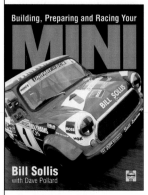

Building, Preparing and Racing Your Mini
by Bill Sollis
with Dave Pollard
ISBN 1 85960 621 0

Race and Rally Car Source Book (4th Edition)
The guide to building or modifying a competition car
by Allan Staniforth
ISBN 1 85960 846 9

Tuning the A-Series Engine (3rd Edition)
The definitive manual on tuning for performance and economy
by David Vizard
ISBN 1 85960 620 2

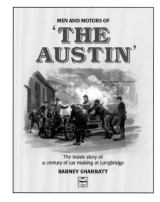

Men and Motors of 'The Austin'
The inside story of a century of car making at Longbridge
by Barney Sharratt
ISBN 1 85960 671 7

SU Carburettors
by A. K. Legg
ISBN 1 85010 506 5

New MINI
by Graham Robson
ISBN 1 85960 874 4